Public Policy-Making

Basic Concepts in Political Science

William A. Welsh, GENERAL EDITOR

PUBLIC POLICY-MAKING

James E. Anderson

PRAEGER PUBLISHERS
New York • Washington

Published in the United States of America in 1975
by Praeger Publishers, Inc.
111 Fourth Avenue, New York, N.Y. 10003

© 1975 by Praeger Publishers, Inc.

Library of Congress Cataloging in Publication Data

Anderson, James E.
    Public policy-making.

    (Basic concepts in political science)
    Bibliography: p.
    1. United States—Politics and government—1945–
2. Policy sciences.   I. Title.
JK271.A65   320'.2   73-8174
ISBN 0-275-19690-9
ISBN 0-275-84680-6 (pbk.)

Printed in the United States of America

Contents

Series Editor's Introduction

This book is one of a series of volumes, published and forthcoming, written for introductory and intermediate undergraduate courses in political science. In one sense, the purpose of these books is to introduce students to the field of political science. The core volume in the series, *Studying Politics,* presents an overview of the concepts, approaches, and subject matter of the discipline, together with an introduction to elements of critical thinking about the study of politics. Each of the other volumes in the series focuses on one or two central concepts used to describe major areas of political activity. These concept volumes provide definitions of important terms, summarize basic approaches, and describe what political scientists have discovered about the involvement of human beings in these activities—political socialization, the exercise of power and influence, conflict, policy-making, political leadership, the development of political culture, the formation and activities of political groups. By using various combinations of these relatively short books, instructors can structure, as broadly or as selectively as they wish, an introduction to the study of politics for undergraduate students.

In another sense, the purpose of this series is both less "academic" and more ambitious. For this series proceeds from the premise that what political scientists do *qua* political scientists has relevance well beyond the relatively narrow confines of a scholarly discipline. As political science has labored toward greater precision, rigor, and theoretical maturity, it has developed new ways of organizing and studying information about politics. By now, there is substantial agreement that these new approaches and techniques have—on balance—improved the scientific status of the discipline. But what of those who are not committed to becoming professional political scientists, but who nevertheless seek a sound, reliable understanding of politics, simply because political activity is so central to the management of human affairs? Does the development of systematic perspectives in the field of political science contribute only to the advancement of science, yielding no benefits for the thoughtful layman?

If one of the goals of science is to provide understanding of our environment, then scientists and nonscientists alike surely share that concern. If this is the case, then our progress as political scientists should hold the promise of improved understanding for nonscientists as well. In short, what political scientists have learned about how to study politics—especially about the close relationship between *what* we know and *how* we find out—ought to be useful to anyone who wants to understand politics. That belief constitutes the principal motivation for this series of books.

In pursuit of that goal, these books attempt to do four things. First, they introduce students to the language and approaches of political science—not merely as elements of a scholarly discipline, but as useful ways of looking at the world we live in. Second, relatedly, these books raise some basic methodological issues involved in studying politics—not as abstract issues in scholarship but as problems of how we obtain and critically analyze information available to us. Third, the concept-based volumes in this series introduce the student to concrete aspects of political activity through the use of unifying concepts that cut across both traditional subfields of the discipline and formal institutions, or structures, of government. They treat politics as a blend of several types of human behavior. Fourth, the books in the series attempt to overcome the student's natural parochialism—the limitations imposed by his much greater familiarity with the political practices and structures of the society in which he lives—by providing frequent examples of political activity from a variety of cultural settings. In short, the series seeks to be both systematic and concrete. It is designed to provide useful perspectives on an exciting area of human activity, and to present these perspectives in a way that is meaningful for students who are beginning their formal study of the subject.

The task is ambitious, and the accomplishment doubtless will be less than perfect. But the effort seems worthwhile, if we hope to establish the relevance of the discipline of political science not only to theory-building in social science but also to sound, reliable understanding of politics on the part of concerned citizens.

WILLIAM A. WELSH

Public Policy-Making

1. The Study of Public Policy

As a consequence of American military intervention in Southeast Asia during the 1960's and early 1970's, more than 45,000 American soldiers lost their lives, many thousands more were wounded, and tens of billions of dollars were expended on the Indochina war effort. Protests and demonstrations against the war occurred, many young men went to prison or to Canada to avoid being drafted, and cynicism and distrust toward government increased. It is really difficult to estimate the impact that American Southeast Asia policy has had on the United States, let alone Southeast Asia and the rest of the world.

As a consequence of the Nixon Administration's policies following the development of the energy crisis, gasoline prices rose sharply and many motorists spent hours waiting in lines to purchase fuel. Whether rationing and price controls would have produced more satisfactory results is certainly open to argument. The point is, however, that what happened was not "natural," was not simply a matter of events following their normal course; public policy gave shape to the events that occurred.

In our daily lives and in our academic activities, such as political science courses, we make many references to public policy. The term may be used quite broadly, as in "American foreign policy," "Soviet economic policy," or "agricultural policy in Western Europe." It may also be employed with more specific referents, as when we speak of the national government's policy toward conglomerate mergers, the state policy of Texas on farm-to-market roads, or the policy of New York City on snow removal. Although public policy may seem rather abstract or we may think of it as something that "happens" to someone else, this is clearly not the case, as the preceding two examples should indicate. All of us are profoundly affected by a myriad of public policies in our daily lives.

Generally, the term "policy" is used to designate the behavior of some actor (e.g., an official, a group, a government agency) or set of actors in a given area of activity. Such usage may be adequate for ordinary speech, but, since the concern in this book is with the systematic analysis of public policy and its formation, we need a more precise definition, or concept, of public policy in order to communicate more effectively with one another.

WHAT IS PUBLIC POLICY?

The literature of political science is full of definitions of public policy. Sooner or later, it seems, almost everyone gives in to the urge to define public policy and does so with greater or lesser success in the eyes of his critics. A few such definitions will be noted and their utility for analysis remarked upon. To be really useful and to facilitate communication, an operational definition (or concept, as I am using the two words somewhat interchangeably) should indicate the essential characteristics of the concept under discussion.

One definition of public policy holds that, "broadly defined," it is "the relationship of a government unit to its environment."[1] Such a definition is so broad as to leave most students uncertain of its meaning; it could encompass almost anything. Another definition states that "public policy is whatever governments choose to do or not to do."[2] There is a rough accuracy to this definition, but it does not adequately recognize that there may be a divergence between what governments decide to do and what they actually do. Moreover, it could be taken to include such actions as personnel appointments or grants of licenses, which are usually not thought of as policy matters. Richard Rose has suggested that policy be considered "a long series of more-or-less related activities" and their consequences for those concerned rather than as a discrete decision.[3] Though somewhat ambiguous, Rose's definition nonetheless embodies the useful notion that policy is a course or pattern of activity and not simply a decision to do something. Finally, let us note Carl Friedrich's definition. He regards policy as

. . . a proposed course of action of a person, group, or government within a given environment providing obstacles and opportunities which the policy was proposed to utilize and overcome in an effort to reach a goal or realize an objective or a purpose.[4]

To the notion of policy as a course of action, Friedrich adds the requirement that policy is directed toward the accomplishment of some purpose or goal. Although the purpose or goal of government actions may not always be easy to discern, the idea that policy involves purposive behavior seems a necessary part of a policy definition. Policy, however, should designate what is actually done rather than what is proposed in the way of action on some matter.

Taking into account the problems raised by these definitions, we offer the following as a useful concept of policy: *A purposive course of action followed by an actor or set of actors in dealing with a problem or matter of concern.* This concept of policy focuses attention on what is actually done as against what is proposed or intended, and it differentiates a policy from a decision, which is a choice among competing alternatives.

Public policies are those policies developed by governmental bodies and officials. (Nongovernmental actors and factors may, of course, influence policy development.) The special characteristics of public policies stem from the fact that they are formulated by what David Easton has called the "authorities" in a political system, namely, "elders, paramount chiefs, executives, legislators, judges, administrators, councilors, monarchs, and the like." These are, he says, the persons who "engage in the daily affairs of a political system," are "recognized by most members of the system as having responsibility for these matters," and take actions that are "accepted as binding most of the time by most of the members so long as they act within the limits of their roles."[5]

At this point it would be well to spell out some of the implications of our concept of public policy. First of all, purposive or goal-oriented action rather than random or chance behavior is our concern. Public policies in modern political systems are not, by and large, things that just happen. Second, policy consists of courses or patterns of action by governmental officials rather than their separate discrete decisions. For example, policy involves not only the decision to enact a law on some topic but also subsequent decisions relating to its implementation and enforcement. Third, policy is what governments actually do in regulating trade, controlling inflation, or promoting public housing, not what they intend to do or say they are going to do. If a legislature enacts a law requiring employers to pay no less than the stated minimum wage but nothing is done to enforce the law, and consequently no change occurs in economic behavior, then it is fair to contend that public policy in this instance is really one of nonregulation of wages. It seems nonsensical to regard an intention as policy without regard for what subsequently happens. Fourth, public policy may be either positive or negative in form. Positively, it may involve some form of government action to affect a particular problem; negatively, it involves a decision by government officials not to take action, to do nothing, on some matter on which governmental involvement is sought. Governments, in other words, can follow a policy of *laissez faire,* or hands off, either generally or in particular areas. Such inaction may have major consequences for a society or some of its groups. Lastly, public policy, at least in its positive form, is based on law and is authoritative. Members of a society accept as legitimate that taxes must be paid, import controls obeyed, and antitrust laws complied with unless one wants to run the risk of fines, jail sentences, or other legally imposed sanctions or disabilities. Public policy thus has an authoritative, potentially legally coercive quality that the policies of private organizations do not have.

The nature of public policy as a course of action can be better or more fully understood if it is broken down into a number of categories, these being policy demands, decisions, statements, outputs, and outcomes. In practice they will not necessarily occur in neat sequential order.

Policy demands are those demands or claims made upon public officials by other actors, private or official, in the political system for action or inaction on some perceived problem. Such demands may range from a general insistence that government ought to "do something" to a proposal for specific action on the matter. For instance, prior to the passage of the Landrum-Griffin Act of 1959 (formally, the Labor-Management Reporting and Disclosure Act), some groups merely voiced a general desire for curbs on the power of labor unions; others called for the prohibition of particular union practices they found objectionable.[6] The demands that help give rise to public policy, and which it is designed to satisfy, at least in part, are important items for consideration in the study of public policy formation.

Policy decisions are decisions made by public officials that authorize or give direction and content to public policy actions. Included are decisions to enact statutes, issue executive orders or edicts, promulgate administrative rules, or make important judicial interpretations of laws. Thus, the decision by Congress to enact the Sherman Antitrust Act in 1890 was a policy decision; so was the ruling of the Supreme Court in 1911 that the Act prohibited only unreasonable restraints of trade rather than all restraints of trade. Each was of major importance in shaping that course of action called antitrust policy. Such decisions may be contrasted with the large numbers of relatively routine decisions made by officials in the day-to-day application of public policy. The Veterans Administration makes hundreds of thousands of decisions every year on veterans' benefits; most, however, fall within the bounds of settled policy.

Policy statements are the formal expressions or articulations of public policy. Included are legislative statutes, executive orders and decrees, administrative rules and regulations, and court opinions, as well as statements and speeches by public officials indicating the intentions and goals of government and what will be done to realize them. Policy statements are sometimes ambiguous. Witness the conflicts that arise over the meaning of statutory provisions or judicial holdings, or the time and effort expended analyzing and trying to divine the meaning of policy statements made by national political leaders such as the President of the United States or France or the rulers of the Soviet Union. Also, different levels, branches, or units of government may issue conflicting policy statements, as on environmental pollution controls or energy usage.

Policy outputs are the "tangible manifestations" of public policies, the things actually done in pursuance of policy decisions and statements. Simply stated, policy outputs are what a government does, as distinguished from what it says it is going to do. Here our attention is focused on such matters as taxes collected, highways built, welfare benefits paid, restraints of trade eliminated, ports blockaded, or foreign-aid projects undertaken. An examination of policy outputs may indicate that policy in actuality is somewhat or greatly different from what policy statements indicate it should be. Many laws on the statute books, such as local "blue laws" regulating work and amusements on Sundays, go entirely unenforced and thus policy is clearly not what the law states in such instances.

Policy outcomes are the consequences for society, intended or unintended, that flow from action or inaction by government. Welfare policies in the United States can be used to illustrate this concept. It is fairly easy to measure welfare policy outputs—amount of benefits paid, average level of benefits, number of people aided, and the like. But what are the outcomes (or consequences) of these actions? Do they increase personal security and contentment? Do they reduce individual initiative? In the case of aid to families with dependent children (AFDC), do they have the effect of encouraging promiscuity and illegitimacy, as some allege? Questions such as these may be quite difficult to answer, but they direct our attention to the impact of public policies, an item that should be of central concern to us as policy analysts. Among other things, we want to know whether policies accomplish what they are intended to accomplish. This is the task of policy evaluation that will be discussed in a later chapter.

WHY STUDY PUBLIC POLICY?

Political scientists, in their teaching and research, have customarily been most concerned with political processes, such as the legislative or electoral process, or with elements of the political system, such as interest groups or public opinion. This is not to say, however, that political scientists have been unconcerned with policy. Foreign policy and policy relating to civil rights and liberties have attracted much attention. So has what Robert Salisbury calls constitutional policy, that is, "decisional rules by which subsequent policy actions are to be determined."[7] Illustrative of the procedural and structural "givens" that make up constitutional policy are legislative apportionment, the use of the city-manager form of government, and federalism. Each helps to shape decisions or substantive policy. Also, some political scientists with a normative bent manifest concern with what governments *should* do, with "proper" or "correct" public policy. Their value-oriented approach, however, has placed them outside the mainstream of political science in recent decades because political science as a "science" is supposed to be value-free. We will return to this particular matter a little later on.

Currently, political scientists are giving increased attention to the study of public policy—to the description, analysis, and explanation of the causes and effects of governmental activity. As Thomas Dye aptly states:

This involves a description of the content of public policy; an assessment of the impact of environmental forces on the content of public policy; an analysis of the effect of various institutional arrangements and political processes on public policy; an inquiry into the consequences of various public policies for the political system; and an evaluation of the impact of public policies on society, both in terms of expected and unexpected consequences.[8]

One is thus directed to seek answers to such questions as: What is the actual content of antitrust policy? What effects do urbanization and industrialization have on welfare policies? How does the organization of Congress help shape agricultural policy? Do elections affect the direction of public policies? Do welfare programs contribute to political quiescence or stability? Who is benefited and who is not by current tax policies or urban renewal programs?

This leads us to the question posed in the heading of this section: Why study public policy? Or to put it another way: Why engage in policy analysis? It has been suggested that policy can be studied for scientific, professional, or political reasons.[9]

Scientific Reasons. Public policy can be studied in order to gain greater knowledge about its origins, the processes by which it is developed, and its consequences for society. This, in turn, will increase our understanding of the political system and society generally. Policy may be regarded as either a dependent or an independent variable for purposes of this kind of analysis. When it is viewed as a *dependent variable,* our attention is placed on the political and environmental factors that help determine the content of policy. For example, how is policy affected by the distribution of power among pressure groups and governmental agencies? How do urbanization and national income help shape the content of policy? If public policy is viewed as an *independent variable,* our focus shifts to the impact of policy on the political system and environment. How does policy affect support for the political system or future policy choices? What effect does policy have on social well-being?

Professional Reasons. Don K. Price makes a distinction between the "scientific estate," which seeks only to discover knowledge, and the "professional estate," which strives to apply scientific knowledge to the solution of practical social problems.[10] We will not concern ourselves here with the issue of whether political scientists should help prescribe the goals of public policy. Although by no means all political scientists would agree, many argue that political scientists as political scientists have no particular skills beyond those of laymen for this endeavor. Whatever the answer here may be, it is quite correct to contend that if we know something about the factors that help shape public policy, or the consequences of given policies, then we are in position to say something useful concerning how individuals, groups, or governments can act to attain their policy goals. Such advice can be directed toward indicating either what policies can be used to achieve particular goals or what political and environmental factors are conducive to the development of a given policy. It puts us in the position of saying, for example, *if* you want to prevent economic monopoly, *then* you should do such and such. Questions of this sort are factual in nature and are open to, indeed require, scientific study. Certainly factual knowledge is a prerequisite for prescribing on, and dealing with, the problems of society.

Political Reasons. As was noted above, at least some political scientists do not believe that political scientists should refrain from helping to prescribe policy goals. Rather, they say that the study of public policy should be directed toward ensuring that governments adopt appropriate policies to attain the "right" goals. They reject the notion that policy analysts should strive to be value-free, contending that political science cannot be silent or impotent on current political and social problems. They want to improve the quality of public policy in ways they deem desirable, notwithstanding that substantial disagreement exists in society over what constitute "correct" policies or the "right" goals of policy. The efforts of these political scientists usually generate both heat and light in some proportion.

We should now explicitly distinguish between *policy analysis* and *policy advocacy.* Policy analysis is concerned with the examination and description of the causes and consequences of public policy. We can analyze the formation, content, and impact of particular policies, such as on civil rights or international trade, without either approving or disapproving of them. *Policy advocacy,* on the other hand, is concerned especially with what governments *should* do, with the promotion of particular policies through discussion, persuasion, and political activism. The candidate for public office serves as a good prototype of the policy advocate. Richard Nixon and George McGovern as Presidential candidates in 1972 each had his notions of what the government should do in foreign and domestic policy. In this book the focus will be on policy analysis.

To conclude this discussion we shall again call on Professor Dye, who states that policy analysis encompasses three basic considerations:

1. A primary concern with explanation rather than prescription.
2. A rigorous search for the causes and consequences of public policies [through] the use of scientific standards of inference.
3. An effort to develop and test general propositions about the causes and consequences of public policy and to accumulate reliable research findings of general significance. The object is to develop general theories about public policy which are reliable and which apply to different governmental agencies and different policy areas.[11]

So conceived, policy analysis can be both scientific and "relevant" to current political and social problems. Analysts with normative orientations do not have a corner on relevance.

THEORIES OF DECISION-MAKING

Political and social scientists have developed many models, theories, approaches, concepts, and schemes for the analysis of policy-making and its component, decision-making. Indeed, political scientists have often shown much more facility and verve for theorizing about public policy than for actually studying policy. Nonetheless, concepts and models are necessary and useful to guide policy analysis, as they help clarify and direct our inquiry on policy-making, facilitate communication, and suggest possible explanations for policy actions. Clearly, when we set out to study policy we need some guidelines, some criteria of relevance, to focus our efforts and to prevent aimless meandering through the fields of political data. What we find depends partly upon what we are looking for; policy concepts and theories give direction to our inquiry.

In this and the subsequent section, we will examine a number of concepts and models for the study of public policy, without trying to determine which is "best." Before doing this we need to distinguish between decision-making and policy-making, something that is not always done with clarity, if at all, by students of public policy. Decision-making involves the choice of an alternative from among a series of competing alternatives. Theories of decision-making are concerned with how such choices are made. A policy, to recall our earlier definition, is "a purposive course of action followed by an actor or set of actors in dealing with a problem or matter of concern." Policy-making typically involves a pattern of action, extending over time and involving many decisions, some routine and some not so routine. Rarely will a policy be synonymous with a single decision. To use a mundane example: A person is not accurate in saying it is his policy to bathe on Saturday night when, in fact, he bathes only with great infrequency, however elegant the decision-making process that results in his doing so on a particular Saturday. It is the course of action that defines policy, not the isolated event, and in this example the policy involved is essentially one of not bathing.

Three theories of decision-making that focus on the steps or activities involved in making a decision will be discussed here. To the extent that they describe how decisions are made by individuals and groups, they are empirical. Viewed as statements of how decisions should be made, they are normative. It is not always easy to separate these two qualities in decision theories, as one will discover.

The Rational-Comprehensive Theory

Perhaps the best-known theory of decision-making, and also perhaps the most widely accepted, is the rational-comprehensive theory. It usually includes the following elements:

1. The decision-maker is confronted with a given problem that can be separated from other problems or at least considered meaningfully in comparison with them.

2. The goals, values, or objectives that guide the decision-maker are clarified and ranked according to their importance.

3. The various alternatives for dealing with the problem are examined.

4. The consequences (costs and benefits) that would follow from the selection of each alternative are investigated.

5. Each alternative, and its attendant consequences, can be compared with the other alternatives.

6. The decision-maker will choose that alternative, and its consequences, that maximizes the attainment of his goals, values, or objectives.

The result of this process is a rational decision, that is, one that most effectively achieves a given end.

The rational-comprehensive theory has had substantial criticism directed at it. Charles Lindblom contends that decision-makers are not faced with concrete, clearly defined problems. Rather, they have first of all to identify and formulate the problems on which they make decisions. For example, when prices are rising rapidly and people are saying "we must do something about the problem of inflation," what is the problem? Excessive demand? Inadequate production of goods and services? Administered prices by powerful corporations and unions? Inflationary psychology? Some combination of these? One does not, willy-nilly, attack inflation but the causes of inflation, and these may be difficult to determine. Defining the problem is, in short, often a major problem for the decision-maker.

A second criticism holds that rational-comprehensive theory is unrealistic in the demands it makes on the decision-maker. It assumes that he will have enough information on the alternatives for dealing with a problem, that he will be able to predict their consequences with some accuracy, and that he will be capable of making correct cost-benefit comparisons of the alternatives. A moment's reflection on the informational and intellectual resources needed for acting rationally on the problem of inflation posed above should indicate the barriers to rational action implied in these assumptions —lack of time, difficulty in collecting information and predicting the future, complexity of calculations. Even use of that modern miracle, the computer, cannot fully alleviate these problems.

The value aspect of the rational theory also receives some knocks. Thus it is said that the public decision-maker is usually confronted with a situation in which value conflict rather than agreement exists, and the conflicting values do not permit comparison or weighting. Moreover, the decision-maker might confuse his personal values with those of the public. And, finally, the rationalistic assumption that facts and values can be readily separated does not hold up in practice. Note how facts and values become intermingled in the following situation:

> Public controversy . . . has surrounded the proposal to construct a branch of the Cook County Hospital on the South Side in or near the Negro area. Several questions of policy are involved in the matter but the ones which have caused one of the few public debates of an issue

in the Negro community concern whether, or to what extent, building such a branch would result in an all-Negro or "Jim Crow" hospital and whether such a hospital is desirable as a means of providing added medical facilities for Negro patients. Involved are both an issue of *fact* (whether the hospital would be segregated, intentionally or unintentionally, as a result of the character of the neighborhood in which it would be located) and an issue of *value* (whether even an all-Negro hospital would be preferable to no hospital at all in the area). In reality, however, the factions have aligned themselves in such a manner that the fact issue and the value issue have been collapsed into the single issue of whether to build or not to build. Those in favor of the proposal will argue that the facts do not bear out the charge of "Jim Crowism"—"the proposed site . . . is not considered to be placed in a segregated area for the exclusive use of one racial or minority group"; or "no responsible officials would try to develop a new hospital to further segregation"; or "establishing a branch hospital for the . . . more adequate care of the indigent patient load . . . does not represent Jim Crowism." At the same time these proponents argue that, whatever the facts, the factual issue is secondary to the overriding consideration that "there is a here-and-now need for more hospital beds. . . . Integration may be the long-run goal, but in the short-run we need more facilities."[12]

Finally, there is the problem of "sunk costs." Previous decisions and commitments, investments in existing policies and programs, may foreclose many alternatives from consideration on either a short-run or a long-run basis. A decision to institute a system of socialized medicine represents a commitment to a particular mode of medical care that is not easily reversed or significantly altered in the future. An airport, once constructed, cannot be easily moved to the other side of town.

The Incremental Theory

The incremental theory of decision-making, or, more simply, incrementalism, is presented as a decision theory that avoids many of the problems of the rational-comprehensive theory and, at the same time, is more descriptive of the way in which public officials actually make decisions.[13] Incrementalism can be summarized in the following manner:

1. The selection of goals or objectives and the empirical analysis of the action needed to attain them are closely intertwined with, rather than distinct from, one another.

2. The decision-maker considers only some of the alternatives for dealing with a problem, and these will differ only incrementally (i.e., marginally) from existing policies.

3. For each alternative only a limited number of "important" consequences are evaluated.

4. The problem confronting the decision-maker is continually redefined. Incrementalism allows for countless ends-means and means-ends adjustments that have the effect of making the problem more manageable.

5. There is no single decision or "right" solution for a problem. The test of a good decision is that various analysts find themselves directly agreeing on it, without agreeing that the decision is the most appropriate means to an agreed objective.

6. Incremental decision-making is essentially remedial and is geared more to the amelioration of present, concrete social imperfections than to the promotion of future social goals.[14]

Lindblom contends that incrementalism represents the typical decision-making process in pluralist societies such as the United States. Decisions and policies are the product of "give and take" and mutual consent among numerous participants ("partisans") in the decision process. Incrementalism is politically expedient because it is easier to reach agreement when the matters in dispute among various groups are only modifications of existing programs rather than policy issues of great magnitude or an "all or nothing" character. Since decision-makers operate under conditions of uncertainty with regard to the future consequences of their actions, incremental decisions reduce the risks and costs of uncertainty. Incrementalism is also realistic because it recognizes that decision-makers lack the time, intelligence, and other resources needed to engage in comprehensive analysis of all alternative solutions to existing problems. Moreover, people are essentially pragmatic, seeking not always the single best way to deal with a problem but, more modestly, "something that will work." Incrementalism, in short, yields limited, practicable, acceptable decisions.

Mixed-Scanning

Sociologist Amatai Etzioni agrees with the criticism of the rational theory but also suggests there are some shortcomings in the incremental theory of decision-making.[15] For instance, decisions made by incrementalists would reflect the interests of the most powerful and organized interests in society, while the interests of the underprivileged and politically unorganized would be neglected. Moreover, by focusing on the short-run and seeking only limited variations in current policies, incrementalism would neglect basic social innovation. Great or fundamental decisions, such as declaration of war, do not come within the ambit of incrementalism. Although limited in number, fundamental decisions are highly significant and often provide the context for numerous incremental decisions.

Etzioni presents mixed-scanning as an approach to decision-making, which takes into account both fundamental and incremental decisions and provides for "high-order, fundamental policy-making processes which set basic directions and . . . incremental processes which prepare for fundamental decisions and work them out after they have been reached." He provides the following illustration of mixed-scanning:

> Assume we are about to set up a worldwide weather observation system using weather satellites. The rationalistic approach would seek an exhaustive survey of weather conditions by using cameras capable of detailed observations and by scheduling reviews of the entire sky as often as possible. This would yield an avalanche of details, costly to analyze and likely to overwhelm our action capacities (e.g., "seeding" cloud formations that could develop into hurricanes or bring rain to arid areas). Incrementalism would focus on those areas in which similar patterns developed in the recent past and, perhaps, on a few nearby regions; it would thus ignore all formations which might deserve attention if they arose in unexpected areas.
>
> A mixed-scanning strategy would include elements of both approaches by employing two cameras: a broad-angle camera that would cover all parts of the sky but not in great detail, and a second one which would zero in on those areas revealed by the first camera to require a more in-depth examination. While mixed-scanning might miss areas in which only a detailed camera could reveal trouble, it is less likely than incrementalism to miss obvious trouble spots in unfamiliar areas.[16]

Mixed-scanning permits decision-makers to utilize both the rational-comprehensive and incremental theories in different situations. In some instances, incrementalism will be adequate; in others, a more thorough approach along rational-comprehensive lines will be needed. Mixed-scanning also takes into account differing capacities of decision-makers. Generally speaking, the greater the capacity of decision-makers to mobilize power to implement their decisions, the more scanning they can realistically engage in; and the more encompassing is scanning, the more effective is decision-making.

Mixed-scanning is thus a kind of "compromise" approach that combines use of incrementalism and rationalism. It is not really clear from Etzioni's discussion, however, just how it would operate in practice. This is something on which the reader can ponder and speculate. Certainly, though, Etzioni does help alert us to the significant facts that decisions vary in their magnitude (e.g., scope, impact) and that different decision processes may be appropriate as the nature of decisions varies.

A Note on Decision Criteria

Whether the decision process they select is rational-comprehensive, incremental, or mixed-scanning in nature, those who make choices among alternatives must have some basis for doing so. While some "decisions" may be the product of chance, inadvertence, random selection, or inaction that permits particular actions to prevail, most decisions will involve conscious choice. The question then becomes: What kinds of criteria (values or standards) influence the actions of decision-makers? Of course, many factors appear to impinge upon political decision-makers—political and social pressures, economic conditions, procedural requirements (e.g., due process), previous commitments, the pressure of time, and so on. In our concern with these, however, we should be careful not to neglect the values of the decision-maker himself, notwithstanding that they may be difficult to determine and impossible to isolate in many instances.

Most of the values that may serve to guide the behavior of decision-makers may be summarized in four categories.

Political Values. The decision-maker may evaluate policy alternatives in terms of their import for his political party or the clientele groups of his agency. Decisions are made on the basis of political advantage, with policies being viewed as means for the advancement or achievement of political party or interest group goals. Political scientists have often studied and evaluated policy-making from this perspective. Particular decisions will be "explained" as being made for the benefit, say, of organized labor, wheat farmers, or a given political party. The decision of the Eisenhower Administration to raise farm-price supports just prior to the 1956 Presidential election did appear to have a partisan hue. So did the enthusiasm of many congressional Democrats for campaign finance reform, including expenditure limits, prior to the 1972 election campaigns.

Organization Values. Decision-makers, especially bureaucrats, may also be influenced by organizational values. Organizations, such as administrative agencies, utilize many rewards and sanctions in an effort to induce their members to accept, and act on the basis of, organizationally determined values. To the extent this occurs, the individual's decisions may be guided by such considerations as the desires to see his organization survive, to enhance or expand its programs and activities, or to maintain its power and prerogatives. Many bureaucratic struggles between rival agencies, such as the Army Corps of Engineers and the Bureau of Reclamation in the water-resource policy area, stem from their desire to protect or expand their programs and activities.

Personal Values. The urge to protect or promote one's physical or financial well-being, reputation, or historical position may also serve as a decision criterion. The politician who accepts a bribe to make a particular decision, such as the award of a license or contract, obviously has personal benefit in mind. On a different plane, the President who says he is not going to be "the first President to lose a war," and who acts accordingly, is also being influenced by personal considerations, such as concern for his "place in history."

Policy Values. Neither the discussion to this point nor cynicism should lead us to conclude that political decision-makers are influenced only by considerations of political, organizational, or personal benefit. Decision-makers may well act on the basis of their perceptions of the public interest or beliefs concerning what is proper or morally correct public policy. A legislator who votes in favor of civil rights legislation may well do so because he believes it is morally correct and that equality is a desirable goal of public policy, notwithstanding that his vote may cause him some political risk. Studies of the Supreme Court indicate that the justices are influenced by policy values in deciding cases.[17]

Ideological Values. Ideologies are sets of logically related values

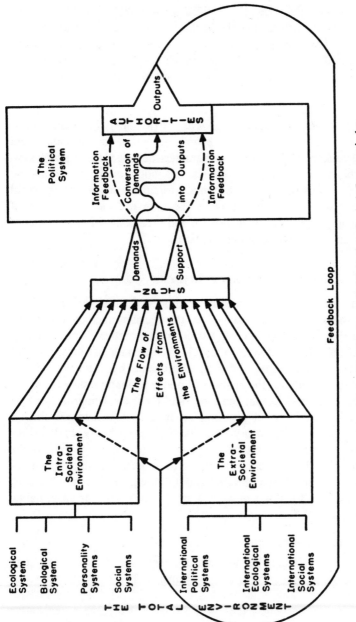

Easton's "Dynamic Response" Model of a Political System. From *A Framework for Political Analysis* (Englewood Cliffs, N.J.: Prentice-Hall, 1965), p. 110.

and beliefs which present simplified pictures of the world and serve as guides to action for people. In the Soviet Union, Marxist-Leninist ideology has served at least in part as a set of prescriptions for social and economic change. Although the Soviets have sometimes departed from Marxist-Leninist ideology, as in the use of economic incentives to increase production, it still serves as a means for rationalizing and legitimizing policy actions by the regime. In many of the developing countries in Asia, Africa, and the Middle East, nationalism—the desire of a people or nation for autonomy and deep concern with their own characteristics, needs and problems— has been an important factor shaping both foreign and domestic policies. Nationalism has become particularly important in world politics in the twentieth century, because it fueled the desire of colonial peoples for independence and created and intensified con- flicts among both old and new nations.

Some Approaches to Policy Analysis

Just as political scientists have created theories and models to help them understand and explain the decision-making process, so have they also developed a variety of theoretical approaches to assist them in the study of the political behavior of entire political systems. Although most of these approaches have not been devel- oped specifically for the analysis of policy formation, they can read- ily be converted to that purpose. The theoretical approaches that will come under brief examination here include systems theory, group theory, elite theory, functional process theory, and institu- tionalism. Such theoretical approaches are useful in, and to the extent, that they direct our attention to important political phenom- ena, help clarify and simplify our thinking, and suggest possible explanations for political activity or, in our particular case, public policy.

Political Systems Theory

Public policy may be viewed as the response of a political system to demands arising from its environment. The *political system,* as defined by Easton, is composed of those identifiable and interre- lated institutions and activities in a society that make authoritative decisions (or allocations of values) that are binding on society.[18] *Inputs* into the political system from the environment consist of demands and supports. The *environment* consists of all those conditions and events external to the boundaries of the political system. *Demands* are the claims made by individuals and groups on the political system for action to satisfy their interests. *Support* is rendered when groups and individuals abide by election results, pay taxes, obey laws, and otherwise accept the decisions and actions of the authoritative political system made in response to demands. These authoritative allocations of values constitute public policy. The concept of *feedback* indicates that public policies (or outputs) may subsequently alter the environment and the demands generated therein, as well as the character of the political system itself. Policy outputs may produce new demands, which lead to further policy outputs, and so on in a continuing, never ending flow of public policy.

The usefulness of systems theory for the study of public policy is limited by its highly general nature. It does not, moreover, say much concerning how decisions are made and policy is developed within the "black box" called the political system. Nonetheless, systems theory is a useful aid in organizing our inquiry into policy formation. It also alerts us to some significant aspects of the political process, such as: How do environmental inputs affect the content of public policy and the nature of the political system? How does public policy affect the environment and subsequent demands for action? What forces or factors in the environment act to generate demands upon the political system? How is the political system able to convert demands into public policy and preserve itself over time?

Group Theory

According to the group theory of politics, public policy is the product of the group struggle. As one writer states: "What may be called public policy is the equilibrium reached in this [group] struggle at any given moment, and it represents a balance which the contending factions or groups constantly strive to weight in their favor."[19]

Group theory rests on the contention that interaction and struggle among groups is the central fact of political life. A group is a collection of individuals that may, on the basis of shared attitudes or interests, make claims upon other groups in society. It becomes a political interest group "when it makes a claim through or upon any of the institutions of government."[20] And, of course, many groups do just that. The individual is significant in politics only as he is a participant in, or a representative of, groups. It is through groups that individuals seek to secure their political preferences.

Public policy, at any given time, will reflect the interests of dominant groups. As groups gain and lose power and influence, public policy will be altered in favor of the interests of those gaining influence against the interests of those losing influence.

The role of government ("official groups") in policy formation has been described in the following manner by one proponent of group theory:

> The legislature referees the group struggle, ratifies the victories of the successful coalitions, and records the terms of the surrenders, compromises, and conquests in the form of statutes. Every statute tends to represent compromises because the process of accommodating conflicts of group interests is one of deliberation and consent. The legislative vote on any issue tends to represent the composition of strength, i.e., the balance of power, among the contending groups at the moment of voting. . . . Administrative agencies of the regulatory kind are established to carry out the terms of the treaties that the legislators have negotiated and ratified. . . . The judiciary, like the civilian bureaucracy, is one of the instrumentalities for the administration of the agreed rules.[21]

Group theory, while focusing attention on one of the major dynamic elements in policy formation, especially in pluralist societies such as the United States, seems both to overstate the importance of groups and to understate the independent and creative role that public officials play in the policy process. Indeed, many groups have been generated by public policy. The American Farm Bureau Federation, which developed around the agricultural extension program, is a notable example, as is the National Welfare Rights Organization. Public officials also may acquire a stake in particular programs and act as an interest group in support of their continuance. In the United States some welfare agency employees, including social workers, prefer current programs, with their emphasis on supervision and services (as well as benefits), to a guaranteed annual income, which would probably eliminate some of their jobs. In the Soviet Union, the bureaucracy has even been depicted as a "new class" that benefits from and supports the current system of state planning and controls.

Finally, we should note that it is rather misleading and inefficient to try to explain politics, or policy formation in terms of group struggle without giving attention to the many other factors—for example, ideas and institutions—that abound. This sort of reductionism, or unicausal explanation, should be avoided.

Elite Theory

Approached from the perspective of elite theory, public policy can be regarded as the values and preferences of a governing elite. The essential argument of elite theory is that it is not the people or the "masses" who determine public policy through their demands and action; rather, public policy is decided by a ruling elite and carried into effect by public officials and agencies.

Thomas Dye and Harmon Zeigler, in *The Irony of Democracy,* provide a summary of elite theory:

1. Society is divided into the few who have power and the many who do not. Only a small number of persons allocate values for society; the masses do not decide public policy.

2. The few who govern are not typical of the masses who are governed. Elites are drawn disproportionately from the upper socioeconomic strata of society.

3. The movement of non-elites to elite positions must be slow and continuous to maintain stability and avoid revolution. Only non-elites who have accepted the basic elite consensus can be admitted to governing circles.

4. Elites share a consensus on the basic values of the social system and the preservation of the system. [In the United States, the elite consensus includes private enterprise, private property, limited government, and individual liberty.]

5. Public policy does not reflect demands of the masses but rather the prevailing values of the elite. Changes in public policy will be incremental rather than revolutionary. [Incremental changes permit responses to events that threaten a social system with a minimum of alteration or dislocation of the system.]

6. Active elites are subject to relatively little direct influence from apathetic masses. Elites influence masses more than masses influence elites.[22]

So stated elite theory is a rather provocative theory of policy formation. Policy is the product of elites, reflecting their values and serving their ends, one of which may be a desire to provide for the welfare of the masses. Thomas Dye has argued that development of civil rights policies in the United States during the 1960's can be suitably explained through the use of elite theory. These policies were "a response of a national elite to conditions affecting a small minority of Americans rather than a response of national leaders to majority sentiments." Thus, for example, the "elimination of legal discrimination and the guarantee of equality of opportunity in the Civil Rights Act of 1964 was achieved largely through the dramatic appeals of middle-class black leaders to the conscience of white elites."[23]

Elite theory does focus our attention on the role of leadership in policy formation and on the fact that, in any political system, a few govern the many. Whether the elites rule, and determine policy, with little influence by the masses is a difficult proposition to handle. It cannot be proved merely by assertions that the "establishment runs things," which has been a familiar plaint in recent years. Political scientist Robert Dahl argues that to defend the proposition successfully one must identify "a controlling group, less than a majority in size, that is not a pure artifact of democratic rules; . . . a minority of individuals whose preferences regularly prevail in cases of differences of preferences on key political issues."[24] It may be that elite theory has more utility for the analysis and explanation of policy formation in some political systems, such as developing or Communist-bloc countries, than in others, such as the pluralist democracies of the United States and Canada.

Functional Process Theory

Another way to approach the study of policy formation is to focus on the various functional activities that occur in the policy process. Harold Lasswell has presented a scheme involving seven categories of functional analysis that will serve as the basis for discussion here.[25]

1. *Intelligence:* How is the information on policy matters that comes to the attention of policy-makers gathered and processed?

2. *Recommendation:* How are recommendations (or alternatives) for dealing with a given issue made and promoted?

3. *Prescription:* How are general rules adopted or enacted, and by whom?

4. *Invocation:* Who determines whether given behavior contravenes rules or laws and demands application of rules or laws thereto?

5. *Application:* How are laws or rules actually applied or enforced?

6. *Appraisal:* How is the operation of policies, their success or failure, appraised?

7. *Termination:* How are the original rules or laws terminated or continued in modified or changed form?

Although Lasswell refers to this as the "decision process," it goes beyond the making of a particular choice and really involves "the course of action on some matter" definition of policy that was presented earlier in the chapter. In the later stages of the process, policy-makers may seek and utilize new information in order to change the original policy process.

This scheme of analysis is not tied to particular institutions or political arrangements and lends itself readily to comparative analysis of policy formation. One can inquire how these different functions are performed, to what effect, and by whom in different political systems or government units, for that matter. Its emphasis on functional categories, however, may lead to neglect of the politics of policy formation and the effect of environmental variables on the process. Obviously, policy formation is more than an intellectual process.

Institutionalism

The study of government institutions is one of the oldest concerns of political science. Political life generally revolves around governmental institutions such as legislatures, executives, courts, and political parties; public policy, moreover, is initially authoritatively determined and implemented by governmental institutions. It is not surprising, then, that political scientists would devote much attention to them.

Traditionally, the institutional approach concentrated on describing the more formal and legal aspects of governmental institutions

—their formal organization, legal powers, procedural rules, and functions or activities. Formal relationships with other institutions might also be considered. Usually little was done to explain how institutions actually operated, as apart from how they were supposed to operate, to analyze public policies produced by institutions, or to try to discover the relationships between institutional structure and public politics.

Subsequently, we should note, political scientists turned their attention in teaching and research to the political processes within governmental or political institutions, concentrating on the behavior of participants in the process and on political realities rather than formalism. To use the legislature as an example, concern shifted from simply describing the legislature as an institution to analyzing and explaining its operation over time, from its static to its dynamic aspects. In the curriculum the course on the "legislature" often became one on the "legislative process."

Institutionalism, with its emphasis on the formal or structural aspects of institutions, can nonetheless be usefully employed in policy analysis. An institution is a set of regularized patterns of human behavior that persist over time. (Some people, unsophisticated of course, seem to equate institutions with the physical structures in which they exist.) It is their differing sets of behavior patterns that really distinguish courts from legislatures, from administrative agencies, and so on. These regularized patterns of behavior, which we often call rules, structures, and the like, can affect decision-making and the content of public policy. Rules and structural arrangements are usually not neutral in their impact; rather, they tend to favor some interests in society over others, some policy results rather than others. For example, it is contended that some of the rules (and traditions, which often have the effect of rules) of the Senate, such as those relating to unlimited debate and action by unanimous consent, favor the interests of minorities over majorities. In a federal system, which disperses power among different levels of government, some groups may have more influence if policy is made at the national level, other groups may benefit more if policy is made at the state or provincial level. Civil rights groups in the United States during the 1960's received a better response in Washington, D.C., than they did in Montgomery, Alabama, or Columbia, South Carolina, for example.

In summary, institutional structures, arrangements, and procedures can have a significant impact on public policy and should not be ignored in policy analysis. Neither should analysis of them, without concern for the dynamic aspects of politics, be considered adequate.

Although individual political scientists often manifest a preference for one or another of these or other theoretical approaches, it is not really possible to say which is the "best" or most satisfactory. Each focuses attention on different aspects of politics and policy-making and seems more useful for some purposes or some situations than others. Generally, one should not permit oneself to be bound too rigidly or dogmatically to a particular model or theoretical approach. A good rule is to be eclectic and flexible and use those theories as organizing concepts that seem most useful for the satisfactory analysis and explanation of a particular public policy or political action. It is my belief that the explanation of political behavior, rather than the validation of a given theoretical approach, should be the main purpose of political inquiry and analysis. Each of the theoretical approaches discussed in this section can contribute to our understanding of policy-making.

THE PLAN OF THIS BOOK

At this point it seems fair to give the reader some idea of what to expect in the remainder of the book. Our central concern will be with the policy process, which is a shorthand way of designating the various processes by which public policy is actually formed.[26] There is, it should be stressed, no one single process by which policy is made. Variations in the subject of policy will produce variations in the manner of policy-making. Foreign policy, taxation, railroad regulation, aid to private schools, professional licensing, and reform of local government are each characterized by distinguishable policy process. Furthermore, it makes a difference whether the primary institutional location of policy-making is the legislature, executive, judiciary, or administrative agencies. And certainly the process of forming, for instance, tax policy differs in the United States, the Soviet Union, and, say, Ethiopia.

All of this should not be taken to mean that each policy-making situation is unique and that it is impossible to develop generalizations on policy formation. Given the complexity and diversity in policy processes, it is not now possible to develop a "grand theory" of policy formation. But a useful start can be made toward what political scientists call "theory building" by seeking to generalize on such matters as who is involved in policy formation, on what kinds of issues, under what conditions, in what ways, and to what effect. Nor should we neglect the question of how policy problems develop. Such questions are really not as simple as they may first appear.

To provide a conceptual framework to guide our discussion, the policy process will be viewed as a sequential pattern of action involving a number of functional categories of activity that can be analytically distinguished, although in various instances this distinction may be difficult to make empirically. The categories will be presented briefly here.[27]

1. *Problem formation:* What is a policy problem? What makes it a public problem? How does it get on the agenda of government?

2. *Formulation:* How are alternatives for dealing with the problem developed? Who participates in policy formulation?

3. *Adoption:* How is a policy alternative adopted or enacted? What requirements must be met? Who adopts policy?

4. *Implementation:* What is done, if anything, to carry a policy into effect? What impact does this have on policy content?

5. *Evaluation:* How is the effectiveness or impact of a policy measured? Who evaluates policy? What are the consequences of policy evaluation? Are there demands for change or repeal?

Within this framework policy formation and implementation are perceived as political in that they involve conflict and struggle among individuals and groups having conflicting desires on issues of public policy. Policy-making is "political," it involves "politics," and there is no reason either to resist or to denigrate this conclusion, or to imitate those who dismiss policies they do not like with such phrases as "It's just a matter of politics."

This framework has a number of advantages. In actuality, policy-making often does chronologically follow the sequence of activities listed above. The sequential approach thus helps capture the flow of action in the policy process. Second, the sequential approach is open to change.[28] Additional steps can be introduced if experience indicates they are needed. The various forms of data collection and analysis—whether quantitative, legal, normative, or whatever—are compatible with it. Third, it yields a dynamic and developmental rather than cross-sectional or static view of the policy process. Moreover, it emphasizes the relationships among political phenomena rather than simply listing factors or developing classification schemes. Fourth, the sequential approach is not "culture-bound," and it can be readily utilized to study policy-making in foreign policy-making systems. Also, it lends itself to manageable comparisons, as of how problems get on the policy agenda in various countries or of the ways in which policies are adopted.

In presenting this framework for the analysis of policy-making, I will concentrate upon national domestic policies in the United States, though not to the total exclusion of foreign policy or other political systems. The discussion that follows is intended to provide the reader both with an understanding of the policy process and with some tools for his own analysis of policy-making.

Notes

1. Robert Eyestone, *The Threads of Public Policy: A Study in Policy Leadership* (Indianapolis: Bobbs-Merrill, 1971), p. 18.
2. Thomas R. Dye, *Understanding Public Policy* (Englewood Cliffs, N.J.: Prentice-Hall, 1972), p. 18.
3. Richard Rose (ed.), *Policy Making in Great Britain* (London: Macmillan, 1969), p. x.
4. Carl J. Friedrich, *Man and His Government* (New York: McGraw-Hill, 1963), p. 79.
5. David Easton, *A Systems Analysis of Political Life* (New York: Wiley, 1965), p. 212.
6. Alan K. McAdam, *Power and Politics in Labor Legislation* (New York: Columbia University Press, 1964).
7. Robert H. Salisbury, "The Analysis of Public Policy: A Search for Theories and Roles," in Austin Ranney (ed.), *Political Science and Public Policy* (Chicago: Markham, 1968), p. 159.
8. Dye, *op. cit.*, p. 3.
9. The following discussion is based on Austin Ranney, "The Study of Policy Content: A Framework for Choice," in Ranney (ed.), *Political Science and Public Policy* (Chicago: 1968), pp. 13–18.
10. Don K. Price, *The Scientific Estate* (Cambridge, Mass.: Harvard University Press, 1965), pp. 122–35.
11. Dye, *op. cit.*, p. 6. Italics in original have been deleted.
12. James O. Wilson, *Negro Politics* (New York: Free Press, 1960), p. 89, as quoted in Amitai Etzioni, "Mixed-Scanning: A 'Third' Approach to Decision-Making," *Public Administration Review*, XXVII (December, 1967), pp. 385–92.

13. The leading proponent of incrementalism undoubtedly is Charles Lindblom. See his "The Science of 'Muddling Through,'" *Public Administration Review,* XIX (1959), pp. 79–88; *The Intelligence of Democracy* (New York: Macmillan, 1964); *The Policy-Making Process* (Englewood Cliffs, N.J.: Prentice-Hall, 1968); and, with David Braybrooke, *The Strategy of Decision* (New York: Free Press, 1963).
14. This summary draws primarily on Lindblom's "The Science of 'Muddling Through,'" *op. cit.,* and *The Intelligence of Democracy, op. cit.,* pp. 144–48.
15. Amitai Etzioni, "Mixed-Scanning: A 'Third' Approach to Decision-Making," *Public Administration Review,* XXVII (December, 1967), pp. 385–92.
16. *Ibid., p.* 389.
17. Glendon Schubert, *Judicial Policy-Making* (Chicago: Foresman, 1965).
18. David Easton, "An Approach to the Analysis of Political Systems," *World Politics,* IX (April, 1957), pp. 383–400. Cf. Easton, *A Framework for Political Analysis* (Englewood Cliffs, N.J.: Prentice-Hall, 1965), and *A Systems Analysis of Political Life* (New York: Wiley, 1965). Those wishing to explore systems theory in depth should consult these works.
19. Earl Latham, *The Group Basis of Politics* (New York: Octagon Books, 1965), p. 36.
20. David Truman, *The Governmental Process* (New York: Knopf, 1951), p. 37.
21. Latham, *op. cit., pp.* 35–36, 38–39.
22. Thomas R. Dye and L. Harmon Zeigler, *The Irony of Democracy* (Belmont, Calif.: Wadsworth, 1970), p. 6. This book examines American politics from the perspective of elite theory.
23. Dye, *op. cit.,* pp. 39, 66.
24. Robert A. Dahl, "Critique of the Ruling Elite Model," *American Political Science Review,* LII (June, 1958), p. 464.
25. Harold D. Lasswell, *The Decision Process* (College Park, Md.: Bureau of Governmental Research, University of Maryland, 1956).
26. Here it is useful to distinguish an *Institutional Process,* such as the legislative process, from the policy process. Cf. Charles O. Jones, *An Introduction to the Study of Public Policy* (Belmont, Calif.: Wadsworth, 1970), pp. 4–5.
27. This framework obviously draws on Lasswell's scheme, discussed earlier in the chapter. It also benefits from Jones, *op. cit.*
28. See, generally, Richard Rose, "Concepts for Comparison," *Policy Studies Journal,* I (Spring, 1973), pp. 122–27.

2. The Policy-Makers and Their Environment

This chapter will survey the environment within which policy-making occurs and some of the official and unofficial participants in policy formation and implementation. This discussion is not intended to be exhaustive; rather, the purpose is to give the reader some notion of who participates in the policy process and in what ways, as well as of what factors usually influence policy behavior.

THE POLICY ENVIRONMENT

Systems theory suggests that policy-making cannot be adequately considered apart from the environment in which it takes place. Demands for policy actions are generated in the environment and transmitted to the political system; at the same time, the environment places limits and constraints upon what can be done by policy-makers. Included in the environment are such geographical characteristics as natural resources, climate, and topography; demographical variables like population size, age distribution, and spatial location; political culture; social structure; and the economic system. Other nations become a significant part of the environment for foreign and defense policy. The discussion here will focus on two of these environmental factors that political scientists have given much attention to (though not always from a policy analysis perspective), namely, political culture and socio-economic variables.

Political Culture

Every society has a culture that differentiates the values and life-styles of its members from those of other societies. The anthropologist Clyde Kluckhohn has defined culture as "the total life way of

29

a people, the social legacy the individual acquires from his group. Or culture can be regarded as that part of the environment that is the creation of man."[1] Most social scientists seem agreed that culture shapes or influences social action, but that it does not fully determine it. It is only one of many factors that may affect human behavior.

What is of interest to us here is that portion of the general culture of a society that can be designated as political culture—widely held values, beliefs, and attitudes concerning what governments should try to do and how they should operate, and the relationship between the citizen and government.[2] Political culture is transmitted from one generation to another by a socialization process in which the individual, through many experiences with parents, friends, teachers, political leaders, and others, learns politically relevant values, beliefs, and attitudes. Political culture, then, is acquired by the individual, becomes a part of his psychological make-up, and is manifested in his behavior. Within a given society, variations among regions and groups may result in distinctive subcultures. In the United States there are noticeable variations in political culture between North and South, black and white, young and old. One political scientist contends there are three identifiable political cultures—moralistic, individualistic, and traditionalistic—and mutations thereof scattered throughout the United States.[3] Where such variations exist, they clearly compound the tasks of description and analyses.

No attempt will be made here to provide a full statement of the political culture of the United States or any other society. Rather, discussion will be confined to indicating and illustrating some of the implications and significance of political culture for policy formation.

A well-known sociologist, Robin W. Williams, has identified a number of "major-value orientations" in American society. These include individual freedom, equality, progress, efficiency, and practicality.[4] Values such as these—and others, such as democracy, individualism, and humanitarianism—clearly have significance for policy-making. For example, the general approach of Americans to regulation of economic activity has been practical or pragmatic, emphasizing particular solutions to present problems rather than long-range planning or ideological consistency. Moreover, concern with individual freedom has created a general presumption against restriction of private activity in favor of the broadest scope possible for private action. Stress on individualism and private property finds expression in the notion that a person should generally be free to use his property as he sees fit.

Differences in public policy and policy-making in various countries can be explained at least partially in terms of political cultural variations. Public medical care programs are of longer standing and more numerous and extensive in Western European countries than in the United States because there has been greater public expectation and acceptance of such programs in Western Europe. Again, few people in Great Britain disapprove of government ownership, whereas few in the United States approve of it.[5] This being so, it is not surprising to find considerably more government ownership of business and industry in Great Britain. Americans much prefer government regulation to ownership when control seems necessary.

Karl Deutsch suggests that the time orientation of people—their view of the relative importance of the past, the present, and the future—has implications for policy formation. A political culture oriented more to the past than to the present or future may better encourage preservation of monuments than the making of innovations. It may enact legislation on old-age pensions years before expanding public higher education. Thus, Great Britain passed an old-age pension law in 1908, but it did not significantly expand public higher education until after 1960. In contrast, Deutsch notes that the United States, with a more future-oriented culture, adopted legislation in 1862 providing for land-grant colleges and in 1935 for Social Security.[6]

Almond and Verba have differentiated between parochial, subject, and participant political cultures.[7] In a *parochial* political culture, citizens have little awareness of, or orientation toward, either the political system as a whole, the input process, the output process, or the citizen as a political participant. The parochials expect nothing from the system. It is suggested that some African chiefdoms and kingdoms and tribal societies, and modern-day Italy, are illustrative of parochial political cultures. In a *subject* political culture, like that of Germany, the citizen is oriented toward the political system and the output process; yet, he has little awareness of input processes or himself as a participant. He is aware of governmental authority, he may like or dislike it, but he is essentially passive. He is, as the term implies, a subject. In the *participant* political culture, which Almond and Verba found the United States to be, citizens have a high level of political awareness and information and have explicit orientations toward the political system as a whole, its input and output processes, and meaningful citizen participation in politics. Included in this orientation is an understanding of how individuals and groups can influence decision-making. Some of the implications of these differences in political culture for policy formation seem readily apparent. Obviously, citizen participation in policy formation in a parochial political culture is going to be essentially nonexistent, and government will be of little concern to most citizens. The individual in a subject political culture may believe that he can do little to influence public policy, whether he likes it or not. This may lead to passive acceptance of governmental action that may be rather authoritarian in style. In some instances, frustration and resentment may build until redress or change is sought through violence. In the participant political culture, individuals may organize into groups and otherwise seek to influence government action to rectify their grievances. Government, and public policy, is viewed as controllable by citizens. Also, one can assume that more demands will be made on government in a participant political culture than in either a parochial or a subject culture.

To return to an earlier point, political culture helps shape political behavior; it "is related to the *frequency* and *probability* of various kinds of behavior and not their rigid determination."[8] Common values, beliefs, and attitudes inform, guide, and constrain the actions of both decision-makers and citizens. Political culture differences help ensure that public policy is more likely to favor economic competition in the United States because individual opportunity is a widely held value, while it is more likely to tolerate industrial cartels in West Germany, because economic competition has not been highly valued there. Some political scientists shy away from using political culture as an analytic tool because they see it as too imprecise and conjectural. Notwithstanding some truth to this view, political culture still has utility for the analysis and explanation of policy.

Socio-economic Conditions

The term socio-economic conditions is used here because it is often impossible to separate social and economic factors as they impinge on or influence political activity. This will become quite apparent as the discussion proceeds.

Public policies can be usefully viewed as arising out of conflicts between different groups of people, private and official, possessing differing interests and desires.[9] One of the prime sources of conflict, especially in modern societies, is economic activity. Conflicts may develop between the interests of big business and small business, employers and employees, debtors and creditors, wholesalers and retailers, chain stores and independents, consumers and sellers, farmers and the purchasers of farm commodities, and so on. Groups that are underprivileged or dissatisfied with their current relationships with other groups in the economy may seek governmental assistance to improve their situation. Customarily, it is the weaker or disadvantaged party (at least in a comparative sense) in a private conflict that seeks government involvement in the matter. The dominant group, the one that is able to achieve its goals satisfactorily by private action, has no incentive to bring government into the fray and usually will oppose government action as unnecessary or improper. Thus, it has been labor groups, dissatisfied with the wages resulting from private bargaining with employers, that have sought minimum-wage legislation.

Satisfactory relationships between groups may be disrupted or altered by economic change or development, and those that feel adversely affected or threatened may demand government action to protect their interests or establish a new equilibrium. Rapid industrialization and the growth of big business in the United States in the latter part of the nineteenth century produced new economic conditions. Farmers, small businessmen, reformist elements, and aggrieved others called for government action to control big business. The eventual result was the enactment of the Sherman Antitrust Act by Congress in 1890.

It is a truism to state that a society's level of economic development will impose limits on what government can do in providing public goods and services to the community. Nonetheless, it is something that is sometimes overlooked by those who assume that the failure of governments to act on problems is invariably due to recalcitrance or unresponsiveness rather than limited resources. Clearly, one factor that affects what governments can do in the way of welfare programs is available economic resources. The scarcity of economic resources will, of course, be more limiting in many of

the less developed (or "underdeveloped") countries of the world
than in an affluent society such as the United States. Still, government in the United States does not have available economic resources to do everything that everyone wants done. Moreover,
resources are very unequally distributed among state and local
governments.

Social conflict and change also provoke demands for government
action. Recently in the United States, growing concern about wom-
en's rights and the increased use (and acceptance) of marijuana,
especially by middle-class people, have produced demands for alteration in public policies to provide greater protection for women's
rights (including the right to have abortions) and lesser penalties
for the use of marijuana. Those with conflicting interests and values
have opposed such demands, with the consequences that public
officials often find themselves hard-pressed to devise acceptable
policy solutions.

The ways in which socio-economic conditions influence or constrain public policies in the American states have recently been sub-
jected to considerable analysis by political scientists. Controversy
has developed over the relative influence of political variables and
of socio-economic variables on policy. This matter clearly merits
some discussion here.

One of the most prominent efforts on this question has been
Dye's study of policy outputs in the fifty states.[10] He contended that
the level of economic development (as measured by such variables
as per capita personal income, per cent urban population, median
level of education, and industrial employment) had a dominant influence on state policies on such matters as education, welfare,
highways, taxation and public regulation. The impact of economic
development was compared with the impact of the political system.
He found that political variables (voter participation, interparty
competition, political party strength, and legislative apportionment)
had only a weak relationship to public policy. Dye summed up the
findings of his involved statistical analysis in the following manner:

> Much of the literature in state politics implies that the division of the
> two-party vote, the level of interparty competition, the level of voter
> participation, and the degree of malapportionment in legislative
> bodies all influence public policy. Moreover, at first glance the fact
> that there are obvious policy differences between states with differ-
> ent degrees of party competition, Democratic dominance, and voter

participation lends some support to the notion that these system characteristics influence public policy. . . .

However, partial correlation analysis reveals that these system characteristics have relatively little *independent* effect on policy outcomes in the states. Economic development shapes both political systems and policy outcomes, and most of the association that occurs between system characteristics and policy outcomes can be attributed to the influence of economic development. Differences in the policy choices of states with different types of political systems turn out to be largely a product of differing socioeconomic levels rather than a direct product of political variables. Levels of urbanization, industrialization, income, and education appear to be more influential in shaping policy outcomes than political system characteristics.[11]

It should be noted that Dye argued not that political variables do not have *any* impact on state policy, but rather that they are clearly subordinated to socio-economic factors.

Another study attempting to demonstrate the stronger impact of socio-economic than political factors on policy was done by Dawson and Robinson.[12] They analyzed the effect of interparty competition and some economic variables on public welfare policy to determine whether party competition had a significant influence on welfare policy (especially expenditures). They concluded that environment factors had a greater impact than party competition. "The level of public social welfare programs in the American states seems to be more a function of socio-economic factors, especially per capita income."[13]

The conclusions of these and similar studies were quickly accepted by some political scientists. One declared that such research provides "a devastating set of findings and cannot be dismissed as not meaning what it plainly says—that analysis of political systems will not explain policy decisions made by those systems."[14] Is public policy really an outcome, primarily, of some kind of socio-economic determinism? Are studies such as those just cited really conclusive on this issue? Two scholars have recently cautioned against a "simple acceptance" of such a conclusion.[15] While not discounting the importance of socio-economic factors in influencing policy outputs, they indicate there are a number of problems and limitations in these studies.

First, there is a tendency to exaggerate the strength of the economy-policy relationship. Thus, "Dye reports 456 coefficients of simple correlations between policy measures and his four economic measures of income, urbanism, industrialization and education, but only 16 of them (4 per cent) are strong enough to indicate that an economic measure explains at least one-half the interstate variation in policy."[16] This leaves quite a bit unexplained statistically. Second, the political variables used in such studies have been of limited scope, focusing only on a few aspects of the political process. Third, there is a tendency to overlook variations in the influence of economic factors on policy-making. Officials of local governments appear more strongly influenced than state officials by economic factors. Further, local officials are not equally influenced by the character of the local economy:

> Where the locality has adopted reformed government structures there is less of an economy-policy linkage than where local government has an unreformed structure. The principal features of a reformed local government structure are a professional city manager, nonpartisan elections for local offices, and a council selected at-large rather than by wards. These features seem to depoliticize the social and economic cleavages within a community, permitting local officials to make their policy decisions with less concern for economics.[17]

Another limitation is that most of these studies are concerned with the statistical relationships between various political and socio-economic variables and public policy. If, when condition A exists, policy B usually occurs with it, and the relationship is not caused by some third factor, then we can predict that, when A exists, B will occur. Such a prediction, however, is not an explanation, and we are still left with the task of explaining *how* political decisions are actually made. If per capita income is directly related to the level of welfare spending, then we must try to explain the relationship. This is neither an insignificant task nor an easy one. Glib answers should be avoided.

Two conclusions can be fairly drawn from this discussion. One is that to understand how policy decisions are made and why some decisions are made rather than others, we must consider social and economic as well as political factors. The second is that whether socio-economic factors are more important than political factors in shaping public policy is still an open question. Most of the research along this line has been focused on the American states, and it is less than conclusive.

THE OFFICIAL POLICY-MAKERS

Official policy-makers are those who possess legal authority to engage in the formation of public policy. (I recognize, of course, that some who have the legal authority to act may, in fact, be controlled by others, such as political party bosses or pressure groups.) These include legislators, executives, administrators, and judges. Each performs policy-making tasks at least somewhat different from the others'.

It is useful to differentiate between primary and supplementary policy-makers. Primary policy-makers have direct constitutional authority to act; for example, Congress does not have to depend upon other governmental units for authorization to act. Supplementary policy-makers, such as national administrative agencies, must gain their authority to act from others (primary policy-makers) and hence are at least potentially dependent upon or controllable by them. Administrative agencies who derive their operating authority from congressional legislation will typically feel a need to be responsive to congressional interests and requests. Congress, in turn, has less need to be responsive to the agencies. This distinction between primary and supplementary policy-makers probably will not hold in countries without a coherent constitution (e.g., some African nations), or where there is little respect for the constitution (e.g., some Latin American countries).

The conflict between the President and Congress during the second Nixon Administration over whether the President could refuse to spend appropriated funds and act on his own to terminate previously authorized programs illustrates the importance of the distinction between primary and supplementary policy-makers. If the President lacked constitutional authority for impounding funds, as many in Congress contended, then Congress could ultimately control spending. The conflict over constitutional authority was essentially a conflict over whether the President could act as a primary policy-maker, which would increase the independence and power of the executive vis-à-vis Congress. Given the different interests and constituencies of the two branches, how such a controversy is resolved has profound policy implications.

The following survey of official policy-makers is intended only to be suggestive, that is, to convey a notion of their general role in policy formation, not to catalogue all of their powers and activities.

Legislatures

The easy response to the question "What do legislatures do?" is to say that they legislate, that is, that they are concerned with the central political tasks of lawmaking and policy formation in a political system. It cannot be assumed, however, that a legislature, merely because it bears that formal designation, really has independent decision-making functions. This is a matter to be determined by empirical investigation rather than by definition.

Investigation would indicate that legislatures in American government do indeed often legislate in an independent decisional sense. In Congress, for example, the standing committees possess life-or-death authority over proposed legislation and may even act in opposition to a majority of the members of the house in which they exist. Policies on such matters as taxation, civil rights, welfare, and labor relations tend to be shaped in substantial part by Congress. In contrast, in the area of foreign policy Congress is more likely to defer to Presidential leadership. In the instance of the famous Tonkin Gulf Resolution of 1964, which served as the legal justification for the subsequent expansion of the Vietnam war by the Johnson Administration, Congress hastily approved what was recommended by the President without alteration and with little deliberation.

Within the American states, the role of the legislature often varies with the nature of the issue involved. Many state legislatures, because of their limited sessions, rather "amateur" membership, and inadequate staff assistance, are often unable to act independently on complex, technical legislative matters. They may simply enact bills agreed upon elsewhere. For example, the Texas legislature passed a law in 1965 dealing with pooling (or unitization) for the common development of oil fields almost in the identical form in which it was introduced after having been agreed to and drafted by representatives of the major and independent petroleum producers organizations. The legislature did not really have the capacity to do otherwise. On other matters, such as criminal legislation, the legislature clearly does "legislate." The Texas legislature is not atypical among state legislatures.

The British Parliament has been said to consent merely to laws that are originated by political parties and interest groups, drafted by civil servants, and steered through the House of Commons by the government (the Prime Minister and Cabinet). This over-simplifies the situation. The government usually gets what it wants from Commons partly because it knows what Commons will accept and requests only measures that are acceptable. In the course of approving legislation, Commons performs a vital function of deliberation, scrutinizing, criticizing, and publicizing government policies and activities and their implications for the public.

In comparison, the Russian national legislature, the Supreme Soviet, often merely ratifies or confirms decisions made by high officials within the Communist Party. So too, many Latin American legislatures are dominated by the executive and do little, if anything, in the way of independent decision-making. (The Chilean legislature is one of a few exceptions.) For such political systems, the student of policy formation may be wasting his time if he gives much attention to legislative organization and processes.

To conclude with a global generalization, legislatures are more important in policy formation in democratic than in dictatorial countries; within the democratic category, legislatures generally tend to have a larger role in Presidential systems (like the United States) than in parliamentary systems (like Great Britain). In some countries such as Oman, there is no legislature in existence.

The Executive

We live in what has been called an "executive-centered era," in which the effectiveness of government depends substantially upon executive leadership, both in policy formation and in policy execution. Consider the case of the President of the United States.

The President's authority to exercise legislative leadership is both clearly established and accepted as a necessity. The fragmentation of leadership in Congress resulting from the committee system and lack of strong party leadership renders that body incapable of developing a legislative program. Consequently, Congress in the twentieth century has come to expect the President to present it with proposals for legislation. This does not mean, however, that Congress does whatever the President recommends; such is by no means the case, and not a few Presidential proposals are either rejected or modified in important respects before enactment.

Legislation often delegates significant policy-making authority to the President. Foreign-trade legislation, for example, gives the President discretionary authority to raise or lower tariff rates on imported goods. The Economic Stabilization Act of 1970 essentially gave the President a free hand, if he so chose, to institute price and wage controls to combat inflation. The result was the price-wage freeze announced in August, 1971, the subsequent Phases II, III, and IV control programs, and then the end of controls.

In the areas of foreign and military policy, which are often difficult to differentiate, the President possesses greater constitutional power and operating freedom than in domestic policy. U.S. foreign policy is largely a creation of Presidential leadership and action. American policy concerning Vietnam, as we well know, has been shaped by the Presidents in office during the past two decades. Again, the decision to seek more open and friendly relations with Communist China was President Nixon's. Foreign policy is to a great extent the domain of the executive. This is true not only for the United States but for all national political systems. Can anyone think of a country in which foreign policy is dominated by the legislature?

In the developing countries (e.g., Ghana, Iraq, Thailand), the executive probably has even more influence in policy-making than in modern countries. Yehezkel Dror explains:

> Because there are few policy issues, a larger proportion of them can reach the cabinet level in developing countries; because there is often no professional civil service, the executive plays a larger role in forming public policies about most issues; because power is more highly concentrated, the political executive is free to establish policies on many more issues without worrying as much about having to build coalitions.[18]

The policy-making structure, in short, is rather simple in many developing countries; executive policy-making prevails. In such countries, too, interest groups have little impact on policy-making because of their limited independence from existent political institutions.

Reflective of the important policy-making role of the executive is that in evaluating an executive—whether the President, a state governor, or some other chief executive—our focus is on his policy-making rather than his administrative activities.

Administrative Agencies

Administrative systems throughout the world differ with respect to such characteristics as size and complexity, hierarchical organization, and degree of autonomy. Although it was once common doctrine in political science that administrative agencies only carried into effect, more or less automatically, policies determined by the "political" branches of government, it has now become axiomatic that politics and administration are blended, and that administrative agencies are often significantly involved in the development of public policy. This is particularly so given the concept of policy as what government actually does concerning particular matters. Administration can make or break a law or policy made elsewhere. For example, in the eighteenth century, Catherine II of Russia decreed the abolition of a large part of the institution of serfdom. The landowning aristocracy, which really controlled the administration of the government, was largely able to prevent the implementation of the decision. In the United States, the effectiveness of state pollution-control laws has often been blunted by heel-dragging and nonenforcement in many instances by the administering agencies.

In complex industrial societies especially, the technicality and complexity of many policy matters, the need for continuing control, and the legislators' lack of time and information, have led to the delegation of much discretionary authority, often formally recognized as rule-making power, to administrative agencies. Consequently, agencies make many decisions that have far-reaching political and policy consequences. Illustrations include the choice of weapons systems by the Department of Defense, the development of air-safety regulations by the Federal Aviation Agency, the location of highways by state highway departments, and the regulation of the volume of petroleum production by such agencies as the Texas Railroad Commission. As Professor Norman Thomas comments: "It is doubtful that any modern industrial society could manage the daily operation of its public affairs without bureaucratic organizations in which officials play a major policy-making role."[19]

Agencies are also a major source of proposals for legislation in such political systems as the United States and Great Britain. Moreover, American agencies typically not only suggest needed legislature but actively lobby and otherwise seek to exert pressure for its adoption. Thus the Department of Agriculture has been known to round up pressure-group support for its price-support proposals, thereby in effect lobbying the lobbyists.

In all, there is much accuracy in the view that "policy is at the mercy of administrators."

The Courts

Nowhere do the courts play a greater role in policy formation than in the United States. The courts, notably national and state appellate courts, have often greatly affected the nature and content of public policy through exercise of the powers of judicial review and statutory interpretation in cases brought before them.

Basically, judicial review is the power of courts to determine the constitutionality of actions of the legislative and executive branches and declare them null and void if such actions are found to be in conflict with the Constitution. Clearly, the Supreme Court was making policy when, in various cases up to 1937, it held that no legislature, state or national, had constitutional authority to regulate minimum wages. After 1937, the Constitution was found (i.e., interpreted) to permit such legislation. Clearly, too, in recent years the Court has helped shape public policy by holding that segregated school systems, prayers in public schools, and malapportionment of state legislatures were unconstitutional. The thrust of policy is importantly affected by such decisions. Although the Court has used its power of judicial review somewhat sparingly, the very fact it has such power may affect the policy-making activities of the other branches. Congress may hesitate to act on some matter if there is some expectation that its action would be found unconstitutional. State supreme courts also have the power of judicial review but frequently have less discretion in its exercise because of the detailed and specific nature of most state constitutions.

Courts are also called upon to interpret and decide the meaning of statutory provisions that often are generally stated and permit conflicting interpretations. When a court accepts one interpretation rather than another, the consequence of its action is to give effect to the policy preference of the winning party. In 1954, the Supreme Court held, counter to the wishes of the Federal Power Commission and others, that the Natural Gas Act of 1938 not only authorized but required the agency to regulate the wellhead (or field) price of natural gas. This was a policy decision with far-reaching consequences.

The judiciary has played a major role in the formation of economic policy in the United States. Much of the law relating to such matters as property ownership, contracts, corporations, and employer-employee relationships has been developed and applied by the courts in the form of common law and equity. These are systems of judge-made law fashioned over the years on a case-to-case basis. They originated in England but have been adapted to American needs and conditions by American judges. Much of this law was developed by the state courts, and much of it is still applied by them.[20]

Judicial activism is nothing new, although in the past it was confined mostly to the areas of economic regulation and law enforcement. In the last two decades, and especially in the last few years, the courts have ventured into many areas of social and political activity that previously had been considered pretty much off-limits. Legislative apportionment, the rights of welfare recipients, the operation of public institutions such as prisons and hospitals, and the location of public facilities are primary examples. Not only are the courts getting involved but they are playing a more positive role in policy formation, specifying not only what government cannot do but also what it must do to meet legal or constitutional obligations. For instance, the Supreme Court, in a 1973 case, declared several states' abortion-control laws at issue unconstitutional. It then went on to specify the standards future laws would have to meet if they are to be constitutional. The growing impact of government on people's lives, the refusal or failure of the legislative and executive branches to act on many problems, the willingness of the courts to become involved, and the increasing litigiousness of at least some segments of the population probably guarantee a continuation of extended judicial involvement in policy formation in the future.

Although courts in such other countries as Canada, Australia, and West Germany have some power of judicial review, their impact on policy has been much less than that of the American courts. In the developing countries, the courts appear to have no meaningful policy-making role. The American practice of settling many important policy issues in the courts remains unique.

UNOFFICIAL PARTICIPANTS

In addition to the official policy-makers, many others may participate in the policy process, including interest groups, political parties, and individual citizens. They are designated as unofficial participants because, however important or dominant they may be in various situations, they themselves do not usually possess legal authority to make binding policy decisions.

Interest Groups

Interest groups appear to play an important role in policy-making in practically all countries. Depending upon whether they are democratic or dictatorial, modern or developing, countries may differ with respect to how groups are constituted and how legitimate they are. Thus, groups appear to be more numerous and to operate much more openly and freely in the United States or Great Britain than they do in the Soviet Union. In all systems, however, groups perform an interest articulation function, that is, they express demands and present alternatives for policy action. They may also supply public officials with much information, often of a technical sort, concerning the nature and possible consequences of policy proposals. In doing so, they contribute to the rationality of policy-making.

Interest groups, such as those representing organized labor, business, and agriculture, are a major source of demands for policy action by public officials in the United States. Given the pluralist nature of American society, it is not surprising that pressure groups are many in number and quite diverse in their interests, size, organization, and style of operation. This does not mean, however, that some societal interests may not be poorly represented, if at all, by groups. Migrant workers are a case in point. Typically, the concern of an interest group is to influence policy in a specific subject area. Because several groups often have conflicting desires on a particular policy issue, public officials are confronted with the necessity of having to choose from among, or reconcile, conflicting demands. Groups that are well organized and active are likely to fare better than groups whose potential membership is poorly organized and inarticulate.

The influence of interest groups upon decisions depends on a number of factors. These may include (subject to the rule of *ceteris paribus*—other things being equal) the size of the group's membership, its monetary and other resources, its cohesiveness, the skill of its leadership, its social status, the presence or absence of competing organizations, the attitudes of public officials, and the site of decision-making in the political system. (On this last item, recall the discussion of institutionalism in Chapter 1.) Again other things being equal, a large, well-regarded group (e.g., the American Legion) will have more influence than a smaller, less well-regarded group (e.g., the League for Soviet-American Friendship). Or, a union with a large membership will have more influence than one with few members. Also, as a consequence of the factors enumerated here, a group may have a strong or controlling influence on decisions in one policy area and little, if any, influence in another. Whereas, the National Association of Manufacturers has much influence on some economic issues, it has little impact in the area of civil rights.

In a study of the strength of pressure groups generally in the American states, Zeigler and van Dalen focused on the impact of three variables: strength of party competition, legislative cohesion (strength of parties in the legislature), and the socio-economic variables of urban population per capita income and industrial employment.[21] Two patterns emerged from his analysis. Strong pressure groups (their particular purposes aside) seemed to be associated with weak parties, both electorally and legislatively, low urban population, low per capita income, and a higher rate of nonindustrial employment (agriculture, fishing, and forestry). Moderate or weak pressure groups seemed associated with strong, competitive parties and higher rates of urban population, per capita income, and industrial employment. Their study represents a systematic attempt to discover what affects group strength, although the findings should be viewed as suggestive rather than conclusive. Moreover, it should be kept in mind that they were not concerned with the strength of particular groups.

Political Parties

In the United States, political parties are concerned primarily with contesting elections in order to control the personnel of government. They are, in short, concerned more with power than with policy. This situation has often led to the complaint that the Republican and Democratic parties represent a choice between Tweedledee and Tweedledum, and that, so far as public policy is concerned, it makes little difference which party is in office. Although the parties are not highly policy-oriented, such complaints ignore the meaningful impact that the parties have on policy.

Clearly, the parties appeal to different segments of society. Thus, the Democratic Party draws disproportionately from big city, labor, and minority and ethnic voters; the Republican Party draws disproportionately from rural, small town, and suburban areas, Protestants, and businessmen and professionals. The parties often come into conflict on such issues as welfare programs, labor legislation, business regulation, public power projects, public housing, and agricultural price-support legislation. The reader should not have much difficulty in differentiating between the parties on these issues. Given such policy inclinations, and the fact that party members in Congress often vote in accordance with party policy positions, which party controls Congress or the Presidency has important policy implications.

In the American state legislatures, the importance of political parties varies significantly. In one-party states, it is obvious that parties do not exercise much discipline over legislative voting, and the party has little, if any, effect on policy-making, as in the Texas and Louisiana legislatures. In contrast, in such states as Connecticut and Michigan both parties are active and cohesive and have considerable impact on legislative decision-making. When conflict over policy occurs in such states, the function of parties is to provide alternatives. In many cities, an effort has been made to eliminate party influence on policy through the use of nonpartisan elections for city officials. Policy is supposed to be made "objectively." An unintended consequence of nonpartisanship, it might be noted, is a reduction of interest and participation in politics.

In modern societies generally, political parties often perform a function of "interest aggregation"—that is, they seek to convert the particular demands of interest groups into general policy alternatives. The way in which parties "aggregate" interests is affected by the number of parties. In predominantly two-party systems, such as the United States and Great Britain, the desire of the parties to gain widespread electoral support "will require both parties to include in their policy 'package' those demands which have very broad popular support and to attempt to avoid alienating the most prominent groups."[22] In multiparty systems, on the other hand, parties may do less aggregating and act as the representatives of fairly narrow sets of interests, as appears to be the case in France. Generally, though, parties have a broader range of policy concerns than do interest groups; hence, they will act more as brokers than as advocates of particular interests in policy formation. In some one-party systems, such as the Soviet Union, they are the predominant force in policy-making.

The Individual Citizen

In discussions of policy-making, the individual citizen is often neglected in the concern with legislatures, interest groups, and more prominent participants. This is unfortunate, as the individual often does seem to make a difference. Although the task of policy-making is generally assigned to public officials, in various instances citizens still participate directly in decision-making. In some of the American states (notably California) and some countries (such as Switzerland), citizens can and do still vote directly on legislation. Moreover, in most of the states, constitutional amendments are submitted to the voters for approval. In many local jurisdictions, bond issues and increases in tax rates must be authorized directly by the voters. A great many citizens, of course, do not avail themselves of these opportunities to shape policy directly because of inertia or indifference.

This leads to a frequently made point, namely, that citizen participation in policy-making, even in democratic politics, is thin. Many people do not vote, engage in party activity, join pressure groups, or even display much interest in politics. Survey research indicates, moreover, that voters are influenced comparatively little by policy considerations when voting for candidates for public office. Granting this, it still does not hold that citizens have no impact on policy except in the limited situations mentioned in the preceding paragraphs. Let us note some possibilities.

Even in dictatorial regimes, the interests or desires of common citizens are consequential for public policies.[23] The old-style dictator will pay some attention to what his people want in order to keep down unrest. As a Latin American dictator supposedly once said, "You can't shoot everyone." Modern totalitarian regimes, such as the Soviet Union, also seem concerned to meet many citizen wants even as they exclude citizens from more direct participation in policy formation. Thus, in recent years the Soviet regime has increased production of consumer goods and has even indicated a desire to surpass the United States in the level of consumer benefits.

Elections in democratic countries may serve indirectly to reinforce official responsiveness to citizen interests. As Charles Lindblom summarizes the argument:

> The most conspicuous difference between authoritarianism and democratic regimes is that in democratic regimes citizens choose their

top policy makers in genuine elections. Some political scientists speculate that voting in genuine elections may be an important method of citizen influence on policy not so much because it actually permits citizens to choose their officials and to some degree instruct these officials on policy, but because the existence of genuine elections put[s] a stamp of approval on citizen participation. Indirectly, therefore, the fact of elections enforces on proximate policy makers a rule that citizens' wishes count in policy making.[24]

The "rule" Lindblom refers to is sometimes expressed in the aphorism that citizens have a right to be heard and officials have a duty to listen. The effect of such considerations on policy-makers is worth thinking about, although they are not amenable to rigorous measurement, given the present state of political science.

Some citizens, through their intellectual activities, contribute new ideas and directions to the policy process. Thus, Rachel Carson, with her *Silent Spring,* and Ralph Nader, with his *Unsafe at Any Speed,* had a considerable impact on policy in the areas of pesticide control and automobile safety. Others, through political activism, may substantially affect policy action. Social security legislation in the 1930's was certainly affected by the activities of Dr. Francis Townsend and civil rights legislation in the 1960's by those of the Reverend Martin Luther King.

LEVELS OF POLITICS

Not all the participants in policy-making discussed above are involved in all policy-making or decision-making situations. Some matters arouse much attention and attract a wide range of participants. Others will be less visible or affect only a few people and will consequently stir little attention and participation. Following Emmette Redford's categories, we can distinguish three levels of policies, based on the scope of participation normally characteristic of each and, to a lesser extent, the kind of issue involved: micropolitics, subsystem policies, and macropolitics.[25]

Micropolitics involves efforts by individuals, companies, and communities to secure favorable government action for themselves. Subsystem politics is focused on particular functional areas of activity, such as airline regulation or river and harbor improvements, and involve interrelationships among congressional committees, administrative agencies (or bureaus), and interest groups. Macropolitics occurs when "the community at large and the leaders of government as a whole are brought into the discussion and determination of [public] policy."[26]

Micropolitics

Micropolitics often occurs when an individual seeks a favorable ruling from an administrative agency or a special bill exempting him from a requirement of the immigration laws, when a company seeks a favorable change in the tax code or a television broadcasting license, or when a community seeks a grant for construction of an airport or opposes the location of a public housing project in its area. What is involved in each of these instances is the specific, differentiated, and intense interest of one or a few in a society of many individuals, companies, and communities. What is required, or sought, is a decision applicable to one or a few. Typically, only a few persons and officials will be involved in, or even aware of, such decision-making situations, however important they may be for those seeking action, and whatever the ultimate consequences of such decisions or a cluster of them may be.

In the short run at least, micropolitical decisions appear to be distributive and can be made without concern for limited resources. That is, such decisions appear to affect only those immediately concerned and can be made on the basis of mutual noninterference, with each seeking benefits (or subsidies) for himself and not opposing or interfering with the efforts of others to do likewise. Benefits received by one individual or group do not appear to be at the expense of other individuals or groups.

The enactment of special tax provisions by Congress is illustrative of micropolitics. Almost every year Congress enacts a number of laws that make particular changes in the internal revenue code.[27] Their effect is to grant special treatment to particular groups or individuals and enable them not to pay taxes they otherwise would have to pay. A notorious example is the "Louis B. Mayer amendment," which was adopted in 1951 and saved Mayer about $2 million in income taxes by treating income he received at retirement from his company as capital gains. Although written in the form of general legislation, its terms were such that it was assumed that the amendment covered only Mayer and one other person. Such legislation arouses little attention on its way through Congress and becomes law with most of the public completely unaware of its existence. Whether these special tax bills create "loopholes" or correct "inequities" depends upon one's perspective, and whether one benefits from them.

As government programs become more numerous and extensive, as they provide more benefits for, or impose more requirements on, individuals, groups, and communities, both the opportunity and the incentive to engage in micropolitics increases.

Subsystem Politics

In what has become a frequently quoted passage, Ernest Griffith in 1939 called attention to the existence of political subsystems and the value of studying them.

> One cannot live in Washington for long without being conscious that it has whirlpools or centers of activity focusing on particular problems. . . . It is my opinion that ordinarily the relationship among these men—legislators, administrators, lobbyists, scholars—who are interested in a common problem is a much more real relationship than the relationship between congressmen generally or between administrators generally. In other words, he who would understand the prevailing pattern of our present governmental behavior, instead of studying the formal institutions or even generalizations or organs, important though all these things are, may possibly obtain a better picture of the way things really happen if he would study these "whirlpools" of special social interests and problems.[28]

Since Griffith wrote that, political scientists and others have devoted considerable attention to the examination of political subsystems (also variously called subgovernments, policy clusters, and policy coalitions).

Most commonly, a subsystem involves a pattern of relationships among some congressional committees (or subcommittees), an administrative agency or two, and relevant interest groups centered around a particular policy area.[29] For civil aviation, there is a subsystem composed primarily of the congressional committees on commerce and the appropriations subcommittees, the Civil Aeronautics Board and the Federal Aviation Agency, and such groups as the Air Transport Association and the Airline Pilots Association. Another well-known subsystem is centered around river and harbor development activity and features the congressional committees on public works, the Corps of Engineers (within the Department of the Army), and the National Rivers and Harbors Congress. A third subsystem is concerned with sugar prices and import quotas and involves the House Agriculture Committee, the Sugar Division of the Department of Agriculture, and representatives of the sugar industry.[30] The management of the public grazing lands in the Western states is the basis for a subsystem composed essentially of the congressional interior committees and appropriation subcommittees, the Bureau of Land Management, and groups representing Western livestock raisers. This list could be greatly extended.[31]

Subsystems develop because not everyone is interested, nor could everyone be, in every area of public policy. The citizen or official who is intensely interested in civil aviation may have little or no interest in banking regulations or the foreign-aid program. While he wants and seeks to influence policy on civil aviation, he will probably leave banking and foreign aid to those more interested in them. Within Congress and the executive branch, separate units of organization—committees and subcommittees, agencies and bureaus—are set up for each major area of government activity. They develop continuing relationships with one another, as the government's specialists in their field, and with the interest groups that represent those served or regulated by their activity.

These subsystems, because of the diffusion of power and their functional specialization, have a considerable amount of autonomy in the formation and application of policy in their fields. Within the limits of existing legislation, they shape governmental action in their field. They are not, however, independent of all overhead control. When new legislation is needed, for example, they must either secure the approval or avoid the veto or disapproval of Congress and the executive. Still, there is a tendency to defer to them as the experts in their areas.

Macropolitics

Some issues will attract sufficient attention, or become sufficiently controversial, to enter the macropolitical arena. A matter may start at the micropolitical level and escalate into a macropolitical issue. This was the case with the award of a television broadcast license for the Miami area in the 1950's, after it was revealed that one of the contestants had some questionable financial dealings with a member of the Federal Communications Commission. What had begun as a routine matter became one that attracted wide attention and participation. Again, a policy issue may be moved from the subsystem to the macropolitical level by the actions of public officials or others. Senator Mike Monroney made the establishment of the Federal Aviation Agency in the late 1950's a macropolitical issue in an effort to secure a stronger agency to deal with airline safety. Some issues are "born" in the macropolitical arena, such as the steel-price crisis of 1962, a major crisis in labor-management relations like a nationwide railroad strike, or the escalation of the Vietnam war.

The central participants in macropolitics include party and congressional leaders (who may overlap), the President, and the executive departments. The communications media and a variety of group spokesmen are also often deeply involved. The range of participants is thus broad. This level of politics often attracts the most attention in studies of policy-making because it is often both quite visible and salient, as well as spectacular.

Decisions made in the macropolitical arena may be considerably different from what they would be if made at one of the other levels. Among other things, when an issue moves, say, from the subsystem to the macropolitical arena, the conflict over it is broadened. And, as E. E. Schattschneider suggests, this often changes the nature of the settlement, that is, the policy decision.[32] Broad public interests are likely to receive fullest consideration in policy-making at the macropolitical level.

A distinctive characteristic of macropolitics is Presidential involvement. Whether the President more fully represents national interests than Congress as many contend, is at least sometimes debatable. What is true, certainly, is that those interests represented by the President enjoy an advantage in the macropolitical arena. The President, because of the centrality and visibility of his office, because of his capacity to formulate policy alternatives, and because of the resources he has to use in support of his proposals, is the policy leader here. His actions will have a substantial impact on the content and direction of public policy. Compare, for example, the effect of the Johnson Administration and the Nixon Administration on antipoverty policy.

In the next chapter we will look at the formation of policy, especially as it occurs in the macropolitical arena.

NOTES

1. Clyde Kluckhohn, *Mirror for Man* (Greenwich, Conn.: Fawcett, 1963), p. 24.
2. For an extended discussion of political culture, see Gabriel A. Almond and Sidney Verba, *The Civic Culture* (Boston: Little, Brown, 1965), and Donald J. Levine, *The Political Culture of the United States* (Boston: Little, Brown, 1972).
3. Daniel J. Elazar, *American Federalism: A View from the States* (New York: Crowell, 1966), chap. 4.
4. Robin M. Williams, Jr., *American Society*, 2d ed. (New York: Knopf, 1960), Chap. 11.
5. Levine, *op. cit.*, pp. 210–11.
6. Karl W. Deutsch, *Politics and Government* (Boston: Houghton Mifflin, 1970), p. 207.
7. Almond and Verba, *op. cit.*, pp. 11–26.
8. Deutsch, *op. cit.*, 207.
9. Cf. E. E.. Schattschneider, *The Semi-Sovereign People* (New York: Holt, Rinehart & Winston, 1960), chap. 1.
10. Thomas R. Dye, *Politics, Economics, and the Public: Policy Outcomes in the Fifty States* (Chicago: Rand-McNally, 1966). Dye uses the term "policy outcome" to designate what were described as policy outputs in chap. 1, *supra*.
11. Ibid., p. 293.
12. Richard Dawson and James Robinson, "The Relation Between Public Policy and Some Structural and Environmental Variables in the American States," *Journal of Politics*, XXV (May, 1963), pp. 265–89.
13. *Ibid.*, p. 289.
14. Robert H. Salisbury, "The Analysis of Public Policy," in Austin Ranney (ed.), *Political Science and Public Policy* (Chicago: Markham, 1968), p. 164.
15. Ira Sharkansky and Richard I. Hofferbert, "Dimensions of State Policy," in Herbert Jacob and Kenneth N. Vines (eds.), *Politics in the American States* 2d ed., (Boston: Little, Brown, 1972), esp. pp. 318–23.
16. *Ibid.*, p. 320.
17. *Ibid.*, p. 321. Cf. Robert L. Lineberry and Edmund P. Fowler, "Reformism and Public Policies in American Cities," *American Political Science Review*, LXI (September, 1967), pp. 701–16.
18. Yehezkel Dror, *Public Policymaking Reexamined* (Scranton, Pa.: Chandler, 1968), p. 118.
19. Norman C. Thomas, *Rule 9: Politics, Administration, and Civil Rights* (New York: Random House, 1966), p. 6.
20. Emmette S. Redford, *American Government and the Economy* (New York: Macmillan, 1965), pp. 53–54.
21. Harmon Zeigler and Hendrick van Dalen, "Interest Groups in the States," in Herbert Jacob and Kenneth N. Vines (eds.), *Politics in the American States* 2d ed. (Boston: Little, Brown, 1971), pp. 126–27.
22. Gabriel A. Almond and G. Bingham Powell, Jr., *Comparative Politics: A Developmental Approach* (Boston: Little, Brown, 1966), p. 103.
23. This discussion draws on Charles E. Lindblom, *The Policy-Making Process* (Englewood Cliffs, N.J.: Prentice-Hall, 1968), p. 44.
24. *Ibid.*, p. 45.
25. Emmette S. Redford, *Democracy in the Administrative State* (New York: Oxford University Press, 1969), chap. 4–5. See also his *American Government and the Economy*, *op. cit.*, chap. 3. The following discussion draws substantially on these sources.
26. Redford, *Democracy in the Administrative State*, p. 53.
27. Stanley S. Surrey, "The Congress and the Tax Lobbyist—How Special

Tax Provisions Get Enacted," *Harvard Law Review,* LXXX (May, 1957), pp. 1145–82.

28. Ernest S. Griffith, *The Impasse of Democracy* (New York: Harrison-Hilton, 1939), p. 182.
29. The subsystem concept is well-discussed in J. Leiper Freeman, *The Political Process* rev. ed. (New York: Random House, 1965).
30. Douglas Cater, *Power in Washington* (New York: Random House, 1964).
31. Theodore J. Lowi, in *The End of Liberalism* (New York: Norton, 1969), p. 110, argues that, "taking all the agriculture programs within or closely associated with the Department of Agriculture, there are at least ten separate autonomous, local self-governing systems."
32. Schattschneider, *op. cit.,* chap. 4.

3. Policy Formation and Adoption

The nature of public problems and three aspects of policy formation will be considered in this chapter: how public problems come to the attention of policy-makers; how policy proposals are formulated to deal with particular problems; and how a specific proposal is chosen for adoption from among the competing alternatives. The legislature will be the primary institutional focus of the discussion. It should be kept in mind that the items listed are functional categories of activities. While they can be distinguished for the purpose of analysis, in actuality they are often blended. For instance, someone formulating a policy proposal will often do so with the need to win support for its adoption as one of the factors guiding his efforts.

POLICY PROBLEMS

Studies of policy formation usually give little attention to the nature of public problems. They are taken as given, and analysis proceeds from there. Some, indeed, would contend that the substance of policy problems falls outside the concern of political science. Yet, policy analysis that does not consider the dimensions of the problems that stimulate governmental action, and to which policy is directed, is less than complete. The nature of the problem—for example, whether it is foreign or domestic—helps determine the nature of the policy process. Again, the evaluation of policy requires information on the substance of the original problem in order to assess effectiveness, among other things.

For policy purposes, a problem can be formally defined as a condition or situation that produces "a human need, deprivation, or dissatisfaction, self-identified or identified by others, for which relief is sought."[1] Such things as low incomes, unclean air, unwholesome food, the actions of a foreign government, or trial court procedures may become problems if they produce sufficient anxiety, tensions, or dissatisfaction as to cause people to seek relief or redress. The point to be made here is that there are all kinds of needs and problems. Only those that move people to action become policy problems. Thus, when a group, for example, has low income but accepts this condition and neither does anything about it nor somehow elicits actions by others in its behalf, then, according to the stated definition, no problem exists. Problems do not become such if they are not articulated.

This leads to a second point. Matters can be defined as problems, and therefore relief sought, by persons other than those directly affected. Thus, in the mid-1960's, poverty was defined as a public problem, and a war on poverty was declared more because of the actions of public officials and others, such as publicists, than because of the actions of the poor themselves. Of course, there is always the possibility that problems will be defined differently by those directly affected than by others.

Our concern now is not merely with problems but with *public* problems. Thus the question: What characteristics or qualities make a problem public? Most people would agree that the fact that John Smith's car is out of gasoline is a private problem, however disturbing to Smith it might be, whereas the widespread shortage of gasoline in a community or region is a public problem. What distinguishes private from public problems? A good way to begin is with John Dewey:

> We take then our point of departure from the objective fact that human acts have consequences upon others, that some of these consequences are perceived, and that their perception leads to subsequent effort to control action so as to secure some consequences and to avoid others. Following this clew, we are led to remark that the consequences are of two kinds, those which affect the persons directly engaged in a transaction, and those which affect others beyond those immediately concerned. In this distinction, we find the germ of the distinction between the private and the public. . . . The public consists of all those who are affected by the indirect consequences of transactions to such an extent that it is deemed necessary to have those consequences systematically cared for.[2]

Drawing on the differentiation made by Dewey in this statement, we can say that public problems are those that have a broad effect, including consequences for persons not directly involved. Problems that have a limited effect, being of concern only to one or a few persons who are directly involved, can be viewed as private. Admittedly, this is not a very sharp set of definitions. An illustration may help convey the notion. Assume that an individual is unhappy with his tax burden under the existing tax laws. Acting on his own, he may seek a favorable administrative ruling to reduce his burden, or he may try to induce his representative in Congress to sponsor an amendment to the tax laws that will lessen his tax obligation. Our imaginary citizen has a problem, but it is essentially private. As another alternative, he may seek to publicize his problem and enlist in the cause others in a similar situation. A bill may be introduced in the legislature and a campaign for it launched, which actions, in turn, draw opposition. Directly or indirectly, many people become involved or perceive themselves as being affected. A public problem exists.

Many of the problems that are acted upon by government, it should be remarked, are really private problems. To a great extent, the micropolitical level of politics discussed in Chapter 2 is focused on private problems. Moreover, much of the time of many members of Congress is devoted to "case work," which involves providing assistance to individual constituents in their relationships with administrative agencies.

A large number and variety of public problems exist in the United States, and they can be categorized in a variety of ways. One distinction is between procedural and substantive problems. Procedural problems relate to how government is organized, and how it conducts its operations and activities. Substantive problems are concerned with the actual consequences of human activity, whether it involves free speech, the sale of used cars, or environmental pollution. Another distinction, which is based on their origins, can be made between foreign and domestic problems. Within the domestic area, we encounter education, taxation, crime, transportation, welfare, and other problems. These really are sets of problems; for example, what is often referred to as the "welfare problem" is really a variety of problems related to the aged, the working poor, families with dependent children, and so on.

Drawing on Theodore Lowi's work,[3] problems can also be categorized as distributive, regulatory, and redistributive. This classification depends upon the number of people affected and their relationships with one another. Distributive problems involve small numbers of people and can be treated one by one: for example, the quests of communities for flood-control projects, industries for tariff concessions, and companies for governmental contracts. Regulatory problems produce demands for the restriction or limitation of the actions of others. Those who feel aggrieved by the actions of labor unions may call for regulation of their activities to prevent undesired consequences. Redistributive problems are those that call for the transfer of resources among large groups, or classes, in society. Those who define income inequality as a public problem often demand graduated income taxes and other public policies intended to transfer resources from the haves to the have-nots. Proposed policies to deal with redistribution problems are customarily highly productive of conflict and tend to involve class conflict or something akin thereto.

Before leaving this discussion of problems, it should be stressed that whether some condition or situation is regarded as a problem depends not only on its objective dimensions but also, and more importantly, on the way in which it is perceived by people. Take as an illustration the "farm problem" in the United States during the 1950's and 1960's. Essentially, the problem was that of "surplus" production, which would not move in the market at prices agreeable to farmers. (It was not surplus in the sense that no one, anywhere, would not use it at some price). For a great many nations in the world, this abundance would have been viewed as a blessing rather than a "problem." In the United States, given the frame of reference and context in which it was viewed, it was a problem. Again, whether there is an "energy crisis," and whether this is a public problem requiring governmental action, depends on its being publicly defined (or perceived) as such. Petroleum company executives are more likely to see it as a public problem requiring favorable (to them) government action than are critics of the petroleum industry.

This leads us to another topic for consideration—namely, why are some matters, apart from the breadth of their consequences, seen as public problems requiring action, while others are not? Some insight into this question should be provided by the following discussion of the policy agenda.

THE POLICY AGENDA

One constantly hears or reads about demands being made by this group or that individual for action by some governmental body on some problem, whether it be rough streets or crime therein, the high price of meat, or industrial monopoly. Of the thousands and thousands of demands made upon government, only a small portion receive serious attention from public policy-makers. Those demands that policy-makers either do choose or feel compelled to act upon constitute the *policy agenda*.[4] Thus, the policy agenda is distinguishable from political demands generally. It can also be distinguished from the term "political priorities," which usually designates a ranking of agenda items, with some being considered more important or pressing than others.

There will be a number of policy agendas in a political system. Cobb and Elder identify two basic types of agendas: the systemic agenda and the institutional, or governmental, agenda. The systemic agenda "consists of all issues that are commonly perceived by members of the political community as meriting public attention and as involving matters within the legitimate jurisdiction of existing governmental authority."[5] A systemic agenda will exist in every national, state, and local political system. Some items, such as crime in the streets, will appear on more than one systemic agenda, while others, such as whether to recognize the People's Republic of China or build a new convention center, will appear only on the national and local agenda, respectively.

The systemic agenda is essentially a discussion agenda. Action on a problem requires that it be brought before a governmental institution with authority to take appropriate action. An institutional or governmental agenda is composed of those problems to which public officials give serious and active attention. Since there are a variety of points at which policy decisions can be made, there are also a variety of institutional agendas. At the national level, one finds congressional, Presidential, administrative, and judicial agendas. An institutional agenda is an action agenda and will be more specific and concrete than a systemic agenda. Where crime in the streets may be of systemic concern, Congress will be confronted with more specific proposals for dealing with this problem area—for example, financial aid to local law-enforcement agencies.

Institutional agenda items can be separated into old items and new items, to use a not very imaginative pair of categories. Old items are those that appear with some regularity on agendas—for example, public employee pay increases, congressional reform, social security benefit increases, or budget allocations. They are familiar to officials, and the alternatives for dealing with them are somewhat patterned. New items are generated by particular situations or events, such as a nationwide railroad strike or a foreign policy crisis, or by the development of broad support for action on such issues as gun control or air-pollution abatement. Old items, it is suggested, "tend to receive priority from decision-makers, who constantly find their time is limited and that their agenda is overloaded. . . . Decision-makers presume that older problems warrant more attention because of their longevity and the greater familiarity officials have with them."[6] Of course, problems that reach the agenda as new items may, over time, be converted into old items. Environmental pollution and the Vietnam war are illustrative examples.

It should be noted that a policy agenda is not necessarily highly structured or defined. It would probably not be possible to get complete agreement on the content of a particular agenda, whether it is that of Congress or of a city council. Yet, clues to the content of the congressional agenda are provided by Presidential messages, legislation singled out by party leaders for attention, issues discussed in the communication media, and the like. Inability to enumerate all the items on a policy agenda does not destroy the usefulness of the concept for policy analysis.

Some of the ways in which policy problems achieve agenda status were hinted at earlier. More thorough treatment of this topic is now in order. Why do some problems achieve agenda status, while others do not? Or, to state the matter another way, what converts a policy problem into a live political issue?

One possibility is suggested by political scientist David Truman in his book on interest groups. Truman says that groups seek to maintain themselves in a state of reasonable equilibrium, and, if anything threatens this condition, they react accordingly.

> When the equilibrium of a group (and the equilibrium of its participant individuals) is seriously disturbed, various kinds of behavior may ensue. If the disturbance is not too great, the group's leaders will make an effort to restore the previous balance. . . . this effort may immediately necessitate recourse to the government. Other be-

haviors may occur if the disturbance is serious to the point of disruption.[7]

Thus small businessmen, threatened by the development of chain stores and other mass distributors, demand and obtain governmental action to protect their interests. Domestic oil producers, seeing cheaper imported oil as adverse to their price and profit situation, seek limitation on oil imports. Moreover, when one group gets what it wants from government, this success may cause a reaction by other groups, as in the case of organized labor's efforts to secure repeal or modification of the Taft-Hartley Act after 1947. But, as Charles Jones states, group processes cannot account for all of the problems which achieve governmental agenda status.[8]

Political leadership may be an important factor in agenda setting. Political leaders, whether motivated by considerations of political advantage, concern for the public interest, or both, may seize upon particular problems, publicize them, and propose solutions. Of particular importance here is the President because of his prominent role as an agenda-setter in American politics. Presidential legislative recommendations almost automatically go on the congressional agenda, as did the Nixon Administration's recommendations in 1974 to relax some of the pollution-control standards of the Clean Air Act. Members of Congress may also sometimes act as agenda setters. Area redevelopment legislation became a significant issue in the late 1950's and early 1960's largely through the efforts of Senator Paul Douglas, who first encountered the problem of depressed areas while campaigning in southern Illinois. Senator Edmund Muskie has for years been a policy leader in the area of environmental pollution control.

Items may achieve agenda status and be acted upon as a consequence of some kind of crisis or spectacular event, such as a coal mine accident or a natural disaster. This serves to dramatize an issue and attract wide attention, causing public officials to feel compelled to respond. There may be awareness, discussion, and continued advocacy of action on some matter; but, without broad interest being stirred or policy action obtained, some sort of "triggering" event seems needed to push the matter onto the policy agenda.[9] Thus the Soviet launching of the first Sputnik in 1957 helped push space exploration onto the policy agenda in the United States, notwithstanding initial professed lack of concern by some Eisenhower Administration officials. The furor touched off by the revelation that a sedative drug called thalidomide caused birth defects in babies when taken by pregnant women, and that it was not being marketed in the United States only because of the opposition of some officials in the Food and Drug Administration, made strengthening of drug licensing laws a major issue and eventuated in the Food and Drug Amendments of 1962. Indeed, until recently it seems that some kind of crisis event frequently has been required before major food or drug legislation has been enacted.[10]

Protest activity, including violence, is another means by which problems may be brought to the attention of policy-makers and put on the policy agenda.[11] During the 1960's, such actions as the sit-in movement, the voters-right march in Selma, Alabama (and the brutal reaction by the Selma police), and the 1963 "March on Washington" helped keep civil rights issues at the top of the national political agenda. The riots in many Northern cities in the mid-1960's focused attention on the problems of urban blacks. A sociologist, discussing the effects of the 1965 Watts riot, states: "The riot appears to have stemmed, at least in part, from frustrated efforts of the community to call attention to its plight. It seems to have been a call for help . . . where other means to draw attention to the community's distress seemed socially unavailable."[12] In more recent years, groups concerned with women's rights have utilized various kinds of demonstrations in their efforts to move their concerns onto the political agenda, and with some success. Even the gay people have taken to the streets to call attention to their problems.

Particular problems or issues may attract the attention of the communications media and, through their reportage, either be converted into agenda items or, if already on the agenda, be given more salience. A classic example is the activities of the Pulitzer and Hearst newspapers in the 1890's, through their highly colored and often inaccurate reporting, in making Spain's treatment of its colonies, especially Cuba, a major issue and doing much to cause the United States eventually to declare war on Spain.[13] In the mid-1960's, once poverty became a major agenda item, the news media helped keep the war on poverty in the public's eye by reporting fully many of the difficulties and errors in the conduct of the anti-poverty campaign. Minor events, such as a disturbance in a Job Corps camp or the misuse of a comparatively small sum of money, often were treated as major news items. Whether the news media are motivated by a desire to "create" news, report all that is newsworthy, stimulate sales, or serve the public interest is not under consideration here. Whatever their motives, as important opinion-shapers they help structure the political agenda. While both the conventions concerning how the news media are to operate and the compelling force of some events will limit somewhat the discretion the media have in selecting the events they call to the public's attention, they nonetheless do have much leeway.[14]

My purpose here has been to suggest some of the ways in which problems reach the policy agenda in order to illustrate this phase of the policy process.[15] I have not sought to present all the alternatives, assuming that this would be possible. It should also be apparent that all public problems do not reach the policy agenda. Policymakers do not feel compelled to deal with some problems. To account for their inaction, the concept of *nondecision* appears as a useful analytical and explanatory tool.

Nondecision-making has been defined by Peter Bachrach and Morton Baratz as "a means by which demands for change in the existing allocation of benefits and privileges in the community can be suffocated before they are even voiced; or kept covert; or killed before they gain access to the relevant decision-making arena."[16] There are various ways by which problems may be kept off a systemic or institutional agenda. At the local level, particularly, force may be utilized, as in the South during the 1950's and 1960's by various white groups to stifle black demands for equal rights. Another possibility is that prevailing values and beliefs—political culture—may operate to deny agenda status to particular problems or policy alternatives. Public acceptance of the graduated income tax has operated to deny agenda status to demands of the radical right for its repeal. Our beliefs concerning private property and capitalism have kept the issue of railroad nationalization from ever becoming a real agenda item, even in the late nineteenth and early twentieth centuries, when railroad policy was being developed, except when particular facets of railroad operations, such as passenger service (witness Amtrack), become unprofitable for private enterprise.

A third possibility has been suggested by E. E. Schattschneider. "The crucial problem in politics," he states, "is the management of conflict. No regime could endure that did not cope with this problem. All politics, all leadership, all organization involves the management of conflict. All conflict allocates space in the political universe. The consequences of conflict are so important that it is inconceivable that any regime would survive without making an attempt to shape the system." To survive, then, political leaders and organizations must prevent problems or issues that would threaten their existence from reaching the political arena (that is, achieving agenda status). The kinds of problems they are resistant to will depend upon what kinds of leaders and organizations they are, whether, for example, conservative Republicans or independent commissions. They will in any case resist considering some problems, for, as Schattschneider contends, "all forms of political organization have a bias in favor of the exploitation of some kinds of conflicts and the suppression of others because *organization is the mobilization of bias.* Some issues are organized into politics while others are organized out."[17]

In the study of public policy-making it is important to know why some problems are dealt with and others are neglected or suppressed. Recall that public policy is determined not only by what government does do but also by what it does not do. Take the situation of migratory farm workers, whose problems usually receive short shrift from public officials. Why is this the case? What does an answer to this question tell us about who gets what, and why, from the policy process? Is the neglect of migrant workers at least partly due to nondecision-making? Notwithstanding the somewhat imprecise nature of the concept of nondecision, it has utility for the analysis of the policy process.

Two Cases in Agenda Setting

To illustrate the agenda concept further, brief consideration will be given to how two recent problems, of substantially different content and scope, achieved agenda status. One is coal mine safety; the other is environmental pollution control.

Coal mining has long been a highly hazardous occupation, marked by a high rate of accidental injuries and deaths. Initially, coal mining was regulated by the states, but, because of dissatisfaction with their activities, federal regulation was sought by miners and their supporters, and obtained with the Coal Mine Safety Act of 1952. Enforcement of the Act was handled by the Bureau of Mines, which was often criticized as being too favorable toward the interests of mineowners. Frequent accidents continued, but for nearly two decades nothing was really done to strengthen mine-safety policy. Coal mining is concentrated in a few areas of the country, such as West Virginia and Southern Illinois, and most people are both relatively unaffected by, and unaware of, the problems of miners.

Then, on November 20, 1968, an explosion occurred at the Consolidated Coal Company's No. 9 mine in West Virginia. Seventy-nine miners were trapped below the surface, and all died before they could be rescued. This tragedy focused national attention on the miners' plight, which included not only mine explosions and accidents but also black-lung disease, caused by the inhalation of coal dust. The miners staged protest meetings, engaged in wildcat strikes, and conducted other activities, including a march on the West Virginia state capitol, in demand of remedial action. Public officials felt compelled to respond. In March, 1969, the West Virginia legislature enacted a law providing for compensation of victims of black-lung disease.

The miners and their spokesmen continued to press for national legislation, with a nationwide coal strike being repeatedly threatened if action were not forthcoming. President Nixon responded by sending Congress a special message, along with a draft bill, on coal mine safety. The bill was stronger than one previously proposed by President Johnson. In October, the Senate passed a mine-safety bill by a vote of 73 to 0, and a few weeks later the House did so by a 389 to 4 vote. It was subsequently signed into law by President Nixon.

Environmental pollution is a long-standing feature of our society, but only in the past decade has it become a major public problem. Where, for example, belching factory smokestacks were once regarded as a sign of progress, now they are generally viewed as problems requiring control. Both the national and state governments have enacted a variety of pollution-control legislation, and demands for additional, and stronger, legislation continue.

Several factors have contributed to making pollution control an important item on the policy agenda.[18] The affluence of American society contributes in several ways to the problem of pollution. As Davies explains:

> The increase in production has contributed to an intensification of the degree of actual pollution; the increase in the standard of living has permitted people the comparative luxury of being able to be con-

cerned about this; and the availability of ample public and private resources has given the society sufficient funds and skilled manpower to provide the potential for dealing with the problem.

People who are compelled to be continually concerned with securing the necessities of life will probably have little time or inclination to worry about pollution. In the developing countries, one will note little concern for the problem. Indeed, it is probably not perceived as a problem. In an affluent society, on the other hand, the conditions of life contribute to concern over pollution. More leisure time leads to greater demands for recreational resources and aesthetic pleasures, while a higher level of education enables people to understand better the nature and dangers of pollution. One can usefully regard pollution control as a "middle class issue," which helps ensure governmental attention to it.

Pollution control is an attractive public issue. It affects everyone, and a program that does something for everyone tends to be quite attractive politically. Moreover, it is difficult to oppose pollution control—except indirectly, as by contending that pollution standards increase energy use and thus contribute to the energy crisis—because one cannot win many political allies by openly favoring dirty air and water. In addition, pollution control is often tied to public health, which is another popular concern. As the old song has it, "Everybody wants to go to heaven, but nobody wants to die."

Finally, when government acts on the pollution problem, it helps create a demand for additional action. The problem is publicized and given respectability, and the public learns that something can be done to alleviate the problem. Moreover, when agencies are established to administer pollution-control programs, they develop vested interests in drawing attention to the programs. This, in turn, may lead to the development of group support for the program, an institutionalization of concern, and a continuous demand for action. The experience of the National Environmental Protection Agency is a case in point. Pollution control appears highly likely to remain on the policy agenda at all levels of government for years to come.

THE FORMULATION OF POLICY PROPOSALS

Policy formulation involves the development of pertinent and acceptable proposed courses of action for dealing with public problems. Policy formulation does not always result in a proposed law, executive order, or administrative rule. Policy-makers may decide not to take positive action on some problem but, instead, to leave it alone, to let matters work themselves out. In other words, the fact that a public problem is on the policy agenda does not mean that positive government action will be taken. Congress wrestled with the problem of railroad regulation for two decades, and considered many policy proposals, before it finally enacted the Interstate Commerce Act of 1887. Awareness of a problem does not guarantee positive government action, although unawareness or nonconcern pretty much ensures inaction.

Who Is Involved?

In this discussion of who is involved in the development of policy proposals, attention will be focused on the national level in the United States. In the twentieth century, the President and his chief aides and advisers in the Executive Office have been the major source of initiative in the development of policy proposals. The members of Congress have come to expect the President to present policy recommendations to them for consideration. Moreover, they have also come to expect the executive to provide them with draft bills embodying his recommendations. This does not mean that Congress always accepts the President's proposals; such, as you well know, is far from the case. What the members of Congress want is "some real meat to digest."

Many policy proposals are developed by officials—both career and appointed—in the administrative departments and agencies. Concerned with governmental programs in agriculture, health, law enforcement, foreign trade, and other areas, they become aware of policy problems and develop proposals to deal with them. These are transmitted to the executive and Congress for their consideration. Many such proposals will involve modification of existing laws, such as plugging up revealed loopholes. A classic case involves the soil bank legislation of 1956. It was found that the original law did not prohibit persons from leasing government grazing lands at low rates per acre while being paid much higher rates for having taken them out of "production." Corrective legislation was proposed by Department of Agriculture officials and enacted to prohibit this practice.

Special study groups or advisory commissions, composed of private citizens and officials, are sometimes created by the President to examine particular policy areas and develop policy proposals. The President's Committee on Urban Housing (1967–68) was appointed by President Johnson and charged with developing proposals to increase the production of housing for low- and moderate-income families. Many of its proposals were transmitted to Congress by the President. Such advisory commissions are employed both to develop policy proposals and to help win support for them through their usually prestigious membership. Some groups, of course, may be largely designed to give the appearance of concern and action on some problem in order to satisfy demands for action. An example is the Commission on Campus Unrest, appointed in 1970 by President Nixon. It has had no discernible impact on public policy.

It is well to note that some advisory commissions may have a substantial effect on policy in directions other than those intended by their Presidential creator. An interesting glimpse into the policy process is provided by the case of the Committee to Strengthen the Security of the Free World (1962–63), which was appointed by President Kennedy to study the foreign-aid program. Unexpectedly, the Committee, in its report, while defending the program in principle, advocated a reduction in spending for foreign aid. Although this recommendation ran counter to the administration's wishes, it was decided not to reject the report so that General Lucius Clay, the Committee chairman, could testify for the program before Congress. Moreover, rejecting the report might have pushed Clay into the anti–foreign aid camp, which had seized upon the report as support for its position. Thus, President Kennedy reduced his foreign-aid request in accordance with the Committee's recommendation and got Clay to defend the program. Congress not only accepted the President's cut but made still more cuts of its own, all of which added up to the largest reduction in the history of the foreign aid program. In addition, new restrictions were added to the program.[19]

Legislators are also involved in policy formation. In the course of congressional hearings and investigations, through contacts with various administrative officials and interest-group representatives, and on the basis of their own interests and activity, legislators receive suggestions for action on problems and formulate proposed courses of actions. In some policy areas, congressmen have done much of the policy formulation. Such is the case in the area of air and water pollution, where Congress, under the leadership of such individuals as Senator Edmund Muskie and Representative Paul Rogers, has been willing to move more quickly and extensively than has the executive. Tax-reform legislation in 1969 was largely a congressional product, with the Nixon Administration getting on the bandwagon only after it was well under way.

Finally, interest groups often play a major role in policy formulation, sometimes going to the legislature with specific proposals for legislation. Or they may work with legislative and executive officials for the enactment of one officially proposed policy, perhaps with some modifications to suit their interests. Management groups were closely involved in the development of the bill that became the Labor Reform (Landrum-Griffin) Act of 1959. At the state level, interest groups often play an important role in the formulation of legislation, especially on technical and complex matters, because state legislators lack the time and staff resources needed to cope with them. Steiner and Gove report that the Illinois legislature customarily enacts legislation in the area of labor-management relations only after it has been agreed to by representatives of organized labor and industry. Thus, by custom, private groups may become the actual formulators of policy.

Competing proposals for dealings with a given problem may come from these sources. Take the example of national health insurance in the early 1970's.[20] The Nixon Administration presented to Congress a National Health Insurance Partnership Act that provided that employers make approved health-care plans available to their employees, that government-sponsored insurance be available to low-income families with children not protected by employment-based insurance, and that health services be improved through the establishment of health-maintenance organizations. Senator Edward Kennedy and Representative Martha Griffiths, developed and introduced a bill providing for a comprehensive national health insurance system covering all citizens; it would be financed partly by taxes on employers and beneficiaries and partly by general revenue funds. The American Medical Association's entry was the Health Care Insurance Act ("Medicredit"), providing for income-tax credits for the purchase of private health insurance, along with federally subsidized health insurance or group insurance for low-income people. The Health Insurance Association of America, an insurance company interest group, proposed a National Health Care

Act creating an insurance system in which insurance costs were met by employer and employee contributions; the poor would be covered by government subsidized, state-sponsored programs. And there are still other proposals in the arena. Policy-makers, therefore, are not confronted simply with a choice between a government health insurance program or no program at all. Rather, private and official actors have formulated a variety of proposals that compete for acceptance. What is likely to result is the adoption of some compromise course of action based on these proposals. The involvement of both public officials and private interests and compromise are basic characteristics of policy formulation in America (and in most other political systems).

Policy Formulation as Process

Policy formulation can be viewed as involving two types of activities. One is deciding generally what should be done, if anything, concerning a particular problem. Thus, in the above illustration, there is the question "What kind of national health insurance system shall we have?" In other instances, the question may be: "What kind of foreign-aid program shall we have?" or "What should be the minimum wage level and who should be covered by it?" Answers to these questions take the form of general principles. Once such questions have been resolved, the second type of activity involves the actual drafting of legislation (or the writing of administrative rules), which, when adopted, will carry these principles into effect. This is a technical and rather mundane, but nonetheless highly important, task. The way a bill is written, the specific provisions it contains, can have substantial effect on its administration and the actual content of public policy.

An interesting illustration is provided by the National Defense Education Act of 1958. A particular provision of the Act provided that students receiving graduate fellowship assistance had to sign a noncommunist affidavit, or "loyalty oath." This soon created much controversy. Liberals criticized it as unnecessary and an affront to the patriotism of students, among other things. Conservatives defended it as necessary to prevent aid from going to communists and wondered why any loyal American would object to signing such an oath. Some universities announced they would not participate in the fellowship program with the oath requirement. (Apparently few, if any, students who qualified for fellowships declined to sign the oath and take the money.) Eventually, the oath was replaced by a milder and more acceptable loyalty affirmation.

Notwithstanding the controversy sparked by the oath requirement, there was no discussion of it in either the committee hearings or the floor debates on the Act. No one advocated its inclusion in the legislation. How, then, did it get into the law? The answer to this question is not very dramatic, but such is the case with answers to many questions. The person drafting the formal language of the National Defense Education Act copied some of its fellowship provisions from a 1950 statute; one of these provisions was the loyalty oath requirement. It had caused no controversy under the earlier law. But when it was discovered in the 1958 law, the fun started. One moral that can be drawn from this is that it is often easier to get a provision into law than it is subsequently to remove it.

In practice, it is often difficult, if not impossible, to separate neatly policy formulation from policy adoption, which will be discussed in the next section. They are analytically distinct functional activities that occur in the policy process. They do not, however, "have to be performed by separate individuals at different times in different institutions."[21] Those concerned with formulating courses of action will be influenced in what they do by the need to win adoption of their proposals. Some provisions will be included, others excluded, in an effort to build support for a proposed policy. Looking further ahead, the formulators may also be influenced by what they think may happen during the administration of the policy.

Formulating the War on Poverty, 1964

The idea of having his administration wage a war on poverty apparently originated with President John Kennedy himself.[22] During a review of economic conditions with Walter Heller, Chairman of the Council of Economic Advisers, in December, 1962, Kennedy stated: "Now look, I want to go beyond the things that have already been accomplished. Give me the facts and figures on the things we still have to do. For example, what about the poverty problem in the United States?" This comment set in motion staff work within the Executive Office that was to culminate in the war on poverty.

Interest in, and discussion of, the poverty problem continued in the Executive Office during the spring and summer of 1963. Not everyone, however, was enthusiastic about an attack on poverty; in June, in a speech to the Communication Workers of America, Heller spoke of the need "to open more exits from poverty" but elicited no positive response. A subsequent meeting with some journalists stirred little in the way of either interest or news stories. In midsummer, Heller called a meeting of White House aides and other executive officials to discuss the possibility of including antipoverty measures as part of the administration's 1964 legislative program. The reaction reportedly ranged from mild support to outright opposition. Theodore Sorensen, one of Kennedy's leading assistants, thought an antipoverty program would be both morally sound and a good political issue in 1964. On the other hand, some thought it unwise to raise the issue of poverty so close to the 1964 campaign. It was contended, for example, that, since Kennedy had pledged in 1960 to "get the country moving again," a stress on poverty would be a confession of failure.

Both the Council of Economic Advisers and the President remained interested in an antipoverty program. In the fall, a decision for antipoverty legislation began to crystallize. Finally, on November 19, Kennedy responded with a flat yes to Heller's question whether antipoverty measures should be included in the 1964 legislative program and said he wanted to see the proposed measures on which Heller was working in a couple of weeks. Three days later, the President was assassinated in Dallas.

On November 24, Heller met with President Johnson to brief him on the work of the Council of Economic Advisers. Informed of the proposed antipoverty program, he quickly gave it his approval. According to Heller, his words were: "That's my kind of program. It will help people. I want you to move full speed ahead on it." Thus, the decision was made to have a poverty program. In January, 1964, President Johnson announced the declaration of war on poverty by his administration. Now let us look specifically at how the legislation to carry out the war on poverty was formulated.

The initial work in planning an antipoverty program was handled by a task force drawn from the Council of Economic Advisers and the Bureau of the Budget (now the Office of Management and Budget). Efforts were focused first on the informational and analytical needs of designing an attack on poverty without any attempt to devise specific programs. Then, in early November, Heller requested the major domestic departments and agencies to submit suggestions for a legislative program. The result was a veritable flood of proposals, featuring many of their favored ideas—job training and employment programs from Labor, rural development from Agriculture, education and welfare services from Health, Education and Welfare, and so on. By the middle of December, no specific proposal had been fashioned, although a "line item" of $500 million had been decided on for the program for the 1965 budget. The Council-Bureau task force was now confronted with the necessity of selecting from among the many proposals presented concerning how to do this and develop an integrated war on poverty for $500 million.

About this time a Budget Bureau official advanced the idea of making a limited number of general-purpose grants to help localities develop their own community-wide antipoverty programs (or community action programs, as they came to be designated). This proposal was based on the experiences of the Ford Foundation and the President's Commission on Juvenile Delinquency and Youth Crime in making grants for programs directed at the problems of slum areas in large cities. The Council-Bureau task force accepted the community action proposal, finding it attractive for several reasons: It was a way to attack poverty with the limited funds available; it drew upon "grass-roots initiative," which has been a popular orientation; and general grants to local agencies seem a good way to fund and coordinate federal programs at the local level. The desire for coordination, we might note, has been a perennial concern of the Budget Bureau.

The departments and agencies were unhappy with this proposal, although much of the money allocated for the community action programs would be spent through existing federal programs. They wanted to control their own funds and programs and feared a loss of control under the proposed arrangement. They felt that their own proposals had not been adequately considered by the task force. Moreover, there was disagreement over how the new program should be administered—by a new independent agency, by a Cabinet-level council, or what? Matters came to a head at a White House meeting on January 23, 1964, at which it became clear that substantial disagreement existed with regard to how the war on poverty should be conducted.

On February 1, much to everyone's surprise, President Johnson announced that he was appointing Sargent Shriver, then Director of the Peace Corps, to plan the war on poverty. Shriver moved rapidly to begin the development of legislation. He soon discovered that Secretary of Labor Willard Wirtz's desire for a broad-based and multifaceted war on poverty enjoyed wide support among the departments and agencies. Consequently, the Council-Bureau proposal for an antipoverty program featuring a limited number of community action programs was rejected in favor of a bill containing a "package" of programs.

To draft this new legislative package, Shriver assembled a task force of volunteers and others on loan from their departments or agencies. Included were people from the Departments of Labor, Agriculture, Defense, and HEW, the Bureau of the Budget, the Small Business Administration, and other agencies. Some concerned intellectuals, particularly Michael Harrington and Paul Jacobs, were involved. All ideas and proposals were reconsidered. Scores of businessmen, union officials, mayors, welfare officials, and others were consulted or asked for suggestions. At no time, however, were representatives of the poor or the black community involved in formulating the legislative proposal put together by Shriver's group.

Within a few weeks a legislative proposal was developed and, on March 16, President Johnson submitted the draft bill for the Economic Opportunity Act to Congress. As introduced, the bill provided for a Job Corps, a Neighborhood Youth Corps, a work-study program, an expanded community action program, loan programs for low-income rural families and small businessmen, and Volunteers in Service to America, or VISTA. An Office of Economic Opportunity was to administer some of these programs and coordinate the over-all war on poverty. Several of the programs included in the legislation were based on administration bills then pending before Congress. Nonetheless, there was little consultation with members of Congress in preparation of the bill.

Significant policy decisions were made not only in deciding what particular programs to include in the proposed legislation but also in drafting the bill. The community action part of the bill is especially illustrative of the latter. At first, an effort was made to draw up detailed specifications for community action programs on the assumption that this would be necessary to secure congressional approval. But various welfare groups then tried to obtain high priority for their favorite programs, and the legal drafting team decided to resolve the issue by dropping all specifications from the bill. A provision was included that local community action programs should be "developed, conducted, and administered with the maximum feasible participation of the residents of the area and members of the groups served." Little attention was paid to this clause, although it was later to become a major source of controversy in the administration of the program. In considering the bill, Congress did not manifest any concern either about the omission of program specifications or about the inclusion of the "maximum feasible participation" clause.

Controlled as it was by substantial Democratic majorities, Congress acted rapidly on the bill. Hearings were quickly scheduled and were stacked with favorable witnesses. Potential opponents had neither much time to organize nor much opportunity to express themselves. The congressional proceedings, on the whole, were handled in rather partisan fashion, with the Republican minority being given little opportunity to participate in shaping the legislation, especially in the House. Congress did make some changes in the bill. Two new programs were added: aid to migrant farm workers and an adult literacy program. A program of grants to enable nonprofit corporations to buy land, redevelop it into family farms, and sell it to low-income farm families was attacked in the Senate as "socialistic" and akin to "collective farming," and was deleted from the bill. The section dealing with the Job Corps was amended, at the insistence of conservation groups, to require that 40 per cent of Job Corps enrollees be assigned to conservation camps. Another amendment, supported by Congresswoman Edith Green, made girls eligible for the Job Corps. On the whole, Congress did not make really major changes in the bill, although it, too, was clearly involved in the formulation process. On August 20, 1964, President Johnson signed the Economic Opportunity Act into law, and the war on poverty officially got under way. A major piece of social legislation had been formulated and adopted in less than a year's time.

MAKING POLICY DECISIONS

Policy formulation, as we noted, is in practice typically blended with the policy decision stage of the policy process. Formulation is directed toward winning approval of a preferred policy alternative; an affirmative decision is the pay-off of the entire process. In this section, we will focus on how policy decisions are made.

A policy decision involves action by some official person or body to approve, modify, or reject a preferred policy alternative. In positive fashion it takes such forms as the enactment of legislation or the issuance of an executive order. It is well here to recall the distinction made in Chapter 1 between policy decisions, which significantly affect the content of public policy, and routine decisions, which involve the day-to-day application of policy. Furthermore, a policy decision is usually the culmination of a variety of decisions, some routine and some not so routine, made during the operation of the policy process.

What is typically involved at the policy decision stage is not selection from among a number of full-blown policy alternatives but, rather, action on what we have chosen to call a preferred policy alternative—one for which the proponents of action think they can win approval, even though it does not provide all that they might like. As the formulation process moves toward the decision state, some proposals will be rejected, others accepted, still others modified; differences will be narrowed; bargains will be struck, until ultimately, in some instances, the policy decision will be only a formality. In other instances, the question will be in doubt until the votes are counted or the decision is announced.

Although private individuals and organizations also participate in making policy decisions, the formal authority rests with public officials—legislators, executives, administrators, judges. In democracies, the task of making policy decisions is most closely identified with the legislature, which is designed to represent the interests of the populace. One frequently hears that a majority of the legislature represents a majority of the people. Whatever its accuracy as a description of reality, such a contention does accord with our notion that the people should rule in a democracy. Policy decisions made by the legislature are usually accepted as legitimate, as being made in the proper way and hence binding on all concerned. Generally, decisions made by public officials are regarded as legitimate if the officials have legal authority to act and meet accepted standards in taking action.

In the remainder of this chapter, several aspects of policy decision-making will come under examination. These include decision criteria; types of decision-making; majority-building in Congress; Presidential decision-making; and incrementalism.

Decision Criteria

Decision-making can be studied either as an individual or as a collective process. In the first instance, the focus is particularly on the criteria used by individuals in making choices. In the latter, the concern is with the processes by which majorities are built, or by which approval is otherwise gained, for specific decisions. Individual choices, of course, are usually made with some reference to what others involved in the decisional situation are likely to do.

An individual may be subject to a variety of influencing factors when deciding how to vote on or resolve a particular policy question. Which of these forces is most crucial, so far as his choice is concerned, is often hard to assess. Public officials frequently make statements explaining their decisions in the *Congressional Record,* constituency newsletters, speeches, press conferences, court opinions, memoirs, and elsewhere. The reasons they give for their decisions may be those that were really controlling; or they may be reasons that are acceptable to the public at large or to important constituents, while the actual bases for choice go unstated. Nonetheless, it is often possible, through careful observation and analysis, to determine what factors were operative in a given situation, if not necessarily to assign them specific weights. A number of criteria that may influence policy choice are discussed here.

Values. In Chapter 1, some of the values (preferences, standards) that a person may employ in making decisions, including political, organizational, policy, and personal values, were presented. There is no need to repeat that discussion here; rather, some aspects of individual values as decision criteria will be more fully commented upon, because the decision-maker's values are probably the most direct and pervasive criteria for deciding what to do. Officials often develop strong commitments to particular ways of handling given problems, such as public rather than private development of hydroelectric power sites, or the use of monetary rather than fiscal policies in combating inflation. On appropriations for the armed forces, a congressman who is a hawk will probably favor increased funds, while a dove will probably support a reduction in funds. Decisions may also be made on the basis of one's ideology, which may be defined as a coherent set of values and beliefs concerning government and politics. Thus, for example, a legislator, in deciding how to vote on a bill, might only have to determine whether it is a conservative or liberal measure and act accordingly. Of course, it may not always be easy to give a bill or proposal an ideological tag. Probably few officials make decisions solely on ideological grounds.

Political Party Affiliation. Party loyalty is a significant criterion for most members of Congress, although it is often difficult to separate from such other considerations as leadership influence and ideological commitments. Relatively few votes in Congress meet the "90 per cent versus 90 per cent" definition of a party vote, in which 90 per cent or more of the Democrats are lined up against 90 per cent or more of the Republicans. In the past century, party voting, as so defined, was at its peak during the McKinley era, when approximately 50 per cent of the votes in the House were party votes.[23] Since then, party voting has declined, and in recent years only 2–8 per cent of House roll-call votes have been party votes.[24] If, however, the test of a party vote is relaxed to "50 per cent versus 50 per cent," then about half of the House roll-call votes during the 1950's and 1960's qualify as party votes. In comparison, it may be noted that most of the votes in the British House of Commons meet the "90 per cent versus 90 per cent" party vote standard. Party affiliation does remain as the best predictor of how congressmen will vote on issues. If one knows a congressman's party affiliation, and the party positions on issues, and then uses party affiliation as the basis for predicting votes, he will probably be correct more often than he will be using any other single indicator. If the political parties in Congress are not strong, disciplined parties, neither are they unimportant in their impact on legislative decision-making.

Party loyalties or attachments vary in importance among issue areas. Party conflict has developed most consistently on such matters as agricultural price supports, business regulation, labor, and social welfare legislation. In the agricultural area, for example, Democrats have tended to favor high price supports and production controls, while Republicans have preferred lower price supports and fewer controls. Again, Democrats have been more inclined to support the development of new welfare programs, such as medicare, and the expansion or increased funding of existing ones, such as public assistance, than have Republicans. In some other issue areas, such as civil rights, veterans' benefits, public works, and foreign policy, it has often been difficult or impossible to delineate distinct and persistent party differences.

Constituency Interests. A bit of conventional wisdom in Congress holds that, when party interests and constituency interests conflict on some issue, the congressman should "vote his constituency." It is, after all, the voters in his district who hold the ultimate power to hire and fire. In acting for the interests of his constituents, a representative may act as a delegate carrying out the instructions of his constituents, or he may act as a trustee and exercise his best judgment in their behalf when voting on policy questions.[25] Of course, he may try to combine these two styles, acting as a delegate on some issues and as a trustee on others.

In some instances, the interests of his constituents will be rather clear and strongly held, and the representative will act contrary to them at his peril. In the past, Southern congressmen were well aware of the strong opposition among their white constituents to civil rights legislation and voted accordingly. Again, a legislator from a strong labor district will probably have little doubt concerning his constituents' interests on minimum wage and right-to-work legislation. On a great many issues, however, a representative will be hard put to determine what his voters want. Large portions of the electorate have little, if any, knowledge of most issues. How, then, does the representative measure which way the wind is blowing from his district if no air currents are moving? In such situations, the legislator will have to make his decision on the basis of his own values, or on other criteria, such as recommendations from party leaders or the chief executive.

Nonelected public officials, such as administrators, may also act as representatives. Agencies often have well-developed relationships with particular interest groups and strive to represent the latter's interests in policy formation and administration. The Department of Agriculture is especially responsive to the interests of commercial farmers, while the Office of Economic Opportunity has (at least until the 1970's) viewed itself as the representative of the poor in the national administrative system. The decision and actions of the two agencies have reflected the interests of their constituents. Some commentators have contended that administrative agencies may be more representative of particular interests in society than are elected officials.[26] Whatever the validity of this contention, it is clear that legislators are not the only officials influenced by the need or desire to act representatively in making decisions.

Public Opinion. Political scientists have devoted much time and effort to studying the formation, content, and change of public opinion on political issues. The more philosophically inclined have been concerned with what should be the role of public opinion in the governmental process. Our concern here is with the effect of public opinion on the actions of policy-makers. Are the choices of policy-makers shaped or determined by public opinion? Does public opinion serve as a decision criteria? It is well to proceed tentatively in answering such questions, bearing in mind V. O. Key's comment that "to speak with precision of public opinion is a task not unlike coming to grips with the Holy Ghost."[27]

A useful way to approach the problem of the effect of public opinion on policy-making is to distinguish between decisions that shape the broad direction, or thrust, of policy and the day-to-day, often routine, decisions on specific aspects of policy. Public opinion is probably not a significant decision criterion in the second category. To draw on Key again, "Many, if not most, policy decisions by legislatures and by other authorities exercising broad discretion are made under circumstances in which extremely small proportions of the general public have any awareness of the particular issue, much less any understanding of the consequences of the decision."[28] The legislator deciding how to vote on a particular tax amendment or public works bill will probably be unaffected in any direct sense by public opinion. Of course, he may try to anticipate the reaction of the public to such votes, but this will leave him with substantial latitude, given the lack of awareness mentioned above.

Nonetheless, the general boundaries and direction of public policy may be shaped by public opinion. Given existing public attitudes, such actions as the nationalization of the steel industry or the repeal of the Sherman Antitrust and Social Security Acts appear highly unlikely. Conversely, officials may come to believe that public opinion demands some kind of policy action, as was the case with labor-reform legislation in 1959 and tax-reform legislation in 1969. These were generalized rather than specific "demands," which left much discretion on details to Congress. In the area of foreign policy, public opinion appears to accord wide latitude to executive officials, as the conduct of American intervention in Vietnam during the 1960's clearly indicates. Ultimately, however, growing public opposition to the Vietnam war appears to have contributed to President Johnson's decision not to run for re-election in 1968 and the beginning of efforts to "wind down" the war and withdraw.[29]

In summary, policy-makers do not appear unaffected in their choices by public opinion. The relationship between public opinion and policy actions, however, is neither as simple nor as direct as was once assumed. But the elected public official who totally ignores public opinion and does not include it among his decision criteria, should there be an official so foolish, is likely to find himself out of luck at the polls.

Deference. Officials confronted with the task of making a decision may decide how to act by deferring to the judgment of others. The "others" to whom deference is given may or may not be hierarchical superiors. Administrative officials often do make decisions in accordance with the directives of department heads or chief executives. This is how we expect them to act, especially when the directives of superiors are clear in meaning—which, it must be added, they sometimes are not. Administrators may also defer to the suggestions or judgments of members of Congress, as Department of Agriculture officials do when receiving advice from Congressman Jamie Whitten, Chairman of the House Agricultural Appropriations Subcommittee. Because of his influence, Whitten has sometimes been referred to as the "permanent Secretary of Agriculture."[30]

Members of Congress often have to vote on issues that are of little interest to them (because they do not affect their constituents), or on which they have little information, or which are highly complex in nature. On such matters, congressmen often decide how to vote by seeking the advice of other legislators whose judgment they trust, whether party leaders, committee chairmen, or policy experts. When a congressman is unable to decide how to vote on the basis of his own analysis of an issue, deference to someone whose judgment he trusts is a reasonably rational, low-information strategy for making decisions. Donald Matthews argues that, because of the widespread practice of deference to policy experts, "few institutions provide more power to the exceptionally competent member than does the House of Representatives."[31]

Judges, too, make decisions by deference. For example, when they interpret a statute, in the course of either applying it to a particular case or determining its constitutionality, they often defer to the intent of the legislature.[32] Statutory language is often ambiguous and its meaning unclear. In trying to determine what the legislature intends by particular phrases such as "restraint of trade" or "all lawful means," they may refer to such materials as committee hearings and reports and floor debates on the law in question. In the course of debate on bills, legislators often strive to build a record of legislative intent to inform both courts and administration on their intended meaning. Those who argue that legislative debates are meaningless ignore this function of debate.

Decision Rules. Those confronted with the task of making many decisions often develop rules of thumb, or guidelines, to focus attention on particular facts and relationships and thereby both simplify and regularize the decision-making process. There is no set of decision rules common to all decision-makers, although some may be widely utilized. What guidelines, if any, apply in a particular situation is a matter to be determined by empirical investigation. A few examples will be presented here to illustrate the concept.

The rule of *stare decisis* (in effect, "let the precedents stand") is often used by the judiciary in deciding cases. According to this decision rule, or principle, current cases should be decided in the same way as similar cases were in the past. The use of precedents to guide decision-making is by no means limited to the judiciary. Executives, administrators, and legislators also frequently make decisions on the basis of precedents. They are often urged to do so by those who would be affected by their actions, particularly if this will help maintain a desired *status quo*. Those adversely affected by existing precedents are likely to find them lacking in virtue and utility.

In the antitrust area, some *per se* rules have been developed. Certain actions, such as price fixing and market allocation, have been held to be *per se* (in effect, "as such") violations of the Sherman Antitrust Act. If the action is found to exist, that is sufficient to prove violation, and no effort is made to inquire into the reasonableness or other possible justifications of the action. *Per se* rules add simplicity and certainty to antitrust decision-making.

Richard Fenno, in his study of a number of congressional committees, has found that each committee has some decision rules that help shape its decision-making activities. Thus, the House Appropriations Committee, seeking independence of the executive, has a "rule" to the effect that it should reduce executive budget requests, and, in fact, most requests are reduced. Again, the House Post Office and Civil Service Committee have as a decision rule, in Fenno's words, "to support maximum pay increases and improvement in benefits for employee groups and to oppose all rate increases for mail users."[33] Fenno points out that every committee has decision rules, although some rules are easier to discover than others.

Styles of Decision-Making

Most policy decisions of any magnitude are made by coalitions, which often must take the form of numerical majorities, whether one's focus is on Congress, North Dakota State Legislature, the Omaha city council, the Danish Folketing, or the British Parliament after the 1974 elections. Even when a numerical majority is not officially required, the support of others is needed to ensure that the decision is implemented and compliance achieved. The commander can yell "Charge!" and have the bugle blown, but, if the troops all ride off to the cantina, he is apt to experience a trying afternoon with the Indians. More to the point, perhaps, the President is often vested with final authority to make decisions, but he will need to gain the support or cooperation of other officials if his decisions are to be effective. As Richard Neustadt, an astute commentator on the Presidency, has remarked: "Underneath our images of Presidents-in-boots, astride decisions, are the half-observed realities of Presidents-in-sneakers, stirrups in hand, trying to induce particular department heads, or Congressmen or Senators, to climb aboard."[34] President Kennedy sometimes told friends who offered policy suggestions or criticisms, "Well, I agree with you, but I'm not sure the government will."[35] These comments point up the coalitional nature of much Presidential decision-making.

Nowhere, perhaps, is the coalitional nature of decision-making better illustrated than in the Danish Folketing (Parliament), where the 179 seats were divided in 1974 among 10 parties. The Liberal Prime Minister governed on the basis of a coalition formed by his party and the Social Democratic, Democratic Center, and Christian Peoples parties. In taking policy actions, the Prime Minister had always to think first about holding his coalition together, lest he lose his majority and his power to govern.

In this section, three styles of decision-making will be examined —namely, bargaining, persuasion, and command. Our focus will turn from individuals' decisions to decision-making as a collective process.

Bargaining. The most common style of decision-making in the American political system is bargaining. Bargaining can be defined as a process in which two or more persons in positions of power or authority adjust their at least partially inconsistent goals in order to formulate a course of action that is acceptable but not necessarily ideal to the participants. In short, bargaining involves negotiation, give-and-take, and compromise in order to reach a mutually acceptable position. In the private realm, it is epitomized in collective bargaining over the terms of work by union leaders and management officials. For bargaining to occur, the bargainers must be willing to negotiate, they must have something to negotiate about, and each must have something (i.e., resources) that others want or need.

Two factors seem especially important in making bargaining the dominant mode of decision-making in our society. One is social pluralism, that is, the presence of a variety of partially autonomous groups—labor unions, business organizations, professional associations, farm organizations, environmental groups, sportsmen's clubs, civil rights groups, and so on. Although partially autonomous, they are also interdependent and "must bargain with one another for protection and advantage."[36] The second factor to note is the use of such constitutional practices as federalism, the separation of powers, and bicameral legislatures, which serve to fragment and disperse political power among many decision points. Major policy decisions at the national level often require the approval of all branches of government, plus acceptance by state or local governments and affected private groups. Such is the case with current federal aid to education and environmental pollution-control policies.

Bargaining may be either explicit or implicit in nature. When bargaining is explicit, the bargainers (group leaders, party officials, committee chairmen, department heads, executives, and so on) state their agreements (bargains) in clear terms in order to minimize the likelihood of misunderstanding. The U.S. Constitution is a good illustration of explicit bargaining between large and small states, North and South, and other interests. An explicit bargain was struck by Wilbur Mills, Chairman of the House Ways and Means Committee, and President Johnson in 1968 when Mills agreed to go along with the administration's income-tax increase proposed only after the President had agreed to a reduction in expenditures.[37] In international politics, treaties exemplify explicit bargains. Here we can note that bargaining in international politics is widely accepted because the idea of national interests is well accepted. In domestic politics bargaining, however necessary and prevalent, is often looked upon as incompatible with a quest for the "public interest" or, in more crude language, as a "sell out."

More frequently, however, bargaining is probably implicit in nature. In implicit bargaining, the terms of agreement among the bargainers are often vague or ambiguous and may be expressed in such phrases as "future support" or "favorable disposition." Such bargaining frequently occurs in Congress, where one member will agree to support another on a given bill in return for future cooperation. Understandings or gentlemen's agreements may be developed by administrators concerning their responsibilities for the administration of particular programs so as to eliminate conflict among themselves. In some instances, implicit bargaining may be sufficiently nebulous so that it is unclear whether an agreement actually exists.

Two common forms of bargaining are log-rolling and compromise. Log-rolling usually involves a straightforward "mutual exchange of support on two different items. This is a prevalent form of bargaining because not every item on an agenda interests every leader to the same extent."[38] A good illustration of log-rolling involves the Omnibus Rivers and Harbors Bill passed by Congress each year. The legislation includes a substantial number of separate and independent river- and harbor-improvement and flood-control projects. The congressman who wants a project for his state or district in effect agrees to support the projects for other congressmen's states or districts. Farm legislation and, in the past, tariff legislation have also involved much log-rolling.

Compromise usually involves explicit bargaining, is normally centered on a single issue, and involves questions of more or less of something. Here the bargainers regard "half a loaf as better than none" and consequently adjust their differences so as to come into agreement. A classic example is the Missouri Compromise of 1820, which temporarily settled conflict between Northern and Southern interests over the extension of slavery into the Louisiana Territory. To simplify, the North wanted slavery excluded from the Territory, while the South wanted no prohibition. It was finally agreed by

Congress that slavery would be prohibited in the Territory (except Missouri) north of 36′30°. The Civil Rights Act of 1964 involved many compromises between those wanting stronger legislation and those wanting weaker or no legislation, especially on the provisions dealing with public accommodations, equal employment opportunity, and judicial enforcement. Issues involving money—for instance, budgets—are probably the most likely and easiest matters on which to compromise.

Persuasion. Attempts to convince others of the correctness or value of one's position, and thereby cause them to adopt it as their own, involve persuasion. Unlike the bargainer, the persuader seeks to build support for what he wants without having to modify his own position. This may involve trying to convince others of the merits of one's position, or the benefits that will accrue to them or their constituents if they accept it, or some combination of the two. The persuader thus seeks to induce others "to do it his way." Attorneys who argue cases before the Supreme Court not only present their side of the issue but seek to persuade a majority of the Court of the correctness of their position. Presidential meetings with congressional leaders are often sessions in which Presidential programs are explained, their benefits for congressmen and their constituents outlined, and appeals made for congressional leaders' support. Within Congress, appeals by party leaders to the rank and file to the effect that "Your party needs your support on this issue, can't you go along?" are essentially persuasive in content. Statements by officials to the public explaining and justifying particular programs, such as a price freeze, represent efforts to convince the public to comply with them.

Command. Bargaining involves interaction among peers; command involves hierarchical relationships among superordinates and subordinates. It is the ability of those in superior positions to make decisions that are binding upon those who come within their jurisdiction. They may use sanctions in the form of either rewards or penalties—although usually sanctions are thought of as penalties—to reinforce their decisions. Thus, the subordinate who faithfully accepts and carries out a superior's decision may be rewarded with favorable recognition or a promotion, while the one who refuses to comply may be fired or demoted. President Nixon's decision to institute a price-wage freeze in August, 1971, on the basis of authority granted by the Economic Stabilization Act was essentially one of command. The Office of Management and Budget engages in command behavior when it approves, rejects, or modifies agency requests for appropriations and proposals for legislation prior to their transmittal to Congress. On the whole, however, command is more characteristic of decision processes in dictatorial rather than democratic societies and in military rather than civilian organizations because of their greater hierarchical qualities. Command is the primary style of decision-making in many Latin American and African countries.

In practice, bargaining, persuasion, and command often become blended in a given decisional situation. The President, although he has authority to make many decisions unilaterally, may nonetheless also bargain with subordinates, modifying his position somewhat and accepting some of their suggestions, in turn, for more ready and enthusiastic support of his decision. Within agencies, subordinates often seek to convert command relationships into bargaining relationships. A bureau that obtains considerable congressional support may thus put itself into position to bargain with, rather than simply be commanded by, the department head. A pollution-control agency may have the authority to set emission standards and act to enforce them on the basis of its statutory authority. It may, however, bargain with those potentially affected in setting the standards in hope of gaining easier and greater compliance with the standards set. Presidential and gubernatorial efforts to win support for legislative proposals typically involve a combination of persuasion and bargaining.

In summary, bargaining is the most common form of decision-making in the American policy process. Persuasion and command are supplementary to it, being "better suited to a society marked by more universal agreements on values and a more tightly integrated system of authority."[39] Nowhere is the bargaining process better illustrated than in Congress, to which we now turn our attention.

Majority-Building in Congress

The enactment of major legislation by Congress requires the development of a numerical majority or, what is more likely, a series of numerical majorities. These are most commonly created by bargaining. Even if a majority in Congress are agreed on the need for action on some issue, such as labor union reform, they may not agree on the form it should take, thereby making bargaining essential.

A highly important characteristic of Congress, which has much importance for policy formation, is its decentralization of political power. Three factors contribute to this condition. First, the political parties in Congress are weak, and party leaders have only limited power to control and discipline party members. In contrast with party leaders in the British House of Commons, who are strong and have a variety of means to ensure support of party policy proposals by party members, congressional leaders, such as the floor leaders, have few sanctions with which to discipline or punish recalcitrant party members. The party leadership has only "bits and fragments" of power—desired committee assignments, office space, use of the rules, the ability to persuade—with which to influence the rank and file. The member who chooses to defy his party's leadership can usually do so with impunity, and, indeed, not a few people will probably applaud his independence.

Second, the system of geographical representation and decentralized elections contributes to the decentralization of power in Congress. Members of the House and Senate are nominated and elected by the voters in their constituencies and owe little or nothing for their election to the national party organizations or congressional leaders. It is their constituencies that ultimately possess the power to hire and fire them, and it is therefore to their constituencies that congressmen must be responsive, at least minimally, if they wish to remain in Congress. From time to time, important interests in a congressman's district may be adversely affected by party programs. Conventional congressional wisdom holds that, when party and constituency interests conflict, the member should "vote his constituency," as his re-election may depend upon it.

A third factor contributing to the decentralization and dispersion of power in Congress is the system of standing committees, of which there are 21 in the House and 17 in the Senate. Most of the standing committees operate through subcommittees, which serve to disperse power even further. Almost all bills are referred to the appropriate standing committees for consideration before they are brought to the floor of the House or Senate for debate and decision. The standing committees possess vast power to kill, alter, or report unchanged bills sent to them. Most bills referred to committees are never heard from again. The committee chairmen, who gain their positions on the basis of seniority, and the subcommittee chairmen, who usually are selected on the basis of seniority, have much influence over the actions of their committees. They schedule and preside over meetings, set the agenda, schedule hearings and choose their witnesses, decide when votes will be taken, and hire the committee's staff. Moreover, through long experience, they are often highly knowledgeable on the policy matters within the jurisdiction of their committees. The result is that on a given policy issue, whether education, taxation, pollution control, or foreign aid, a few congressmen will possess much potential power. For example, if the Chairman of the House Interior Committee strongly opposes legislation relating to the national forests, that may be sufficient to block it or require changes in its content. Committee and subcommittee chairmen often act as policy leaders and, in so doing, operate independently of the elected party leaders.

The decentralization of power in Congress, together with the complexities of its legislative procedures, usually requires the formation of a series of majorities for the enactment of major legislation. There are a number of decision stages through which a bill must pass in the course of becoming a law.[40] Briefly, these would be, in the House: subcommittee, committee, Rules Committee, and finally floor action; similarly in the Senate: subcommittee, committee, and floor action. Assuming the bill is passed in different versions by the two houses, a conference committee must agree on a compromise version, which then must be approved by the two houses. If the President approves it, the bill becomes law; if, however, he vetoes it, the bill becomes law only if it is passed again by a two-thirds majority in each house. There are thus 10 or 12 stages at which a bill requires the approval of some kind of majority. If it fails to win majority approval at one of these stages, it is probably dead. Should it win approval, its enactment is not assured; rather, its supporters face the task of majority-building at the next stage.

Extraordinary majorities are sometimes needed to get bills through some stages of the process. Reference has already been made to the two-thirds majorities needed to overcome a Presidential veto. Rarely are bills able to get these majorities. During the 1945–1970 period, of 494 bills vetoed only 16 were subsequently enacted into law. In the Senate, the debate on a bill can be effectively terminated only by unanimous consent or by cloture. The cloture rule provides that debate may be terminated upon a motion signed by 16 senators, with the concurrence of two-thirds of the senators "present and voting." Since a single senator can block the ending of debate by unanimous consent, this leaves cloture as the only alternative for shutting off a filibuster. Because of the difficulties in winning cloture, Southern Democrats were consistently able to block the enactment of major civil rights legislation through filibusters or the threat thereof until the adoption of the Civil Rights Act of 1964. In 1965, legislation to repeal the provision of the Taft-Hartley Act authorizing state right-to-work laws passed the House but was defeated in the Senate by a conservative filibuster. Apparently, a majority of the Senate favored repeal, but they were unable to secure the two-thirds vote necessary to close debate.

The multiplicity of stages, or decision points, in the congressional legislative process provide access for a variety of groups and interests. Those who lack access or influence at one stage may secure it at another stage. It becomes quite unlikely that a single group or interest will dominate the process. The complexity of the process, however, has a conservative effect in that it gives an advantage to those seeking to block the enactment of legislation. And it is well to remember that many groups are more concerned with preventing than with securing the enactment of legislation. All they have to do to achieve their preference is to win the support of a majority, or at least of a dominant actor, at one stage of the process. Here is support for a familiar generalization, namely, that procedure is not neutral in its impact.

Much bargaining is necessary for the enactment of legislation by Congress. Those who control each of the decision points may require the modification of a bill as a condition for their approval. Or they may exact future support for some item of interest to themselves. Bargaining is facilitated not only by the many decision points but also by the fact that legislators do not have intense interest on many of the matters on which they must decide. It is no doubt easier for them to bargain on such issues than on issues on which they have strong feelings. At this point, however, it does not seem necessary to elaborate further upon the ubiquity of bargaining in Congress.

Presidential Decision-Making

Apart from his role in the legislative process, the President can be viewed as a policy adopter in his own right. In the area of foreign affairs, much policy is a product of Presidential action, based either on his constitutional powers or broad delegations of legislative authority. The decision, in 1972, to recognize Communist China and to adopt a policy of warmer relations with the Chinese was President Nixon's alone. In the area of domestic policy, some statutory delegations of authority to the President are of a breadth and generality approaching the constitutional. A notable example is the Economic Stabilization Act of 1970, which gave the President almost a blank check to institute a system of price-and-wage controls to combat inflation. Anything really worthy of the designation of public policy under that Act has been a product of Presidential action, whether dubbed Phase I, II, III, IV, or beyond. Presidential action has done more than fill in the details; it has, for all practical purposes, created the basic policy. It is, of course, not always easy to draw neat lines between policy formulation, adoption, and implementation. The argument is simply that it is reasonable to consider the President as a policy adopter, among other things.

By considering some of the general factors that shape and limit Presidential decision-making, we not only can gain useful insight into Presidential decision-making but also can discover another perspective from which to view decision-making in general. Before proceeding further, we must remember that Presidential decision-making is an institutional process. A variety of agencies, aides, and advisers (both official and unofficial) assist the President in the discharge of his responsibilities. But whether he simply approves a recommendation from below or makes his own independent choice, the President alone has the ultimate responsibility for decision.

What factors help shape and limit Presidential decision-making?[41] One is permissibility, an aspect of which is legality. The President is expected to act in conformity with the Constitution, statutes, and court decisions. The lack of a clear constitutional basis certainly contributed to congressional criticism of the Nixon Administration's Cambodian bombing policy in the summer of 1973 and to an agreement by the administration to cease bombing after August 15, 1973, without congressional authorization. Another aspect of permissibility is acceptability. Foreign policy decisions often depend for their effectiveness upon acceptance by other nations, while domestic policy decisions, such as that to eliminate the Office of Economic Opportunity, may depend upon their acceptance by Congress, or executive-branch officials and agencies, or the public.

A second factor is available resources. The President does not have resources to do everything he might want to do, whether by resources one means money, manpower, patronage, time, or credibility. Funds allocated to defense are not available for education or medical research. Only a limited number of appeals to the public for support for his actions can be made without the possibility of diminishing returns. Time devoted to foreign policy problems is not available for domestic matters. While the President has considerable control over the use of his time,[42] he does not have time to concern himself with everything that he might wish. A lack of credibility may also limit the President, as the experience of Presidents Johnson and Nixon attests.

A third factor is available time, in the sense of timing and the need to act. A foreign policy crisis may require a quick response, as was the case with the Cuban Missile crisis in 1962, without all the time for deliberation and fact-gathering one might prefer. Domestic policy decisions may be "forced," as by the need to submit the annual budget to Congress in January or the constitutional requirement to act on a bill passed by Congress within ten days if the President wishes to veto it (barring the possibility of a pocket veto). And, as Sorensen states:

> There is a time to act and a time to wait. By not acting too soon, the President may find that the problem dissolves or resolves itself, that the facts are different from what he thought, or that the state of the nation has changed. By not waiting too long, he may make the most of the mood of the moment, or retain that element of surprise which is so often essential to military and other maneuvers.[43]

Previous commitments may also help shape Presidential decisions. These commitments may be personal—for example, campaign commitments and previous decisions. While too much emphasis can be placed on consistency, the President must avoid the appearance of deception or vacillation if he is to retain his credibility. President Kennedy rejected a tax cut as an antirecessionary measure in the spring of 1961. The economist Paul Samuelson, one of his advisers, later commented: "Whatever the merits of the tax cut, it seemed politically out of the question. The President had run on a platform that asked sacrificing of the American people. How then could he begin by giving them what many would regard as a 'handout'?"[44] Kennedy, of course, later did propose a tax cut, but by 1963 conditions had changed. Commitments may also take the form of traditions and principles, such as that of fighting only if attacked. During the Cuban Missile crisis an air strike without warning on the missile sites was rejected as a "Pearl Harbor in reverse." A "first-strike" strategy has been excluded from American foreign policy generally.

Finally, available information can be an important factor. Many sources of information, official and unofficial, are available to the President and at times, particularly with regard to domestic policy, he may be subject to drowning in a torrent of words and paper. Still, the President may be confronted by a shortage of reliable information, especially in the area of foreign affairs. Reliable information on the possible reactions to a Berlin airlift, the resumption of nuclear testing, or the mining of Haiphong harbor may be scarce because of the need to predict the future—and predicting the future is an uncertain task, except, perhaps, for a few who claim a sixth sense. Domestic policy decisions may also involve uncertainty. This is quite obvious in the area of economic-stability policy. Will a cut in income taxes restore full employment? Will a price-wage freeze destroy the inflationary psychology contributing to inflation? When all the advice is in, the President has to make a choice, which is a calculated one, that the action taken will produce the desired result.

As a leader in policy formation, the President is subject to a variety of pressures and constraints, however great his legal powers may appear to be. Legal authority, by itself, often does not convey the capacity to act effectively. Thus, the President may have to persuade because he cannot command; he may have to bargain because he cannot compel action. President Truman once remarked, "I sit here all day trying to persuade people to do the things they ought to have sense enough to do without my persuading them. . . . That's all the powers of the Presidency amount to."[45] An overstatement, perhaps, yet a remark worth reflecting upon.

Incrementalism

The term incrementalism is used, as we have seen, to designate a decision-making process that is characterized by limited analysis and that yields decisions differing only marginally from previous decisions. The belief that political decision-making in the United States is essentially incremental has gained wide acceptance among political scientists. Not infrequently, incremental theory is given both a prescriptive and a descriptive quality that implies or asserts that this is the way decisions properly should be made as well as how they actually are made. One American government textbook goes so far as to contend that even the New Deal is an illustration of incrementalism, given the historical precedents and events leading up to it. If the New Deal as a whole is incremental, then just about everything since Creation can be regarded as incremental and it too may have been such as it occurred in stages (according to Genesis).

In actuality, if nonincremental decisions or policies are defined as being those that depart sharply from past practice or that require large increases or decreases in the commitment of resources to given policies, in recent decades there have been quite a few nonincremental, or fundamental, policy decisions.[46] Some examples include the Social Security Act, the Marshall Plan, the interstate highway program, Medicare, revenue sharing, the 1961 decision to put a man on the moon, and the 1971 wage-price freeze. Although such decisions may be vastly outnumbered by incremental decisions, they significantly shape the content and thrust of public policy. Rather extensive policy analysis and debate usually precede such decisions.

Nowhere, probably, can incrementalism be better illustrated than in the federal budgetary process. (Budget decisions are typically policy decisions.) Congressional analysis of budget requests is usually limited to items for which increases over the previous year are sought, and total agency budgets tend to change only marginally from one year to another.[47] Nonetheless, within the framework of an agency's total budget substantial (nonincremental) changes may be made in particular programs or policies handled by the agency. A recent study of the Atomic Energy Commission budgets for fiscal years 1958–72 found that the total budget changed only marginally from year to year.[48] Within that context, though, five AEC programs were canceled, and a few experienced either sharp continuing declines or increases, while most fluctuated widely in financial support. As this study clearly hints, policy-making through the budgetary process may not be so stable and incremental as many scholars have contended. It also suggests that "the program director, the operating-level bureaucrat, is a central figure in the determination of public policy."[49]

It is also possible that fundamental changes in public policy may be brought about by incremental means without their ever being considered on their merits. Eidenberg argues, for example, that the United States's involvement in a major land war in Vietnam was the product of an incremental decision process.[50] Step by step American participation expanded from financial and material aid to the use of military "advisers," to the commitment of combat troops, to increasing numbers of combat troops. "When in 1968 Johnson announced he would not run again, he became the victim of his earlier neglect to consider fully the implications and costs of an indeterminate and deepening American involvement in Vietnam." Another example of how a policy can be altered fundamentally by incremental means involves the federal income tax. Over the years, a plethora of particular laws have greatly reduced its progressivity by creating exemptions, opening up loopholes, providing tax credits, and so on for various individuals and groups. Upper-income persons benefit far more than lower-income persons from these added provisions.[51]

Incrementalism is a useful descriptive and analytical decision theory. If, however, it is stretched to include all decisions, it loses its value as an analytical device. We need to recognize that policymaking involves both incremental and fundamental decisions. Further, as policy analysts, we should be careful to avoid making incrementalism a prescriptive theory or a rationalization of the existing state of things in decision-making.

Similar processes and problems of public policy-making are probably encountered by executives and legislatures at every level of government and in every industrialized democratic political system. Many of these processes and problems may also occur in nondemocratic systems. There is evidence to indicate, for example, that bargaining as a decision-style sometimes occurs among elites in some communist political systems, such as the Soviet Union.

NOTES

1. David G. Smith, "Pragmatism and the Group Theory of Politics," *American Political Science Review*, LVIII (September, 1964), pp. 607–10. In this discussion of public problems, I have been much benefited by Charles O. Jones, *An Introduction to the Study of Public Policy* (Belmont, Calif.: Wadsworth, 1970), chaps. 2 and 3.
2. John Dewey, *The Public and Its Problems* (Denver: Swallow, 1927), pp. 12, 15–16.
3. Theodore J. Lowi, "American Business Public Policy: Case Studies and Political Theory," *World Politics*, XVI (July, 1964), pp. 677–715.

4. Cf. Layme Hoppe, "Agenda-Setting Strategies: The Case of Pollution Problems." Unpublished paper presented at the annual meeting of the American Political Science Association, September, 1970.
5. Roger W. Cobb and Charles D. Elder, *Participation in American Politics: The Dynamics of Agenda-Building* (Boston: Allyn and Bacon, 1972), p. 85.
6. *Ibid.*, p. 89.
7. David B. Truman, *The Governmental Process* (New York: Knopf, 1951), p. 30.
8. Jones, *op. cit.*, p. 29.
9. Cf. Cobb and Elder, *op. cit.*, pp. 84–85.
10. Mark V. Nadel, *The Politics of Consumer Protection* (Indianapolis: Bobbs-Merrill, 1971), p. 28 and *passim*.
11. See Michael Lipsky, "Protest as a Political Resource," *American Political Science Review* LXII (December, 1968), pp. 1144–58.
12. Lewis Coser, *Continuities in the Study of Social Conflicts* (New York: Free Press, 1967), p. 101.
13. This is discussed, in fascinating style, in W. A. Swanberg, *Citizen Hearst* (New York: Scribner's 1961), pp. 79–169.
14. Norton E. Long, *The Polity,* ed. by Charles Press (Chicago: Rand-McNally, 1962), pp. 152–54.
15. Those wishing to pursue this topic further should consult the highly informative study by Cobb and Elder, *op. cit.*
16. Peter Bachrach and Morton S. Baratz, *Power and Poverty* (New York: Oxford University Press, 1970), p. 44.
17. E. E. Schattschneider, *The Semi-Sovereign People* (New York: Holt, Rinehart & Winston, 1960), p. 71.
18. This discussion is based on J. Clarence Davies III, *The Politics of Pollution* (Indianapolis: Bobbs-Merrill, 1970), pp. 21–24. The quotation is from p. 21.
19. Thomas R. Wolanin, "The Impact of Presidential Advisory Commissions, 1945–1968." Unpublished paper presented at the annual meeting of the American Political Science Association, September, 1972, p. 22.
20. Various health-care proposals are analyzed in Anne R. Somers, *Health Care in Transition: Directions for the Future* (Chicago: Hospital Research and Educational Trust, 1971).
21. Jones, *op. cit.*, p. 53.
22. A number of accounts of the formulation and adoption of the Economic Opportunity Act are available. This treatment draws mostly on Roger Davidson's account in John F. Bibby and Roger H. Davidson, *On Capitol Hill,* 2d ed. (Hinsdale, Ill.: Dryden Press, 1972), pp. 225–49, and Sar A. Levitan, *The Great Society's Poor Law* (Baltimore: Johns Hopkins Press, 1969).
23. David W. Brady, "Congressional Leadership and Party Voting in the McKinley Era: A Comparison to the Modern House," *Midwest Journal of Political Science* XVI (August, 1972), pp. 439–41.
24. Julius Turner, *Party and Constituency: Pressures on Congress,* rev. ed. by Edward V. Schneier, Jr. (Baltimore: Johns Hopkins Press, 1970), p. 17.
25. A thorough discussion of concepts of representation can be found in John C. Wahlke *et al., The Legislative System* (New York: Wiley, 1962).
26. E.g., Peter Woll, *American Bureaucracy* (New York: Norton, 1963), pp. 139–41.
27. V. O. Key, Jr., *Public Opinion and American Democracy* (New York: Knopf, 1961), p. 14.
28. *Ibid.*, pp. 81–90.
29. Cf. John E. Mueller, "Trends in Popular Support for the Wars in Korea and Vietnam," *American Political Science Review,* LXV (June, 1971), pp. 358–75.

30. Nick Kotz, *Let Them Eat Promises: The Politics of Hunger in America* (Englewood Cliffs, N.J.: Prentice-Hall, 1969).
31. Donald R. Matthews and James A. Stimson, "The Decision-Making Approach to the Study of Legislative Behavior." Unpublished paper presented at the annual meeting of the American Political Science Association, September, 1969, p. 19.
32. Robert H. Salisbury, *Governing America: Public Choice and Political Action* (New York: Appleton-Century-Crofts, 1973), p. 237. Chap. 13 contains a very useful treatment of decision-making.
33. Richard F. Fenno, Jr., *Congressmen in Committees* (Boston: Little, Brown, 1973), pp. 48, 64.
34. Richard E. Neustadt, "White House and Whitehall," *The Public Interest,* II (Winter, 1966), pp. 55–69.
35. As quoted in Roger Hilsman, *The Politics of Policy Making in Defense and Foreign Affairs* (New York: Harper & Row, 1971), p. 1.
36. Robert A. Dahl and Charles E. Lindblom, *Politics, Economics, and Welfare* (New York: Harper & Row, 1953), p. 328. Chaps. 12 and 13 present a thorough and insightful discussion of bargaining in American politics.
37. See the good discussion of this episode in Lawrence C. Pierce, *The Politics of Fiscal Policy Formation* (Pacific Palisades, Calif.: Goodyear, 1971), chap. 7.
38. Lewis A. Froman, Jr., *People and Politics* (Englewood Cliffs, N.J.: Prentice-Hall, 1962), p. 56.
39. Dan Nimmo and Thomas D. Ungs, *American Political Patterns,* 2d ed. (Boston: Little, Brown, 1969), p. 367.
40. A thorough treatment of congressional procedures can be found in Lewis A. Froman, Jr., *The Congressional Process* (Boston: Little, Brown, 1967).
41. In this discussion I will depend substantially on a wise and insightful little book by Theodore C. Sorensen, *Decision-Making in the White House* (New York: Columbia University Press, 1963). Sorensen served as Special Counsel to President Kennedy.
42. Cf. George Reedy, *The Twilight of the Presidency* (New York: World, 1970).
43. Sorensen, *op. cit.,* p. 29.
44. Paul A. Samuelson, "Economic Policy for 1962," *Review of Economics and Statistics,* XLI (February, 1962), p. 3.
45. As quoted in Richard E. Neustadt, *Presidential Power* (New York: Wiley, 1960), pp. 9–10.
46. Cf., Charles L. Schultze, *The Politics and Economics of Public Spending* (Washington, D.C.: Brookings Institution, 1968), pp. 77–79.
47. A leading work is Aaron Wildavsky, *The Politics of the Budgetary Process* (Boston: Little, Brown, 1964).
48. Peter B. Natchez and Irvin C. Bupp, "Policy and Priority in the Budgetary Process," *American Political Science Review,* LXVII (September, 1973), pp. 951–63.
49. *Ibid.,* p. 963.
50. Eugene Eidenberg, "The Presidency: Americanizing the War in Vietnam," in Allen P. Sindler (ed.), *American Political Institutions and Public Policy* (Boston: Little, Brown, 1969), pp. 68–126. The quotation is on pp. 119–20.
51. *U.S. News and World Report,* July 16, 1973, pp. 70–71.

4. The Implementation of Policy

Once the legislative adoption stage of the policy process has been completed, we can begin to refer to something called public policy. It must be kept in mind, however, that the content of policy, and its impact on those affected, may be substantially modified, elaborated, or even negated during the implementation stage. (Such terms as application, administration, and effectuation can be used as synonyms for implementation and will be so employed here.) In actuality, it is often quite difficult, if not impossible, to differentiate neatly the adoption of policy from its implementation, just as earlier it was indicated that policy formation and adoption are hard to demarcate. There is, indeed, much truth in the aphorism that policy is made as it is being administered and administered as it is being made. The policy process has some of the appearance of the proverbial "seamless web" so often invoked in scholarly discussions.

Some policy decisions are essentially self-executing, such as the Nixon Administration's decision to formally recognize the government of the People's Republic of China (which, in doctrinaire days, was called Communist China) or the decision of the Canadian Parliament in 1964 to replace the Red Ensign with the Maple Leaf Flag as the official national flag. But relatively few such decisions, which entail clearcut, one-time action, are made, so that those concerned with the analysis of public policy can ill afford to neglect the implementation stage of the policy process. Much that occurs at this stage may seem at first glance to be tedious or mundane, yet its consequences for the substance of policy may be quite profound. Moreover, closer examination will reveal that highly intense political struggles often occur during the administration of legislation. Civil rights legislation should be a very familiar case in point.

Several aspects of policy implementation will be examined in this chapter: who is involved in policy implementation, the nature of the administrative process, compliance with policy, and the effect of implementation on policy content and impact.

WHO IMPLEMENTS POLICY?

In the United States, as in other modern political systems, public policy is implemented primarily by a complex system of administrative agencies. These agencies perform most of the day-to-day work of government and thus affect citizens more directly in their actions than do any other governmental units. Nonetheless, it would not be necessary for policy analysts to be much concerned with public administration (that is, all those structures and processes involved in the implementation of public policy) were it not for the fact that agencies often have much discretion (that is, the opportunity to make choices among alternatives) in carrying out the policies under their jurisdiction. They do not automatically apply whatever the legislature or other policy adopters decide although at one time it was widely assumed they did.

A classic feature of the traditional literature of public administration was the notion that politics and administration were separate and distinct spheres of activity. Politics, Frank Goodnow wrote in 1900, was concerned with the formulation of the will of the state; it was concerned with value judgments, with determining what government should or should not do, and it was to be handled by the "political" branches of government, that is, the legislature and executive.[1] Administration, on the other hand, was concerned with the implementation of the will of the state, with carrying into effect, more or less automatically, the decisions of the political branches. Administration was concerned with questions of fact, with what *is* rather than what *should be,* and consequently could focus on the most efficient means (or "one best way") of implementing policy. Were this indeed the case, the policy analyst could end his inquiry with the adoption of policy. However, with the possible exception of a few archaic or poorly informed souls, no one today accepts this politics-administration dichotomy.

Administrative agencies often operate under broad and ambiguous statutory mandates that leave them with much discretion to decide what should or should not be done. Thus, the Interstate Commerce Commission is directed to fix "just and reasonable" railroad rates; the Federal Communications Commission, to license television broadcasters for the "public convenience and necessity"; the Forest Service, to follow a "multiple use" policy in the management of national forests that balances the interests of lumber companies, sportsmen, livestock grazers, and other users; and the Environmental Protection Agency, to ensure that the "best practicable" devices for the control of water pollutants are in use by 1977. Such statutory mandates are, in effect, directives to the agencies involved to go out and make some policy. Those who participate in the legislative process frequently are unable or unwilling to arrive at precise settlements of the conflicting interests on many issues. Only by leaving some matters somewhat nebulous and unsettled can agreement on legislation be reached. Lack of time, interest, information, and expertness may also contribute to the delegation of broad authority to agencies. The product of these factors is often a statute couched in general language, such as that noted above, which shifts to agencies the tasks of filling in the details, making policy more precise and concrete, and trying to make more definitive adjustments among conflicting interests. Under these conditions, the administrative process becomes an extension of the legislative process and administrators find themselves immersed in politics.

Although legislatures have delegated much policy-making authority to administrative agencies, especially in the twentieth century, it should not be assumed that legislatures cannot act in rather precise fashion. An illustration is social security legislation, which sets forth in rather definite terms the standards of eligibility, the levels of benefits, the amount of additional earnings permitted, and other considerations. Many administrative decisions on benefits simply involve applying the legislatively set standards to the facts of the case at hand. Under such circumstances, administrative decision-making becomes largely routine and is therefore unlikely to produce controversy.

While administrative agencies are the primary implementors of public policy, many other actors may also be involved, and they should not be neglected in our study of policy-making. Those that will be examined here include the legislature, the courts, pressure groups, and community organizations. They may either be directly involved in policy implementation or act to influence administrative agencies, or both.

The Legislature. Congress may affect administration in a variety of ways. The more detailed the legislation passed by Congress, the less discretion agencies have. Specific limitations on the use of funds, for example, may be written into statutes. The committee reports that accompany bills reported from committees often contain suggestions or statements concerning how the legislation should be implemented. These do not have the force of law but will be ignored by administrators only at their peril. The legislative and appropriations committees often attempt to influence the actions of agencies that fall within their purview. Probably one of the most successful in this regard is the House Agricultural Appropriations Subcommittee chaired by Congressman Jamie Whitten. Whitten, who has the support of a majority of his subcommittee, is sometimes referred to as the "permanent Secretary of Agriculture." Department of Agriculture officials are responsive to his recommendations and often clear proposed actions in advance with him. To offend Whitten is to run the risk of adverse action on departmental requests for funds.[2] Senatorial approval is required for many top-level administrative appointments, and this may be used as a lever to influence policy. A classic example was the Senate's rejection of the reappointment of Leland Olds to the Federal Power Commission in 1949 because of petroleum industry opposition to his position in favor of regulating the field price of natural gas.[3] Finally, we can note that much of the time of many congressmen is devoted to "casework," which quite frequently involves problems that constituents are having with administrative agencies. The constituents, of course, want their congressman to secure favorable action for them.

The Courts. Some laws are enforced primarily through judicial action. Laws dealing with crimes are the most obvious example. Some economic regulatory statutes, such as the Sherman Antitrust Act, are enforced through law suits brought in the federal district courts, many of which are eventually appealed to the Supreme Court. Because of this and the generality of the Sherman Act, the meaning of antitrust policy depends greatly upon judicial interpretation and application of the Act. Generally, though, administrative regulation, in which primary responsibility is assigned to an agency for the enforcement of a statute, is much more commonplace than judicial regulation in the American political system. In the nineteenth century, however, it was quite common for legislatures to enact statutes requiring or prohibiting some action and then to leave it to citizens to protect their rights under the law through proceedings brought in the courts.

In some instances, the courts may be directly involved in the administration of policy. Naturalization proceedings for aliens are really administrative in form, but they are handled by the federal district courts. Bankruptcy proceedings are another illustration. A complex system of trustees, receivers, appraisers, accountants, auctioneers, and others is supervised by federal bankruptcy courts. In all, it is "a large scale example of routine administrative machinery."[4] Many divorce and domestic relations cases handled by state courts also appear essentially administrative, involving matters of guidance and management rather than disputed law or facts.

Most important, however, the courts affect administration through their interpretation of statutes and administrative rules and regulations, and their review of administrative decisions in cases brought before them. Courts can facilitate, hinder, or largely nullify the implementation of particular policies through their decisions. The story of how the Supreme Court destroyed the effectiveness of national railroad regulation under the Interstate Commerce Act of 1887 by unfavorable rulings is familiar history. A recent (1973) ruling by a federal appeals court that the Federal Trade Commission has authority under existing law to issue trade regulation rules should facilitate the Commission's trade regulation and consumer protection activities.

Pressure Groups. Because of the discretion often vested in agencies by legislation, once an act is adopted, the group struggle shifts from the legislative to the administrative arena. Given the operating discretion of many agencies, a group that can successfully influence agency action may have a substantial effect on the course and impact of public policies. Sometimes relationships between a group and an agency may become so close as to lead to allegation that the group has "captured" the agency. In the past, it was frequently stated that the Interstate Commerce Commission was the captive of the railroads,[5] and it is not uncommon now to hear comments to the effect that the Civil Aeronautic Board is unduly influenced by the commercial airlines.

Groups may become directly involved in administration, as when representation of particular interests is specified on the boards of plural-headed agencies. A common illustration of this is state occupational licensing boards, whose governing statutes frequently provide that some or all of the board members must come from the licensed profession. As a consequence, occupational licensing (and regulatory) programs are usually controlled by the dominant elements within the licensed groups.

Advisory groups are another means by which groups may become included in policy administration. Take the case of the National Industrial Pollution Control Council, which was created in April, 1970, by President Nixon. The Council, which is composed of representatives of major corporations and trade associations, provides advice to the White House and to agencies responsible for the implementation of environmental policy. Although it is difficult to judge the impact NIPCC has had on environmental policy, its existence provides big business with a regularized form of access to the policy process not afforded to most other groups concerned with the environment. It is estimated that there are between 1,100 and 1,600 advisory committees located in federal administrative agencies and departments. One observer has remarked that, "as a means for guaranteeing the institutional participation by non-government groups in the administrative process, advisory committees are a commonplace feature of American government."[6]

Community Organizations. At the local level, community organizations have sometimes been utilized for the administration of federal programs. Examples include local draft boards, under the now defunct selective service program; farmer committees, under the price-support and soil-conservation programs of the Department of Agriculture; and Community Action agencies providing for "maximum feasible participation" of the poor, under the Community Action program created by the Economic Opportunity Act of 1964. Participatory democracy of this sort may give those involved considerable influence over the application of programs at the grass-roots level. Thus, local draft boards, especially when only a portion of eligible males were needed to meet military needs, clearly helped shape selective service policy with regard to who got drafted and who did not.[7]

In short, a variety of participants affect the administration of a given policy. In addition to those discussed above, political party officials and executive staff agencies may also become involved. Certainly this is true for the Office of Management and Budget. The range of participants will vary from one policy area to another; hence, policy analysis should include whoever has an impact on the implementation of policy.

THE ADMINISTRATIVE PROCESS

The term "administrative process" is used to designate the movement or operation of the administrative system over time. In our discussion, we will focus on some aspects of the administrative process that seem especially to have consequences for the implementation, content, and impact of policy. These include administrative organization, administrative politics, and administrative policy-making. The matter of compliance—that is, conformity to policy directives, or objectives, by those to whom they apply—will be discussed in the next section.

Administrative Organization

One could say that one administrative agency looks pretty much like another or, in another usage, if you have seen one agency, you have seen them all. If one were indeed to take such a position, he would be making a serious mistake. Agencies, in fact, differ greatly in such respects as their structure, operating styles, political support, expertness, and policy orientation. Those seeking to influence the nature of public policy often show much concern over the particular agency or type of agency that will administer a given policy. Conflict over questions of administrative organization can be every bit as sharp as conflict over substantive policies. The formation of administrative organizations is a political as well as a technical task.

Most public policies are not self-executing; hence, if they are to be carried into effect, responsibility for their implementation must be assigned either to an existing agency or to a new agency established for this purpose. The creation of new agencies is usually handled by the legislature. At the national level, however, some have been created by the executive under administrative reorganization authority that permits the President to propose reorganization plans; such plans go into effect automatically unless disapproved by either house of Congress. The Environmental Protection Agency was created by a Nixon Administration reorganization proposal in 1970 and now handles pollution-control enforcement activities formerly spread among a number of agencies. The effect has been to give a sharper focus to the administration of antipollution policies. A few other agencies, such as the Federal Energy Office, have been set up on the basis of broad substantive authority given by Congress to the executive.

The discussion in this section will be focused on the policy implications of administrative organization. A number of propositions will be presented and illustrated to indicate how organizational considerations affect policy, and, thus, why they should receive the attention of policy analysts.

1. When a new program is adopted, the contending interests may seek to have its administration awarded to an agency they think will be more favorable to their interests. A major consideration during the enactment of the Occupational Safety and Health Act of 1970, the first major general industrial-safety bill passed by Congress, was who should administer it. Organized labor and most liberal Democrats favored locating all standard-setting and enforcement activity in the Department of Labor, which they regarded as sympathetic toward labor. Many Republicans, the Nixon Administration, and business groups wanted an independent board, or boards, to make and enforce standards, to avoid Labor Department control of the program. The result was a compromise. The Department of Labor was given authority to set standards, to enforce them, and to assess penalties; an independent, three-member quasi-judicial Occupational Safety and Health Review Commission was created to hear appeals from Labor Department actions. A National Institute for Occupational Safety and Health was established within the Department of Health, Education, and Welfare to conduct research so as to create an information base for health standards. Both organized labor and business expressed satisfaction with this administration arrangement. What impact it will actually have on policy remains to be seen.

In 1953, an independent Small Business Administration was set up to handle assistance programs for small business, following the dismantling of the Reconstruction Finance Corporation by the Eisenhower Administration. Some argued that control of such programs rested properly with the Department of Commerce. But small-business interests and their congressional supporters argued that the Department of Commerce was too oriented toward big business to administer satisfactorily, from their point of view, small-business programs. The Office of Economic Opportunity was given primary control of administering the War on Poverty partly because it was thought that old-line agencies like the Departments of Labor and Health, Education, and Welfare would not be sufficiently sympathetic and vigorous. "The best way to kill a new idea," President Johnson remarked at one point, "is to put it in an old-line agency."[8]

2. Administrative organization may be used to emphasize the need for, or facilitate action on, particular policy problems. Thus, the Kennedy Administration (unsuccessfully) and the Johnson Administration (successfully) sought creation of a Cabinet-level Department of Urban Affairs to emphasize urban problems and facilitate action thereon. Conservative and rural interests opposed its creation because they were afraid it would indeed have this result. Interestingly enough, some private housing organizations who had opposed it during the Kennedy Administration, when it was to be called the Department of Urban Affairs, supported its establishment during the Johnson Administration as the Department of Housing and Urban Development. One reason for their switch was their belief that inclusion of the word housing in the title of the department would produce stress on housing support programs economically beneficial to them.

Another good example is the struggle over the formation of a Consumer Protection Agency. A bill passed by the House of Representatives in 1971 but defeated by a filibuster in the Senate would have created an independent, non-regulatory agency to represent consumer interests in actions before other agencies and the courts. Another effort to accomplish this was launched in 1973. Its supporters believed that such an agency would provide more effective representation of consumer interests and, consequently, foster policy actions by agencies and courts more favorable toward consumers. Conservatives and business groups opposed the proposal as giving too much power to the proposed agency, notwithstanding the fact that it would have no regulatory or enforcement powers. They, of course, did not openly oppose the protection of the consumer, as this is not a politically popular thing to do.

3. The internal structure of an agency may be fashioned to help secure desired action. Take the case of the National Institutes of

Health, which were set up within the Department of Health, Education, and Welfare in the 1950's. It would have been quite logical to have named the various institutes according to the kind of research they would support, such as pathology, microbiology, biochemistry, and genetics. This is the way university research centers are usually organized. Instead, among the institutes established were the National Cancer Institute, the National Heart and Lung Institute, and the National Institute of Arthritis and Metabolic Diseases. This action was based on the reasoning that, while it might be easy for a congressman to vote against an appropriation for microbiology, he would be highly reluctant to vote against funds for cancer or heart research. This has proved effective, for Congress consistently provides more funds for the NIH than what is requested by the executive budget officials.

4. Independent agencies may, over time, become closely aligned with their clientele, that is, those directly served or regulated by an agency. With respect to independent regulatory commissions, such as the Interstate Commerce Commission and Civil Aeronautics Board, it has been stated: "Deprived of the influences on policy that flow from the give-and-take of other departments, and from the directions of the chief executive, the independent commission gravitates toward an industry point of view."[9] To gain political support needed to survive and to enlist cooperation in the performance of its tasks, the agency may incline toward the policy positions of its clientele. Moreover, since these will be the viewpoints most commonly presented to agency personnel, they may come to appear quite reasonable and acceptable. If regulatory commissions do become the captives of the regulated (and there is evidence to support this contention),[10] then independence—in effect, isolation—as a feature of their organizational structure facilitates this condition, which, in turn, has clear consequences for the thrust of policy.

5. Once a group has developed a satisfactory relationship with an agency, it will oppose changes in the agency's structure or departmental location that might disrupt the relationship. Thus, the railroads have steadfastly opposed locating the Interstate Commerce Commission in an executive department, such as Transportation. Merchant shipping interests have opposed moving the Maritime Administration, which subsidizes ship construction and operations, from the Commerce Department to the Department of Transportation. Such moves might appear logical, but they *could* have the ef-

fect of opening the agencies to competing pressures and ultimately changing their operating patterns and policy. Generally speaking, groups prefer a satisfactory present situation to an unknown future one, which, from their perspective, may bring disagreeable changes.

6. Those who support an existing program may seek to have it moved to another agency to avoid hostile or unfavorable handling of it. Conversely, opponents of a current program may seek to lessen its impact, or even kill it, by getting it reassigned to a hostile agency. A classic illustration of the first possibility involves the Forest Service, which was transferred early in this century from the Department of Interior to the Department of Agriculture at the behest of conservationists. According to Gifford Pinchot, "The national forest idea ran counter to the whole tradition of the Interior Department. Bred into its marrow, bone, and fiber, was the idea of disposing of the public lands to private owners."[11] This policy view was clearly unfavorable to forest conservation. It is, of course, no longer held by the Interior Department, but the Forest Service remains in Agriculture, notwithstanding some attempts by Interior to reacquire it. In 1971, supporters of the Volunteers in Service to America (VISTA) program, a part of the War on Poverty, maintained it was being transferred from the Office of Economic Opportunity to the new ACTION agency in order to kill it. This still has not happened.

When policy, therefore, is viewed as a "course of action," its substance is affected by how it is administered. How it is administered depends, at least partly, on what agency administers it. And, when you have seen one agency, you have *not* seen them all.

Administrative Politics

A statute confers upon an agency only legal authority to take action on some topic. How effective the agency is, what it actually does or accomplishes, will be affected by the political context in which it operates and the amount of political support it has. To put it differently, politics affects how an agency exercises its discretion and carries out its programs.

The environment in which an agency exists may contain many "forces" that, at one time or another, may exert influence on its actions.[12] Among these forces are the following:

Relevant Laws, Rules and Regulations, Accepted Modes of Pro-

cedures, Concepts of Fair Play. These are the basic "rules of the game" that help inform and guide official behavior and to which officials are expected to conform. Public opinion and group pressures may focus adversely on administrators who violate the "rules of the game," as by proposing not to follow a given statutory provision or by enticing someone to violate a law so that he can be prosecuted. Officials who "snoop around" may cause trouble for themselves.

The Chief Executive. Agencies either are located in the Presidential chain of command or are otherwise subject to Presidential control and direction in such forms as personnel appointments, budget recommendations and expenditure controls, and policy directives.

The Congressional System of Supervision. This includes the standing commitees and subcommittees thereof, committee staffs, committee chairmen, influential congressmen. Congressional influence is fragmented and sporadic rather than monolithic and continuous. It emanates from parts of Congress, rarely from Congress as a whole.

The Courts. Agencies may be affected by the Judiciary's use of its powers of judicial review and statutory interpretation. Thus, in 1954, the Supreme Court held that the Federal Power Commission had not only the authority but the duty to regulate the field price of natural gas, something that at the time the Commission preferred not to do.[13] While the Federal Power Commission has been significantly affected by judicial action, the Federal Reserve Board and the Bureau of the Mint are little affected thereby.

Other Administrative Agencies. Agencies with competing or overlapping jurisdictions may exert influence on each other, as, for example, the Department of Agriculture does on the ICC in agricultural rate cases. Water agencies such as the Corps of Engineers and the Bureau of Reclamation have been rivals for the right to control particular projects. Or one agency may aspire to take over a program of another agency. Thus, the Department of Labor and HEW eventually acquired some of the poverty programs, such as the Job Corps and Head Start, initially run by the Office of Economic Opportunity. Agencies not infrequently have imperialistic designs on one another.[14]

Other Governments. State governments, municipal and local governments, or associations of state and local officials may attempt to influence national agency decisions. Associations of state highway officials are much concerned about the activities of the Bureau of Public Roads. The Environmental Protection Agency encounters quite a lot of pressure, criticism, and resistance from state and local governments in the development and implementation of pollution-control standards.

Interest Groups. The role of groups was dealt with earlier in the chapter. Suffice it to say here that an agency that is affected by a variety of groups, such as the Forest Service, will act differently than one affected primarily by a single group, such as the Veterans Administration or one that experiences little group pressure, such as the Government Printing Office.

Political Parties. The role of party organization has declined in recent years, but appointments to administrative positions as well as agency decisions may be influenced by considerations of party welfare and party policy orientation. It makes a difference whether the White House is controlled by the Democrats or the Republicans. Witness the decline of OEO under the Nixon Administration.

Communications Media. The mass communications media have an independent role apart from their use as forums for pressure groups and others. The media may play an important role in shaping public opinion toward an agency by revealing and publicizing its actions, favorably or unfavorably. Agencies evidence much concern with maintaining a "good press" or a favorable public image. Some of OEO's political difficulties were due to the extensive press coverage of its administrative difficulties, however minor in terms of the amount of money or number of persons involved.

Each of these forces is multiple rather than monolithic in nature. A variety of pressure groups, state and local governments, or congressional actors may focus on a single agency. Conflicting viewpoints may be held either by members of the same category or by those in different categories. A number of forces operate on an agency pushing and pulling against each other with varying intensity and growing and ebbing over time.

The field of forces surrounding an agency will be drawn from the above categories and will form the *constituency* of the agency, that is, "any group, body, or interest to which [an administrator] looks for aid or guidance, or which seeks to establish itself as so important (in his judgment) that he 'had better' take account of its preferences even if he finds himself averse to those preferences."[15]

(Note that this is a broader concept than that of clientele, referred to earlier.) The constituency of an agency is dynamic rather than static. Some "constituents" will be concerned with the agency only as particular issues arise or are settled; others will be more or less continually involved and will compose the stable core of the agency's constituency. For example, the stable core of the Civil Aeronautics Board's constituency includes the commercial airlines and the congressional commerce and appropriations committees. The chief executive, Department of Commerce, congressional small-business committees, and state aeronautics agencies are intermittently involved with the CAB. Other things being equal, those constituents that continually interact with an agency will probably have the most success in influencing agency action.

The nature of an agency's constituency will affect its power and capacity to make policy decisions and carry policy into effect. The relationship of an agency to one part of its constituency will depend on the kinds of relationships it has with other parts. For example, an agency with strong Presidential support tends to be less responsive to pressure groups than an agency without such support. On the other hand, strong congressional and group support may lessen Presidential influence, as in the case of the Army Corps of Engineers. An agency encountering criticism from state and local government officials may find its congressional support waning also. In general, it can be said that agency policy-making and implementation activities will reflect the interests supported by the dominant elements within its constituency, whether they are hostile or supportive.

An agency's clientele is an important part of its constituency. Some agencies benefit from having large active clienteles, such as the Veterans Administration and the Department of Agriculture. But size alone is not enough. Consumers are a vast group, but, because they are poorly organized and lack self-consciousness as a group, they provide little support to consumer agencies, such as the Food and Drug Administration. If the FDA has been unduly responsive to food and drug manufacturers, it is partly because of lack of consumer support and partly because the agency both needs the cooperation of and encounters organized pressure from food and drug companies. Some agencies have underprivileged or disadvantaged clienteles, such as OEO and most welfare agencies. OEO was hindered in its efforts to administer the War on Poverty by the fact that its clientele, the poor and especially the black poor, did not constitute a good source of political support.

Agencies who provide services to their clientele, rather than regulate them, usually draw more support from their clientele. Most people prefer receiving benefits to being restricted or controlled. An agency with a foreign clientele, such as the Agency for International Development, can draw little political support from its clientele, and the lack of an internal clientele has clearly been to the disadvantage of the foreign-aid program.

An examination of an agency's constituency and clientele can provide considerable insight into, and explanation of, why an agency acts as it does. It should not, however, be assumed that an agency is an inert force at the mercy of its constituency or the dominant elements therein. Agencies, because of their expertise, organizational spirit, or administrative statecraft, can exert independent control over events and help determine the scope of their power.[16]

Any bureaucratic agency has some expertise in the performance of its assigned tasks, whether those involve garbage collection or foreign policy. All bureaucratic skills, however, do not receive equal deference from society. Agencies whose expertise is derived from the natural and physical (i.e., "hard") sciences will receive more deference than those drawing from the social sciences, which are less highly regarded in society. Compare the situations of the National Aeronautics and Space Administration and Atomic Energy Commission with the Office of Education and the Office of Economic Opportunity. Considerable deference is shown to the military as "specialists in violence," and Congress often defers to the judgment of the Department of Defense and the Joint Chiefs of Staff in the military and defense policy areas. Professional diplomats, on the other hand, no longer receive the deference in foreign policy that they once did. Power based on expertise may vary considerably from one time to another as conditions and attitudes change.

Some agencies are more able than others to generate interest in, and enthusiasm for, their programs from both their own members and the public. This can be designated as organizational spirit. Its existence "depends to a large extent upon the development of an appropriate ideology or sense of mission on the part of an administrative agency, both as a method of binding outside supporters to the agency and as a technique for intensifying the loyalty of the organization's employees to its purposes."[17] The Marine Corps, the Peace Corps, the Forest Service, and the Office of Economic Opportunity (in its early years) are agencies served with considerable fervor and commitment by their members. Many agencies display substantial zeal in their early years, only to ease into bureaucratic routine as the years go by, as has happened in some national regulatory commissions.

Leadership, or what Francis Rourke calls administrative statecraft, can also contribute to an agency's power and effectiveness. Although agency leadership, like all organizational leadership, is situational, being shaped significantly by factors in the environment other than the leader himself, still leadership can have a significant impact on agency operation and success. Some agency leaders will be more effective than others in dealing with outside interest groups, cultivating congressional committees, opening the organization to new ideas, and communicating a sense of purpose to agency personnel. The recent revitalization of the Federal Trade Commission has been aided by the leadership of first Casper Weinberger and then Miles W. Kirkpatrick as chairman.[18] John Connally, former governor of Texas, was a capable and vigorous Secretary of the Treasury during the first Nixon Administration and, under his leadership, the Department had a major role in economic policy development. The State Department played a diminished role in foreign policy formation during the first Nixon Administration because of the rather quiescent leadership of then Secretary of State William Rogers.

Administrative Policy-Making

Although administrative agencies are often deeply involved in policy formation at the legislative stage, attention here will be on how agencies shape policy through the implementation of legislation. Two facets of agency action will be examined: characteristics of agency decision-making and the ways in which agencies develop policy. It is well to keep in mind here the distinction between decisions and policy.

In agency decision-making, hierarchy is of central importance. Although in legislatures, all members have an equal vote at the voting stage, within agencies those at upper levels have more authority over final decisions than those at lower levels. To be sure, factors such as the decentralization of authority, the responsiveness of subunits to outside forces (such as pressure groups), and the participation of professionals in administrative activity work against hierarchical authority, but the importance of hierarchy should nonetheless not be underestimated. Complexity, size, and the desire for economical operation and more control over the bureaucratic apparatus all contribute to the development of hierarchical authority. As for its consequences for decision-making, it is a means by which discrete decisions can be coordinated with one another and conflicts among officials at lower levels of decision can be resolved. Hierarchy also means that those at the upper levels have a larger voice in agency decisions because of their high status, even though lower-level officials may have more substantive expertness. A separation of power and knowledge may thus threaten the rationality of administrative decisions.[19] Hierarchy can also adversely affect the free flow of ideas and information in an organization, because subordinates, for example, may hesitate to advance proposals they think may run counter to "official" policy or antagonize their superiors.

Administrative agencies constitute "a governmental habitat in which expertise finds a wealth of opportunity to exert itself and to influence policy."[20] Agencies in their decision-making are clearly affected by political considerations and also by the wish to protect their own power. Thus, the Department of Commerce is unlikely to make policy decisions which sharply conflict with important business interests. Agencies nonetheless do provide a context within which experts and professionals, official and private, can work on policy problems. Technical considerations and professional advice play an important part in most administrative decision-making. Whether it is the Federal Aviation Agency considering adoption of a rule pertaining to aircraft safety, the Environmental Protection Agency setting emission standards, or the President confronted with a major choice on military policy, each needs good information on the technical feasibility of proposed alternatives. Decisions that are made without adequate consideration of their technical aspects, or which run counter to strong professional advice, may be deemed bad on both technical and political grounds. President Nixon's decision to institute Phase III of his price-and-wage control program, which provided for a freeze on many prices, ran counter to much professional economic advice and proved to be both economically ineffective and politically disadvantageous.

Secrecy also plays a role in administrative decision-making. In comparison with that of legislatures, administrative decision-making is a relatively invisible part of government. Agencies may hold public hearings, issue press releases, and the like, but they exercise considerable control over what information becomes available on their internal deliberations and decisions, and, consequently, much of what they do is little noticed by the public or reported by the news media. This secrecy, or invisibility, can contribute to the effectiveness of decisions by providing an environment for presentation and discussion of policy proposals that might otherwise be avoided as publicly unpopular. Deliberations by Kennedy Administration officials during the 1962 Cuban missile crisis were more effective because of their private nature.[21] Secrecy may also facilitate the bargaining and compromise often necessary to reach decisions and take action, because officials will find it easier to move away from privately stated than publicly stated positions. On the other hand, the private nature of administrative deliberation may mean that some pertinent facts are not considered, and that significant interests are not consulted. While secrecy contributed to the effectiveness of the Cuban missile-crisis decisions, it had the opposite effect with regard to the Bay of Pigs invasion the previous year. Secrecy is, on the whole, more characteristic of administrative deliberations in the foreign policy area than in domestic matters.

Finally, administrative decision-making is very frequently characterized by bargaining. Experts and facts are important in administrative decision-making, as has been noted, but so also are accommodation and compromise. Some agencies may be less involved in bargaining than others. The National Bureau of Standards and the Patent Office come to mind as two agencies whose decisions seem primarily expert decisions based on factual records. Economic regulatory agencies, such as the Interstate Commerce Commission and Environmental Protection Agency, often find it necessary to bargain with those whom they regulate. In setting emission standards, EPA has had to bargain with both polluters and state and local officials in order to reach tolerable decisions and secure compliance. A notable example of bargaining involves the consent decrees used by the Antitrust Division of the Department of Justice to close most civil antitrust cases. Negotiated in privacy—it should be observed—by representatives of the Division and of the alleged offender, the consent decree provides that the Division will drop its formal proceedings in turn for the alleged offender's agreeing to stop certain practices, such as price-fixing or proposed acquisition of a competitor. Negotiations with foreign countries for tariff reductions are another good illustration of bargaining, in this instance with foreign administrators.

Turning now to the second concern of this section, administrative decisions may be productive of policy (recall how it was defined in Chapter 1) in several ways—namely, rule-making, adjudication, law enforcement, and program operations.

Rule-Making. A rule may be defined as an agency statement of general applicability and future effect that concerns the rights of private parties and has the force and effect of law. Some rules fill in the details of general statutory provisions; others define the meaning of words such as "small business" or "discriminate" that appear in statutes; still others state how an agency will act in certain matters, as in the location of highways. Many national administrative agencies have been delegated rule-making (or legislative) authority by Congress. Thus, the Securities and Exchange Commission is authorized to make certain rules governing the stock exchanges "as it seems necessary in the public interest or for the protection of investors," and the Occupational Safety and Health Administration is empowered to make rules setting health and safety standards for working conditions that employers must meet. The initial set of rules issued by OSHA occupied several hundred pages of small print. In each of these instances, policy is to a substantial extent the product of agency rule-making. Collectively, the volume of rules made in a year's time by national administrative agencies and reported in the *Federal Register* is greater than the legislation enacted by Congress and recorded in the *U.S. Statutes-at-Large.*

Adjudication. Agencies can make policy when they apply existing laws or rules to particular situations by case-to-case decision-making. In so doing, they act in much the same manner as courts, just as they act in legislative fashion when engaged in rule-making. In the past, the Federal Trade Commission has made policy by applying the legislative prohibition of unfair methods of competition to specific cases. Over time, these cases marked out public policy and indicated the kinds of practices banned by the general prohibition. Again, an agency may make policy when it gives a particular interpretation to a statutory provision in the course of applying it in a case. Thus, the National Labor Relations Board, which administers labor-management relations legislation, makes statutory interpretations in deciding unfair-practices cases that then serve to inform its action in future cases. In such instances NLRB opinions become policy statements of much interest to those concerned with policy in this area.

Much of the adjudication engaged in by administrative agencies is rather routine, such as the hundreds of thousands of decisions made annually by the Veterans Administration and the Social Security Administration on applications for benefits. Still, within the framework of statutory language, seemingly routine decisions may shift the direction or affect the impact of policy. Noteworthy in this regard is the operation of the Internal Revenue Service, which routinely closes most cases of disputed income-tax returns by informal adjudication (and bargaining). IRS statistics for fiscal year 1972, for example, show that, in cases that did not end up in the courts— and most do not—the agency settled for 67 per cent of the amounts owed in the $1–$999 range, while settling for an average of 34 per cent when $1 million or more was allegedly owed. Moreover, settlements varied widely from district to district, ranging from 12 per cent of the amount alleged by IRS in the St. Paul district to 76 per cent in Pittsburgh.[22] Obviously, such actions significantly affect policy content and impact.

Law Enforcement. Agencies may also make policy through their general law-enforcement actions. A statute may be enforced vigorously or even rigidly, in a lax manner, or not at all; it may be applied in some situations and not in others, or to some persons or companies and not to others. Everyone is familiar with the discretion possessed by the police officer on the beat or, what is more likely, in the patrol car. A ticket may be issued to a speeder, or he may be let off with a warning. If no one is ticketed unless he exceeds posted speed limits by a certain rate, this amounts to an amendment of public policy. Even when statutory provisions are quite precise, thus seeming to eliminate discretion in their interpretation, enforcement officers still have some discretion with respect to whether they will be enforced.

The Hepburn Act of 1906, which dealt primarily with railroads, also authorized the Interstate Commerce Commission to regulate the rates charged by pipeline companies. Except for requiring the filing of rates, however, the ICC took no action by itself on the subject until 1934. It did not actually complete a pipeline rate proceeding until 1948, and then no effective action resulted. Since then, the ICC has continued to do little to carry out this authorization,[23] essentially substituting a policy of no regulation for the legislatively declared policy of regulation. The ICC's reluctance to carry out congressional intent illustrates an aspect of the administrative process that needs more systematic attention from policy analysts. Policy may be shaped by administrative inaction or apathy as well as by agency action and zeal. Inaction often affects only the inarticulate general public and consequently may pass unnoticed.

Agency enforcement activity depends not only on the attitudes and motives of agency officials, as well as external pressures, but also on the enforcement techniques available to the agency. Opponents unable to block the legislative enactment of a law may seek to blunt its impact by handicapping its enforcement. Take the case of the equal-employment opportunity provisions of the Civil Rights Act of 1964, which prohibit firms or unions representing 25 or more employees from discriminating against individuals because of their race, color, religion, national origin, or sex. Along with the rest of the Act, these provisions were adopted over strong opposition. The Equal Employment Opportunity Commission was established to enforce them through investigations, conferences, and conciliation, which means essentially voluntary action. If this failed, the EEOC could recommend civil action in the federal courts, which would require the cooperation of the Department of Justice. Moreover, the law provided that EEOC could not act on complaints from states in which there was an anti-discrimination law and an agency to enforce it, unless the state agency was unable to complete action within 60 days. Complaints had to be filed "in writing under oath," which is not a customary requirement for a law violation complaint. This undoubtedly had a chilling effect on many Southern blacks as well as others. Whatever the intent behind these provisions, they clearly limited the effectiveness of the law by making the successful completion of cases a slow, tedious process. After 1964, the EEOC and many supporters of stronger enforcement advocated giving the agency authority to issue "cease-and-desist orders"[24] in discrimination cases and then on its own initiative to seek their enforcement in the federal courts. Opposition to this change was particularly strong from conservatives and Southerners. In 1972, the EEOC was finally empowered to initiate court action on its own, but not to issue cease-and-desist orders when conciliation of complaints was not successful. Though perhaps not as much as hoped, this new authority will undoubtedly strengthen enforcement and the effectiveness of the anti–job discrimination policy.

Program Operations. Many agencies are involved in the operation of loan, grant, benefit, insurance, service, or construction policies and programs that are usually not thought of as being law enforcement in nature because they are not designed *directly* to regulate or shape people's behavior. How such programs are administered helps determine policy. A couple of examples should clarify what is involved here. Since the 1930's, the Federal Housing Administration has administered a mortgage insurance program under which the risks of nonpayment and foreclosure are assumed by the government rather than by private lending agencies. Until 1967, one regulation provided that housing loans, to be FHA-insured, had to be based on the criterion of "economic soundness." Consequently, low-income people in slum or deteriorating areas usually could not secure loans because of the "excessive risk" involved. Interest costs were also high relative to the income of the poor. Because of these operating requirements, the mortgage insurance policy was much more beneficial to middle- and upper-income persons than to the poor. In 1964, only 2.4 per cent of FHA loans on homes went to families with incomes below $4,800 annually. Not surprisingly, FHA gained a reputation of being unfriendly to the poor. Legislation enacted in 1968 was designed to reorder FHA priorities and make public policy in this area more helpful to low-income people.[25]

To take another case, the elementary and Secondary Education Act of 1965, under its Title I, provided financial aid for the education of disadvantaged children in urban and rural poor areas.[26] For fiscal year 1973, these funds, which are handled by the Office of Education, amount to about $1.5 billion. In the view of social-reform elements among its supporters, this policy was designed to help eliminate poverty by improving the educational facilities and opportunities of poor children. The Office of Education, however, has generally not acted with much vigor or effectiveness to see that local school districts actually use the funds as intended. Consequently, it is unclear to what extent funds are actually expended on disadvantaged children, and whether they buy services beyond the level of those provided other children in the aided districts. The program in operation has taken on something of the appearance of general aid to education.

Several factors have contributed to this. Although the legislation clearly specified disadvantaged children as its focus, its legislative history "provided the semblance if not the reality of general aid." This ambiguity, together with the fact that the reformers supporting the legislation did not concern themselves with its implementation, meant that officials in the Office of Education were left to interpret the legislation as they saw fit. Second, the orientation of the Office of Education is to provide assistance and advice to state and local education agencies; it is not inclined to regulate and police their activities. Third, state and local agencies have traditionally dominated the field of education, and they have strong political support in this regard. This makes it very difficult for national officials to impose directives that conflict with local priorities. Because of the manner in which it has been administered, the Title I program has not achieved the results hoped for by its supporters.

COMPLIANCE

All public policies are intended to influence or control human behavior in some way, to induce people to act in accordance with governmentally prescribed rules or goals, whether reference is to policy or such diverse matters as patents and copyrights, open housing, interest rates, night-time burglary, agricultural production, or military recruitment. If compliance with policy is not achieved, if people continue to act in undesired ways, if they do not take desired actions, or if they cease doing what is desired, to that extent policy becomes ineffective or, at the extreme, a nullity. (Foreign policy also depends for its effectiveness on compliance by the affected foreign countries and their officials.) To make consideration of this problem more manageable, we will focus primarily, but not exclusively, on compliance with domestic economic policies.

Except, perhaps, for crime policies, social scientists have not given much attention to the problem of compliance. Perhaps this is partly due to our traditional legalistic approach to government, with its assumption that people have an absolute duty to obey the law. Too, those concerned with securing action on public problems often lose interest therein or shift their attention elsewhere once they secure the enactment of legislation. Such was the case with the Elementary and Secondary Education Act of 1965 referred to above. Political scientists have certainly been far more interested in the legislative and executive formation and adaption of policy than in its administration, which is where compliance comes in. A complete study of policy-making must be concerned not only with the events leading up to a policy decision but also with what is done to implement it and, ultimately, whether people comply with it.

In this section, some of the factors affecting compliance and non-compliance with policy will be examined, along with the role of administrative agencies in securing compliance.[27] Because of a scarcity of empirical data, the discussion must be somewhat speculative.

Causes of Compliance

Substantial respect for authority exists in our society, including authority as expressed in the decisions of governmental agencies. Statements to the effect that Americans are a lawless people appear as exaggerations and should not be permitted to obscure this fact. Respect for, and deference to, authority is built into our psychological make-up by the process of socialization. Most of us are taught from birth to respect the authority of parents, knowledge, status, the law, and government officials, especially if these forms of authority are considered to be reasonable. Consequently, we grow up generally believing it to be morally right and proper to obey the law. Disobedience of the law may produce feelings of guilt or shame. Prior conditioning and force of habit thus contribute to policy.

Compliance with policy may also be based on some form of reasoned, conscious acceptance. Even some whose immediate self-interest conflicts with a particular policy may be convinced that it is reasonable, necessary, or just. Most people undoubtedly would rather not pay taxes, and many do try to avoid or evade paying. But when people believe that tax laws are reasonable and just, or perhaps that taxation is necessary to provide needed governmental services, such beliefs will in all likelihood contribute to compliance with tax policy. Are not factors such as this and the one discussed in the preceding paragraph contributory to the high degree of compliance with the national income tax in the United States?

Another possible cause of compliance is the belief that a governmental decision or policy should be obeyed because it is legitimate, in the sense that it is constitutional, or was made by officials with proper authority to act, or that correct procedures were followed. People would probably be less inclined to accept judicial decisions as legitimate if the courts utilized decision procedures akin to those of legislatures. Courts gain legitimacy and acceptance for their decision by acting as courts are supposed to act. Some people in the South were willing to comply with the Supreme Court's 1954 school desegregation decision because they viewed it as legitimate, as within the Court's competence, even though they disagreed with its substance.

Self-interest is often an important factor in compliance. Individuals and groups may directly benefit from acceptance of policy norms and standards. Thus, farmers have complied with production limitations in the form of acreage allotments and marketing quotas in order to qualify for price supports and benefit payments. Securities regulation is accepted by responsible members of the securities business as a way of protecting themselves and the reputation of their business against unethical practices by some dealers. Businessmen engage in industrial-plant modernization in order to receive investment tax credits. Milk price–control laws have long been sought and complied with by dairy interests as a way of improving their economic well-being. Compliance thus results because private interests and policy prescriptions are harmonious, a fact sometimes ignored. Or, to put it differently, compliance may yield positive rewards. This situation, we should note, is not likely to occur outside the economic policy area.

For any given piece of legislation, such as a minimum-wage law or a Sunday closing law, there will not be simply supporters and opponents. Rather, many points of view will exist, ranging from strong support, through indifference, to intense opposition. A considerable proportion of the population will often be indifferent or neutral toward the legislation in question, if, indeed, they feel affected by it at all. This group, given the general predisposition toward obedience, would seem especially subject to the authority of the law. Here, in effect, the law becomes a "self-fulfilling prophecy"; by its very existence it operates to create a climate of opinion conducive to compliance with it.

The possibility of punishment in the form of fines, imprisonment, and other sanctions also works to secure compliance. A number of recent studies indicate that law-abiding persons, as compared to law violators, considerably overestimate the risks of detection, convention, and punishment for criminal actions.[28] The threat or imposition of sanctions alone, however, is not always sufficient, even given overestimation of the likelihood of their use. "The strong disposition in this country to believe that any behavior can be controlled by threatening punishment has filled American statute books with hundreds of unenforced and unenforceable laws."[29] The experience with national prohibition, World War II price and rationing controls, many Sunday blue laws, and, recently, penalties for marijuana use shows that the threat of punishment is inadequate to cause compliance in the face of widespread violations.

Although many people may comply with policies because they fear punishment, the main function of sanctions is to reinforce and supplement other causes of compliance. To a great extent, policies depend for their effectiveness upon voluntary, that is, noncoerced compliance, because those concerned with enforcement cannot effectively handle, and apply sanctions in, large numbers of cases. The Internal Revenue Service would find itself at an impasse if several millions of people decided not to file returns. If those who would normally comply with policies see others benefiting from noncompliance, they, too, may become violators. Here the application of sanctions to some violators may be an effective promoter of compliance. Thus, the IRS does prosecute flagrant and prominent tax evaders to prove by example that punishment awaits the tax evader.

In many instances, sanctions are effective more because people desire to avoid being stigmatized as lawbreakers than because they fear the penalties involved. In criminal proceedings for antitrust violations, for example, the fines levied have usually been quite nominal, given the economic resources of the violators. Not until 1961 did a businessman actually spend time in jail for an antitrust violation, although this punishment had been possible since the adoption of the Sherman Act in 1890. The real deterrent in these cases is probably the adverse publicity that flows from the proceedings. Legislators and judges are often reluctant to create or impose jail sentences and other severe penalties on businessmen because of their social status and because of the often diffuse and complex impact of law violations such as embezzlement or the misuse of "in-side information" in stock deals. In other situations, sanctions may be more severe and uncertain and have more powerful deterrent effect.

Finally, acceptance of most policies seems to increase with the length of time they are in effect. As time passes—and it always does —a once controversial policy becomes more familiar, a part of the accepted state of things, one of the conditions of doing business. Further, increasing numbers of persons come under the policy who have had no experience with the prepolicy situation. Because "freedom is (in part) a state of mind, such men feel the restrictions to rest more lightly upon them."[30] Although at one time the Wagner Act (1935) was found highly objectionable by businessmen and the Taft-Hartley Act (1947) was vigorously opposed by labor unions, today these statutes have lost much of their controversial quality. They have become a fixed part of the environment of labor-management relations, and businessmen and labor-union officials have "learned to live with them." Predictably, environmental pollution-control policies will seem less restrictive or intrusive a decade from now than they do at present.

Causes of Noncompliance

It will be readily apparent even to the most casual observer that all persons affected by public policies do not comply with them. Statistical information on reported violations is readily obtainable, as in the Federal Bureau of Investigation's Uniform Crime Reports. In addition, a lot of violations go undetected or unreported. Why do some people, or in some situations many people, deviate from officially prescribed norms of behavior? As the obverse of compliance, noncompliance may result when laws conflict too sharply with the prevailing values, mores, and beliefs of the people generally or of particular groups. The extensive violations of national prohibition and wartime price and rationing controls can be attributed in considerable measure to this cause as may much of the noncompliance in the South with the 1954 school desegregation decision and related policy. In such instances, the general predisposition to obey the law is outweighed by strong attachment to particular values and practices.

It is not very useful, however, to ascribe noncompliance to a broad conflict between law and morality. Those who proclaim that "you can't legislate morality" not only oversimplify but also ignore the fact that morality is frequently legislated with considerable success. Failure to comply results when a particular law or set of laws conflicts with particular values or beliefs in a particular time and situation. The law-value conflict must be stated in fairly precise terms if it is to have operational value in explaining noncompliance. Thus, there was considerable noncompliance with the Supreme Court's 1948 decision that "released time" programs of religious instruction in public schools violated the constitutional requirement of separation of church and state.[31] Such released time programs were continued in many school systems where local citizens and school officials wanted them, despite their unconstitutionality.

The concept of selective disobedience of the law is closely related to the law-value conflict.[32] Some laws are felt to be less binding than others on the individual. Those who strongly support and obey what are ordinarily designated as criminal laws sometimes have a more relaxed or permissive attitude toward economic legislation and regulations or laws regulating the behavior of public officials. (In this regard, one should consider the behavior of former Vice-President Spiro T. Agnew.) Many businessmen apparently believe that laws relating to banking operations, trade practices, taxation, and environmental pollution control are not as mandatory for individuals as laws prohibiting robbery, burglary, and embezzlement. This may be, in part, because legislation regulating economic activity developed later than criminal laws. Moreover, economic legislation often runs counter to the businessman's ideology favoring nonintervention by government in the economy, and he may consider it bad law. In addition, the same social stigma usually is not attached to violation of economic policy as it is to criminal laws. Professor Marshall Clinard comments: "This selection of obedience to law rests upon the principle that what the person may be doing is illegal, perhaps even unethical, but certainly not criminal."

One's associates and group memberships may contribute to noncompliance (or, under other conditions, we should note, to compliance). Association with persons who hold ideas disrespectful of law and government, who justify or rationalize law violation, or who violate the law may cause the individual to acquire deviant norms and values that dispose him to noncompliance. In a study of labor relations policy, Lane found that the rate of law violations varied with the community in which the firms studied were located. It was "fairly conclusive" that one reason for these differential patterns was "difference in attitude toward the law, the government, and the morality of illegality. Plant managers stated they followed community patterns of behavior in their labor relations activities."[33] Attorneys for some of the defendant executives in the great price-fixing conspiracy in the electrical industry in the late 1950's attempted to explain and justify their actions, in the hope of lessening their punishment, as being in accord with the "corporate way of life."[34]

The desire to "make a fast buck," or something akin thereto, is often stated as a cause of noncompliance. This would certainly seem to be the case in many instances of fraud and misrepresentation, such as short-weighting and passing one product off for another in retail sales, the promotion of shady land sales and investment schemes, and price-fixing agreements. (Price-fixing is both the most obvious and the most common violation of the Sherman Antitrust Act.) It is really not possible, however, to determine how widespread greed is as a motive for noncompliance. By itself it often seems inadequate as an explanation. If two companies have equal opportunities to profit by violating the law, and one violates the law while the other does not, what is the explanation? One explanation may be that companies that are less profitable or in danger of failure are more likely to violate in an effort to survive than are more financially secure firms.[35] One should be careful, however, in attributing noncompliance to pecuniary motives. Many violations of labor-management relations policy stem from a desire to protect the prerogatives of management, while noncompliance with industrial health-and-safety standards may rest on the conviction that they are unnecessary or unworkable.

Noncompliance may also result from such factors as ambiguities in the law, a lack of clarity, or conflicting policy standards. Income-tax violations often stem from the ambiguity or complexity of provisions of the Internal Revenue Code, which someone once described as a "sustained essay in obscurity." In other instances, persons or companies may believe that a given practice is not prohibited by existing law, only to find upon prosecution that it is. Such a situation may arise because the frames of reference of businessmen and public officials are different, thus each interpreting the law differently. Violations may also result from difficulties in complying with the law, even when its meaning is understood. For example, insufficient time may be allowed for filing complicated forms or for making required changes in existing patterns of action, such as in the installation of pollution-control devices. Sheer ignorance of the existence of laws or rules regulating conduct cannot be discounted as a cause of noncompliance. While ignorance of the law may be no excuse, it often does account for violations. In sum, noncompliance may stem from structural defects in the law and its administration, and from ignorance and lack of understanding of the law, as well as from behavior that is more consciously or deliberately deviant.

Administration and Compliance

The burden of securing compliance with public policies rests primarily with administrative agencies; the courts play a lesser role. The broad purpose of administrative enforcement activities, such as conferences, persuasion, inspection, and prosecution, is to obtain compliance with policies rather than merely to punish violators.

Conscious human behavior involves making choices among alternatives—deciding to do some things and not to do others. For purposes of discussion, we can assume that there are essentially three ways in which administrative agencies, or other governmental bodies, concerned with implementing public policy can influence people to act in the desired ways—to select behavioral alternatives that result in policy compliance. First, to achieve a desired result agencies can strive to shape, alter, or utilize the values people employ in making choices. Educational and persuasional activities are illustrative of this type of activity. Second, agencies can seek to limit the acceptable choices available to people, as by attaching penalties to undesired alternatives and rewards or benefits to desired alternatives. Third, agencies can try to interpret and administer policies in ways designed to facilitate compliance with their requirements. More than one of these alternatives are normally used in seeking compliance with a given policy.

Administrative agencies engage in a wide range of educational and persuasional activities intended to convince those directly affected, and the public generally, that given public policies are reasonable, necessary, socially beneficial, or legitimate, in addition to informing them of the existence and meaning of those policies. The effectiveness of public policies depends considerably on the ability of agencies to promote understanding and consent, thereby reducing violations and minimizing the actual use of sanctions. This is in keeping with our earlier comment on the importance of voluntary compliance. When changes are made in the coverage and level of the federal minimum-wage law, for example, the Department of Labor seeks to acquaint the public, and especially affected employers and employees, of their nature and implications by the distribution of explanatory bulletins, reference guides, and posters, announcements through the news media, meetings with affected groups, appearances at conventions, direct mailings, telephone calls, and the like. After the changes become effective, press releases and mailed materials are used to provide information on enforcement activities and legal interpretations of the law. The Federal Deposit Insurance Corporation relies heavily on advice and warnings to banks, based on inspections, to get them to bring their operations into accord with banking regulations. Formal proceedings are initiated only when persuasion appears ineffective.

Agencies may also use propaganda appeals in support of compliance. (Propaganda is used here not in a pejorative sense but rather to denote efforts to gain acceptance of policies by identifying them with widely held values and beliefs.) Appeals to patriotism were used to win support and acceptance of the military draft. Agricultural programs have been depicted as necessary to ensure equality for agriculture and to help preserve the family farm as a way of life. Antitrust programs have been described as necessary to maintain our system of free competitive enterprise. The Forest Service utilizes Smokey the Bear to tell us that "only you can prevent forest fires." Propaganda appeals are more emotional than rational in thrust. They can be viewed as attempts either to reduce the moral costs of adapting to a policy or to make compliance desirable by attaching positive values to policies.[36]

In the course of administering policies, agencies may make modifications or adopt practices that will contribute to compliance. Revealed inequities in the law may be reduced or eliminated, or conflicts in policy standards may be resolved, or simplified procedures for compliance may be developed, such as simplified federal income-tax forms for lower-income earners. Administrative personnel may develop knowledge and skill in enforcing policy that enables them to reduce misunderstanding and antagonism. Consultation and advice may be used to help those affected by laws come into compliance without the issuance of citations. Laws may be interpreted or applied to make them more compatible with the interests of those affected. For instance, until 1970 the administration of oil-import controls policy by the Oil Import Administration "was almost wholly in the interests of the petroleum industry."[37] They had little cause for complaint. Many of the health-and-safety standards initially issued by the Occupational Safety and Health Administration (OSHA) were "national consensus standards," meaning that they were developed as a result of agreement among the affected interests, including labor and management.

Sanctions will be resorted to by agencies when the various sociological and psychological factors supporting obedience and the other methods available to agencies fail to produce compliance. Sanctions are penalties or deprivations imposed on those who violate policy norms and are intended to make undesired behavior patterns unattractive. They directly punish violators and serve to deter others who might not comply if they saw violations go unpunished.

Sanctions may be imposed by either administrative agencies or the courts. Common forms of judicial sanctions are fines, jail sentences, award of damages, and injunctions. However, in most areas of public policy (crime policy is a major exception) administrative sanctions are used much more frequently because of their greater immediacy, variety, and flexibility. Among the sanctions that agencies may impose are: threat of prosecution; imposition of fines or pecuniary penalties that have the effect of fines, as by OSHA; unfavorable publicity; revocation, annulment, modification, suspension, or refusal to renew licenses; summary seizure and destruction of goods; award of damages; issuance of cease-and-desist orders; and denial of services or benefits. To be most effective, the severity of sanctions must be geared to the violations against which they are directed. If they are too severe, the agency may be reluctant to use them; if they are too mild, they may have inadequate deterrent effects, as seems the case with most fines for antitrust violations. The Office of Education was handicapped in its administration of Title I of the Elementary and Secondary Education Act because the only sanction it had for state and local violations of the law was the cutting off of funds. Because of the reaction this would cause, it was politically reluctant to do so and, indeed, did not. Agencies clearly need appropriate and effective sanctions to help ensure policy compliance.

Agencies may also seek to induce compliance by conferring positive benefits on compliers, thereby bring self-interest into support for compliance. This method can be referred to as the "purchase of consent." Benefits may take such forms as favorable publicity and recognition for nondiscrimination in hiring, price-support payments for compliance with agricultural production limitations, tax credits for industrial plant modernization, and federal grants-in-aid for the support of state programs of medical aid to the indigent that meet federal standards. It is often difficult, however, to distinguish rewards from sanctions. Does an individual comply with a policy provision to secure a benefit or to avoid losing it? Whatever the motives of persons seeking benefits, the government does use rewards extensively to gain compliance with policy. They are undoubtedly much more acceptable politically in many situations than would be a clear-cut prohibition or requirement of some action with penalties for noncompliance. Imagine the reaction if, rather than using tax credits, businessmen were required to modernize their plants or else be subject to fines and other penalties. Subsidy payments clearly have made compliance with production controls more palatable to farmers.

Clearly, then, compliance—or noncompliance—with public policy may stem from a variety of factors. It is a complex topic that needs greater attention by policy analysts because of its importance for the actual content and impact of public policy.

NOTES

1. Frank J. Goodnow, *Politics and Administration* (New York: Russell and Russell, 1900).
2. Nick Kotz, *Let Them Eat Promises: The Politics of Hunger in America* (Englewood Cliffs, N.J.: Prentice-Hall, 1969).
3. This story is well told in Joseph P. Harris, *The Advice and Consent of the Senate* (Berkeley: University of California Press, 1953), chap. II.
4. David T. Stanley and Marjorie Girth, *Bankruptcy: Problems Process Reform* (Washington, D.C.: Brookings Institution, 1971), p. 172.
5. See Samuel P. Huntington, "The Marasmus of the ICC," *Yale Law Journal* LXI (1952), pp. 470–509.
6. Henry J. Steck, "Power and the Policy Process: Advisory Committee in the Federal Government." Unpublished paper presented at the annual meeting of the American Political Science Association, September, 1972, p. 4.
7. James W. Davis, Jr., and Kenneth M. Dolbeare, *Little Groups of Neighbors: The Selective Service System* (Chicago: Markham, 1968).
8. Rowland Evans and Robert Novak, *Lyndon B. Johnson: The Exercise of Power* (New York: New American Library, 1966), p. 430.
9. V. O. Key, Jr., "Legislative Control," in Fritz Morstein Marx, Jr., *Elements of Public Administration*, 2d ed. (Englewood Cliffs, N.J.: Prentice-Hall, 1959), p. 321.
10. See, for example, Louis J. Kohlmeier, Jr., *The Regulators* (New York: Harper & Row, 1969).
11. Quoted in V. O. Key, Jr., *Politics, Parties, and Pressure Groups*, 4th ed. (New York: Crowell, 1958), p. 743.
12. This discussion is based on my *Politics and the Economy* (Boston: Little, Brown, 1966), pp. 86–90.
13. *Phillips Petroleum Company* v. *State of Wisconsin*, 347 U.S. 672 (1954).

14. Cf. Matthew Holden, Jr., " 'Imperialism' in Bureaucracy," *American Political Science Review,* LX (December, 1966), pp. 943–51.
15. Holden, *ibid.,* p. 944.
16. This discussion, and that in the first part of the next section, draws on Francis E. Rourke, *Bureaucracy, Politics and Public Policy* (Boston: Little, Brown, 1969), chaps. 4 and 5.
17. *Ibid.,* p. 75.
18. *New York Times,* May 30, 1972, p. 53; *Houston Chronicle,* December 17, 1972, p. 5, Sect. 1.
19. On the separation of the ability to decide from the authority to decide in organization, see Victor Thompson, *Modern Organizations* (New York: Knopf, 1961).
20. Rourke, *op. cit.,* p. 108.
21. Theodore C. Sorensen, *Kennedy* (New York: Harper & Row, 1965), chap. 25. On secrecy in administration generally, see Harold L. Wilensky, *Organizational Intelligence* (New York: Basic Books, 1967), chaps. 3 and 7; and Francis E. Rourke, *Secrecy and Publicity* (Baltimore: Johns Hopkins Press, 1961).
22. *Wall Street Journal,* February 5, 1973, p. 1. This article is based on information pried from the Internal Revenue Service under the Freedom of Information Act of 1967, which is intended to help combat administrative secretiveness.
23. Kenneth Culp Davis, *Administrative Law Treatise* (St. Paul, Minn.: West, 1958), vol. I, pp. 263–65.
24. A "cease-and-desist order" is a civil directive by an agency to someone to stop engaging in a practice held to be in violation of the law. Agencies such as the Federal Trade Commission and the National Labor Relations Board are authorized to issue such orders.
25. Harold Wolman, *Politics of Federal Housing* (New York: Dodd, Mead, 1971), pp. 26–28.
26. This discussion is based on Jerome T. Murphy, "The Education Bureaucracies Implement Novel Policy: The Politics of Title I of ESEA, 1965–72," in Allen P. Sindler (ed.), *Policy and Politics in America,* 2d ed. (Boston: Little, Brown, 1973), pp. 161–98.
27. This discussion draws heavily on my "Public Economic Policy and the Problem of Compliance: Notes for Research," *Houston Law Review* IV (Spring–Summer, 1966), pp. 62–72.
28. For example, Gary F. Jensen, "Crime Doesn't Pay: Correlates of a Shared Misunderstanding," *Social Problems,* XVII (Fall, 1968), pp. 189–201.
29. Herbert A. Simon, Donald Smithburg, and Victor Thompson, *Public Administration* (New York: Knopf, 1950), p. 479.
30. Robert Lane, *The Regulation of Businessmen* (New Haven: Yale University Press, 1954), pp. 69–70.
31. *McCullom* v. *Board of Education,* 333 U.S. 208 (1948). The impact of this case, and a related one, is discussed in Frank J. Sorouf, *"Zorach* v. *Clausen:* The Impact of a Supreme Court Decision," *American Political Science Review,* LIII (September, 1959), pp. 777–91.
32. Marshall B. Clinard, *Sociology of Deviant Behavior* (New York: Holt, Rinehart & Winston, 1957), pp. 168–71.
33. Robert E. Lane, "Why Business Men Violate the Law," *Journal of Criminal Law, Criminology, and Police Science,* XLIV (1953), pp. 151, 154–60.
34. John G. Fuller, *The Gentlemen Conspirators: The Story of the Price-Fixers in the Electrical Industry* (New York: Grove Press, 1962), pp. 88, 109–10.
35. Lane, *The Regulation of Businessmen, op cit.,* chap. 5.
36. Simon, Smithburg, and Thompson, *op. cit.,* p. 457.
37. Roger G. Noll, *Reforming Regulation* (Washington, D.C.: Brookings Institution, 1971), p. 65.

5. Policy Impact, Evaluation, and Change

The final stage of the policy process, viewed as a sequential pattern of activities, is the evaluation of policy. Generally speaking, policy evaluation is concerned with the estimation, assessment, or appraisal of policy, including its content, implementation, and effects. As a functional activity, policy evaluation can and does occur throughout the policy process and not simply as its last stage. For instance, an attempt is usually made to determine, that is, estimate, the consequences of various policy alternatives for dealing with a problem prior to the adoption of one of them. In this chapter, the focus will be primarily but not exclusively on policy evaluation connected with efforts to implement or carry out policies. As we will see, evaluational activity may restart the policy process (problem, formulation, and so on) in order to continue, modify, or terminate existing policy.

Policy evaluation, as a functional activity, is as old as policy itself. Policy-makers and administrators have always made judgments concerning the worth or effects of particular policies, programs, and projects. Many of these judgments have been of the impressionistic, or "seat of the pants," variety, based often on anecdotal or fragmentary evidence, at best, and strongly influenced by ideological, partisan self-interest and other valuational criteria. Thus, a welfare program may be regarded as "socialistic" and hence undesirable by some, regardless of its actual impact. Or a tax cut may be considered necessary and desirable because it enhances the electoral chances of the evaluators' political party. Unemployment compensation may be deemed "bad" because the evaluator "knows a lot of people" who improperly receive benefits. Most of us are quite familiar with this kind of policy evaluation and have undoubtedly done, and enjoyed doing, a bit of it ourselves. Much conflict may result from this sort of evaluation, because different evaluators, employing different value criteria, reach different conclusions concerning the merits of the same policy.

Another common variety of policy evaluation has centered on the operation of particular policies or programs. Questions asked may include: Is the program honestly run? What are its financial costs? Who receives benefits (payments or services) and in what amounts? Is there unnecessary overlap or duplication with other programs? Were legal standards and procedures followed? This kind of evaluation may tell us something about the honesty or efficiency in the conduct of a program, but, like the first kind of evaluation, it will probably yield little, if anything, in the way of hard information on the societal effects of a program. A welfare program, for example, may be ideologically and politically satisfying to a given evaluator, as well as being honestly and prudently conducted. Assuming we are in agreement with this evaluation, it will in all likelihood tell us little about the impact of the program on the poor or its *social* cost-benefit ratio, or whether it is achieving its officially stated objectives.

A third type of policy evaluation, which is comparatively new in usage, and which has been receiving increasing attention within the national government in recent years, is the systematic, objective evaluation of programs to measure their societal impact and the extent to which they are achieving their stated objectives. We shall refer to this as systematic evaluation, for want of a better term. A number of federal agencies have regular policy evaluation staffs. The Department of Health, Education, and Welfare has an Assistant Secretary for Planning and Evaluation. The Office of Economic Opportunity has carried on a variety of evaluational activities, which are classifiable as follows:

Type I—Program Impact Evaluation: an assessment of overall program impact and effectiveness. The emphasis is on determining the extent to which programs are successful in achieving basic objectives and on the comparative evaluation of national programs.

Type II—Program Strategy Evaluation: an assessment of the relative effectiveness of program strategies and variables. The emphasis is on determining which program strategies are most productive.

Type III—Project Monitoring: assessment of individual projects through site visits and other activities with the emphasis on managerial and operational efficiency.[1]

Types I and II illustrate the kind of evaluation I have in mind in this paragraph, whereas Type III is an example of operational evaluation.

Systematic evaluation directs attention to the effects a policy has on the public problem to which it is directed. It permits at least some tentative responses to the question "Is this policy accomplishing anything?" It gives policy-makers and the general public some notion of the actual impact of policy and provides policy discussions with some grounding in reality.

POLICY IMPACT

In discussing impact and evaluation, it is important to have in mind the distinction between policy outputs and policy outcomes. Policy outputs are the things governments do—highway construction, payment of welfare benefits, arrests for burglary, or operation of public schools. These activities may be measured by such standards as per capita highway expenditures, per capita welfare expenditures, arrests for burglary per 100,000 population, per pupil school expenditures, and the like. Such figures tell us little about the outcomes, or impacts, of public policies because, in trying to determine policy outcomes, our concern is with the changes in the environment or political system caused by policy action. Knowing how much is spent on pupils in a school system on a per capita, or some other, basis will tell us nothing concerning the effect schooling has on the cognitive and other abilities of students, let alone the consequences of education for society generally.

Policy evaluation is concerned, then, with trying to determine the impact of policy on real-life conditions. The phrase "trying to determine" is used because, as will become apparent, determining the actual effects, or consequences, of policies is often a very complex and difficult task. At a minimum, policy evaluation requires that we know what we want to accomplish with a given policy (policy objectives), how we are trying to do it (programs), and what, if anything, we have accomplished toward attainment of the objectives (impact or outcomes, and the relation of policy thereto). And, in measuring accomplishment, we need to determine not only that some change in real-life conditions has occurred, such as a reduction in the unemployment rate, but also that it was due to policy actions and not to other factors, such as private economic decisions.

The impact of a policy has several dimensions, all of which must be taken into account in the course of evaluation.[2] These include:

1. The impact on the public problem at which it is directed and on the people involved. Those whom the policy is intended to affect must be defined, whether the poor, small businessmen, disadvantaged school children, petroleum producers, or whatever. The intended effect of the policy must then be determined. If, for example, it is an antipoverty program, is its purpose to raise the income of the poor, to increase their opportunities for employment, or to change their attitudes and behavior? If some combination of such purposes is intended, analysis becomes more complicated because priorities must be assigned to the various intended effects.

Further, it must be noted that a policy may have either intended or unintended consequences, or even both. A welfare program may improve the income situation of the benefited groups, as intended. But what impact does it also have on their initiative to seek employment? Does it decrease this, as some have contended? A public-housing program may improve the housing situation of urban blacks, but it may also contribute to racial segregation in housing. An agricultural price-support program, intended to improve farmers' incomes, may lead to overproduction of the supported commodities.

2. Policies may have effects on situations or groups other than those at which they are directed. These can be called either externalities or spillover effects.[3] The testing of nuclear explosives in the atmosphere may provide needed data for weapons development, but it also generates hazards for the current and future population of the world. This is a negative externality, but externalities may also be positive. When tariffs are lowered at the behest of American exporters to increase their sales abroad, American consumers may benefit from lower prices caused by increased imports that lower tariffs stimulate. Many of the outcomes of public policies can be most meaningfully understood in terms of externalities.

3. Policies may have impacts on future as well as current conditions. Is a policy designed to improve some immediate, short-term situation, or are its consequences to be long-term, stretched over

many years or decades? Is the Head Start program supposed to improve the cognitive abilities of disadvantaged (i.e., poor) children in the short run, or is it to affect their long-range development and earning capacity? Is a price-control program intended only to check incipient price increases, or is it to have a long-term impact on economic behavior, as by helping eliminate the existence of "inflationary psychology"? Did regulation of the price of natural gas at the wellhead, a policy begun in the 1950's, really contribute to the current energy shortage as some now contend (notably, those in the petroleum industry who long opposed the policy)? If so, this would be a long-term effect of the policy and a negative externality (or cost).

4. The direct costs of policies are another element for evaluation. It is usually fairly easy to calculate the dollar costs of a particular policy or program, when it is stated as the actual number of dollars spent on a program, its share of total government expenditures, or the percentage of the gross national product devoted to it. Other direct costs of policies may be more difficult to discover or calculate, such as expenditures for pollution-control devices by the private sector necessitated by an air-pollution control policy. A direct cost of the selective service system (the "draft") was the loss of freedom of choice by those conscripted. The measurement of such costs is no easy matter.

5. Policies may have indirect costs that are experienced by the community or some of its members. Such costs often have not been considered in making policy evaluations, at least partly because they defy quantification. How does one measure the costs of inconvenience, dislocation, and social disruption resulting from an urban-renewal project? Or the aesthetic costs of building a highway through a scenic park? Or the cost of the Vietnam war in internal strife and loss of credibility by public officials?

Of course, it is also difficult to measure the indirect benefits of public policies for the community. Assuming that patent and copyright policies do indeed stimulate inventive and creative activity, and that these contribute to economic growth and social development, how may we assess their benefits quantitatively? The social security program may contribute to social stability and political contentment as well as the retirement incomes of recipients. The problem of measurement is again apparent.

The evaluation of policy becomes even more complex when we

give explicit consideration to the fact that the effects of policy may be symbolic (or intangible) as well as material (or tangible). Symbolic outputs, in the view of Gabriel Almond and G. Powell, "include affirmations of values by elites; displays of flags, troops, and military ceremony; visits by royalty or high officials; and statements of policy or intent by political leaders" and "are highly dependent on tapping popular beliefs, attitudes, and aspirations for their effectiveness."[4] Symbolic policy outputs produce no real changes in societal conditions. No one eats better, for example, because of a Memorial Day parade or a speech by a high public official on the virtues of free enterprise, however ideologically or emotionally satisfying such actions may be for many people. More to the point of our discussion, however, is the fact that policy actions ostensibly directed toward meeting material wants or needs may turn out, in practice, to be more symbolic than material in their impact.

This is well illustrated by the graduated income tax levied by the national government. Based on the principle of ability to pay, which is widely, if not universally, regarded as a standard of fairness in taxation, rates range from 14 per cent to 70 per cent, depending upon the taxpayer's taxable income. Taken at face value, the graduated income tax is a symbol of equality and progressivity in taxation and draws wide support on that basis. In actuality, the impact of the income tax on many people, particularly the wealthy, is greatly reduced by provisions such as those for income splitting, family partnerships, depletion allowances, and capital gains. The result is that the effective tax rates for the rich are substantially lower than imagined. What is symbolically promised is quite different from what materially results. This was brought home to many people in 1973, when it became known that President Nixon had paid, for the years 1970 and 1971, only $1,671 in taxes on an income of more than $400,000. This is a very token payment indeed, or about what would be paid by the average family of four with an annual income of $9,500. (He subsequently agreed to make a much larger tax payment.)

Other public policies that appear to promise more symbolically than their implementation actually yields in material benefits include antitrust activity, public utility rate regulation, and equal-employment opportunity. Even though the actual impact of a policy may be considerably less than is intended or desired, it nonetheless may have significant consequences for society. An antipoverty program that falls short of the mark may nonetheless assure people that the government is concerned about poverty. Equal employment–opportunity legislation assures people that their government, officially at least, does not condone discrimination in hiring on the basis of race, sex, and nationality. Apart from whatever effects such policies have on societal conditions, they may contribute to social order, support for government, and personal self-esteem, which are not inconsequential considerations.

The analysis of public policy is usually focused upon what governments actually do, why, and with what material effects. We should not, however, neglect the symbolic aspects of government, despite their intangible and nebulous nature. The rhetoric of government–what governments say, or appear to say–is clearly a necessary and proper concern for the policy analyst.

PROBLEMS IN POLICY EVALUATION

The most useful policy evaluation for policy-makers and administrators, and policy critics who wish to have a factual basis for their positions, is the systematic evaluation that tries to determine cause-and-effect relationships and rigorously measure the impact of policy. It is, of course, often impossible to measure quantitatively the impact of public policies, especially social policies, with any real precision. In this context, then, to "measure rigorously" is to seek to assess as carefully and objectively as possible the impact of policy.

The burden of the discussion in this section will be to indicate a number of barriers, or obstacles, that may create problems for the evaluation of policy. This is not intended to be a discourse on futility, but policy evaluation is typically neither easy nor simple, and one should be aware of this. Anyone, of course, can express a judgment on policies without really examining them, and many do. The value of such judgments is often directly proportional to their factual basis–almost nothing.

Uncertainty over Policy Goals. When the goals of a policy are unclear, diffuse, or diverse, as they frequently are, determining the extent to which they have been attained becomes a difficult and frustrating task.[5] This situation often is a product of the policy adoption process. Because support of a majority coalition is needed to secure adoption of a policy, it is often necessary to appeal to persons and groups possessing differing interests and diverse values.

Commitments to the preferred policy goals of various groups may be included in legislation in order to secure their votes. The Model Cities Act of 1966 reflects this process. Its goals include, among others, the rebuilding of slum and blighted areas, the improvement of housing, income and cultural opportunities, the reduction of crime and delinquency, lessening dependency on welfare, and the maintenance of historic landmarks. No priorities are assigned to the various goals. Model-cities evaluation research has to try to come to grips with these diverse goals. It may be no easy task to determine what the real goals of a program are. Officials in different positions in the policy system, such as legislators and administrators, or national and state officials, may define them differently and act accordingly.

Causality. Systematic evaluation requires that changes in real-life conditions must demonstrably be caused by policy actions. But the mere fact that action A is taken and condition B develops does not necessarily mean that a cause-and-effect relationship exists. Some things may happen with or without policy action. An anecdote reported by Robert Levine is in point.[6] A few months after the Office of Economic Opportunity began operating, the Census Bureau reported a substantial drop in poverty from 1963 to 1964. Sargent Shriver received a note from a White House staff official that said "Nice going Sarge." But, since the data for both 1963 and 1964 antedated the existence of OEO, it is unlikely the agency had any effect on the poverty reduction. The staff official had carelessly implied a causal relationship where none existed.

To illustrate further the problem of determining causality, let us take the case of crime-control policies. The purpose, or at least one of the purposes, of these policies is the deterrence of crime. Deterrence may be defined as the prevention of an action that can be said to have had a "realistic potential of actualization,"[7] that is, that really could have happened. (This assumption is required in order to avoid the kind of analysis that holds, for example, that consumption of alcoholic beverages prevents stomach worms, since no one has ever been afflicted with them after starting to drink.) The problem here is that "not doing something" is a sort of nonevent, or intangible act. Does the fact that a person does not commit burglary mean that he has been effectively deterred by policy from so acting? The answer, of course, first depends upon whether he was inclined to engage in burglary. If he was so inclined, then was he deterred by the possibility of detection and punishment, by other factors such as family influence, or by the lack of opportunity? As this should indicate, the determination of causality between actions, especially in complex social and economic matters, is a difficult task.

Diffuse Policy Impacts. Policy actions may affect groups other than those at whom they are specifically directed. A welfare program may affect not only the poor but also others, such as taxpayers, public officials, and low-income people who are not receiving welfare benefits. The effects on these groups may be either symbolic or material. Taxpayers may grumble that their "hard-earned dollars are going to support those too lazy to work." Some low-income working people may decide to "go on welfare" rather than continue working at unpleasant jobs for low wages. So far as even the poor who do receive material benefits are concerned, what effects do benefits have on their initiative and self-reliance, on family solidarity, and on the maintenance of social order? We should bear in mind that policies may have unstated goals: Thus, an antipoverty program may be covertly intended to help defuse the demands of black activists; or, to take another case, a beef control program may be intended to appease cattlemen politically, while not really doing much to limit imports.

The effects of some programs may be very broad and long-range in nature. Antitrust is an example. Originally intended to help maintain competition and prevent monopoly in the economy, how does one now evaluate its effectiveness? We can look at on-going enforcement activity and find that particular mergers have been prevented and price-fixing conspiracies broken up, but this will not tell us much about competition and monopoly in the economy generally. It would be nice to be able to determine that the economy is n per cent more competitive than it would have been in the absence of antitrust policy. Given the generality of its goals and the difficulties of measuring competition and monopoly, this just is not possible. Interestingly enough, after more than 80 years of antitrust action, there are still no agreed upon definitions of monopoly and competition to guide policy action and evaluation. No wonder those assessing the effectiveness of antitrust sometimes come to sharply different conclusions.

Difficulties in Data Acquisition. As some previous comments have implied, a shortage of accurate and relevant statistical data and other information may handicap the policy evaluator. Thus, econometric models may predict the effect of a tax cut on economic activity, but suitable data to indicate its actual impact on the economy are hard to come by. Again, think of the problems involved in securing the data needed to determine the effect on criminal law enforcement of a Supreme Court decision such as that in *Miranda* v. *Arizona*,[8] which held that a confession obtained when a suspect had not been informed of his rights when taken into custody was inherently invalid. The members of the President's Crime Commission in 1967 disagreed about its effect. The majority said it was too early to determine its impact. A minority, however, held that, if fully implemented, "it could mean the virtual elimination of pretrial interrogation of suspects. . . . Few can doubt the adverse effect of *Miranda* upon the law enforcement process."[9] An absence of data does not necessarily hinder all evaluators.

For many social and economic programs, a question that typically arises is: "Did those who participated in programs subsequently fare better than comparable persons who did not?" Providing an answer requires an evaluation design utilizing a control group. The task of devising a control (or comparison) group for a manpower program is summed up in the following passage:

A strict comparison group in the laboratory sense of the physical sciences is virtually impossible, primarily because the behavior patterns of people are affected by so many external social, economic, and political factors. In fact, sometimes the legislation itself prevents a proper comparison group from being established. For example, the Work Incentive Program legislation of 1967 required that *all* fathers must be enrolled in the WIN program within 30 days after receipt of aid for their children. Therefore, a comparison group of fathers with comparable attributes to those fathers enrolled in the program could not be established. Even if all the external factors of the economy could be controlled, it would still be impossible to replicate the social and political environment affecting any experimental or demonstration program. Thus, it is easy for a decision-maker to discount the results of almost any evaluation study on the basis that it lacks the precision control group.[10]

Official Resistance. The evaluation of policy, whether it be called policy analysis, the measurement of policy impact, or something else, involves the making of judgments on the merits of policy. This is true even if the evaluator is a university researcher who thinks of himself as objectively in the pursuit of knowledge. Agency and program officials are going to be concerned about the possible political consequences of evaluation. If the results do not come out "right" from their perspective and if the results come to the attention of decision-makers, their program, influence, or careers may be in jeopardy. Consequently, program officials may discourage or disparage evaluation studies, refuse access to data, or keep records that are incomplete. Within agencies, evaluation studies are likely to be most strongly supported by higher-level officials, who must make decisions concerning the allocation of resources among programs and whether to continue given programs. They may, however, be reluctant to require evaluations, especially if their results may have a divisive effect within the agencies. Finally, we should note that organizations tend to resist change, while evaluation implies change. Organizational inertia may thus be an obstacle to evaluation, along with more overt forms of resistance.

POLICY EVALUATION PROCESSES

Within the national government, policy evaluation is carried on in a variety of ways by a variety of actors. Sometimes it is highly systematic, other times rather haphazard or sporadic. In some instances policy evaluation has become institutionalized; in others it is quite informal and unstructured. A few forms of official policy evaluation, including congressional oversight, the General Accounting Office, Presidential commissions, and agency action, will be examined briefly.

There is, of course, a lot of policy evaluation carried on outside government. The communications media, university scholars, private research organizations such as the Brookings Institution and the Urban Institute, pressure groups, and public-interest organizations such as Common Cause and Ralph Nader and his "raiders" all make evaluations of policies that have greater or lesser effects on public officials. They also provide the larger public with information, publicize policy action or inaction, sometimes serve as advocates of unpopular causes, and often effectively represent the unrepresented—for example, the aged confined to negligently run nursing homes, or exploited migrant workers. Limitations of space do not permit discussion of the activities of such groups here, but this should not be taken to mean that they are not important in the policy process. Consider, for example, the impact of television journalism on American policy in Southeast Asia.

Congressional Oversight. One of the primary functions of Congress, although it is not specified in the Constitution, is the scrutiny and evaluation of the application, administration, and execution of laws or policy. Some, agreeing with John Stuart Mill, think that this is the most important function performed by a legislature. Oversight, however, is not a separable, distinct activity; rather, it is a part of almost everything that congressmen do—for example, gathering information, legislating, authorizing appropriations, helping constituents. It may be intended either to control the actions of agencies, as when they sometimes are required to clear actions in advance with particular committees, or to evaluate agency actions, as when individual congressmen or committees seek to determine whether administrators are complying with program objectives established by Congress. It is the evaluative aspect of oversight that is pertinent here.

Oversight may be exercised through a number of techniques, including: (1) casework, that is, intercession with agencies as a consequence of constituent demands and requests; (2) committee hearings and investigations; (3) the appropriations process; (4) approval of Presidential appointments; and (5) committee staff studies. In the course of these activities, and others, congressmen reach conclusions regarding the efficiency, effectiveness, and impact of particular policies and programs—conclusions that can have profound consequences for the policy process. Congressional oversight is, in essence, more fragmented and disjointed than continuous and systematic. Bits and pieces of information, impressionistic judgments, and the congressmen's intuition and values are blended to yield evaluation of policies and those who administer them.

General Accounting Office. This agency, generally regarded as an "arm of Congress," has broad statutory authority to audit the operations and financial activities of federal agencies, evaluate their programs, and report its findings to Congress.[11] In recent years, the GAO has become increasingly concerned with evaluating programs as well as auditing program operations. The Legislative Reorganization Act of 1970 increased the authority of the agency in this area by directing it to "review and analyze the results of government programs and activities carried on under existing law, including the making of cost-benefit studies," and to make personnel available to congressional committees to assist them in similar activities.

Evaluation studies may be undertaken by the GAO on its own initiative, on the basis of directives in legislation, at the request of congressional committees, or sometimes at the request of individual members of Congress. The Comprehensive Health Manpower Training Act of 1971 directed GAO to make a study of health-facilities construction costs. The completed report "dealt in great depth with the objective of reducing the high cost of constructing health facilities and also identifying and evaluating ways for reducing the demand for such facilities."[12] Another study, requested by the Joint Economic Committee, sought to measure the extent to which poor people, living in six selected geographical areas, benefited from various federal welfare programs. A third study found that the testing program of the National Highway Traffic Safety Administration was inadequate to ensure compliance by manufacturers with national motor-vehicle safety regulation. The results of such studies are delivered to Congress for use in its oversight and decision-making activities.

Presidential Commissions. Earlier we dealt with the role of Presidential commissions in policy formulation. Now we will see that they can also be used as a means of policy evaluation. Whether set up specifically to evaluate policy in some area or for other purposes such as fact-finding, making policy recommendations, or simply creating the appearance of concern, most commissions do involve themselves in policy evaluation.

The President's Commission on Income Maintenance Programs was established by President Johnson with a mandate to evaluate existing and proposed income-maintenance programs and to recommend a new income-maintenance program that would better serve the nation's needs. The commission reported twenty-two months later, in November, 1969. On the basis of such criteria as whether existing programs had favorable cost-benefit ratios, clearly defined the rights and duties of potential participants, provided adequate levels of support, were perceived as equitable, had adverse incentive effects, and minimized administrative costs, the commission concluded that existing income-maintenance programs were "simply inadequate for alleviating existing poverty and protecting the non-poor against risks that they are incapable of dealing with themselves."[13] The commission's main recommendation (there were numerous others) was for the creation of a universal federal income-support program making cash payments to all needy persons at a level providing a base income of $2,400 for a family of four. One can only speculate about what impact the commission's report and its recommendations had on the controversy, during 1969 and 1970, surrounding the Nixon Administration's proposed Family Assistance Plan, which, as initially proposed, in August, 1969, provided for a guaranteed income of $2,400 for a family of four.[14]

Generally, it appears that the policy evaluations made by Presidential commissions do not have much immediate effect on policymaking. The impact they have is probably due primarily to factors other than the quality and soundness of their findings. Charles Jones concludes that an evaluation commission is likely to have the largest effect when its report coincides with other supporting events and is in accord with the President's policy preferences, when it includes some members who hold important government positions and are committed to its recommendations, and when commission staff personnel return to government positions from where they can influence the acceptance of its recommendations.[15]

Administrative Agencies. Much program and policy evaluation is engaged in by the administering agencies, either on their own initiative or at the direction or behest of others. A few developments and examples will be commented upon to give some notion of this source of evaluation.

Much attention in the 1960's was given to the Planning-Programming-Budgeting System (PPBS), which was first introduced in the Department of Defense by Secretary Robert McNamara. Essentially, it was intended to facilitate rational choice among policy and program alternatives on the basis of explicit criteria and firm cost and performance data. On August 25, 1965, President Johnson signed an executive order requiring the use of PPBS throughout the national government. In his view, it would enable decision-makers to:

(1) Identify our national goals with precision and on a continuing basis;

(2) Choose among those goals the ones that are most urgent;

(3) Search for alternative means of reaching those goals most effectively and at the least cost;

(4) Inform ourselves not merely on next year's costs, but on the second, and third, and subsequent years' costs of our programs;

(5) Measure the performance of our programs to insure a dollar's worth of service for each dollar spent.

But things did not go well for PPBS within the bureaucracy, and in June, 1971, the rather turgid prose of an Office of Management and Budget memorandum announced its passing: "Agencies are no longer required to submit with their budget submissions the multi-year program and financing plans, program memoranda and special analytic studies . . ."[16]

Many factors contributed to the death of PPBS. Many agency heads and congressmen were not interested in, or were opposed to, program analysis. Legislation often did not clearly specify program goals or provide funds needed to perform needed data collection and analyses. Moreover, there was often a lack of adequate data to develop measures of the costs and benefits of many programs and a scarcity of personnel skilled in policy analysis. Also, many employees were basically resistant to economic analysis and the difficult task of program evaluation.[17]

In 1973, the Office of Management and Budget announced the official birth of another planning and evaluatory technique—Management by Objective (MBO).[18] More modest in its scope than PPBS, MBO requires agencies to determine, subject to Office of Management and Budget and Presidential approval, the most important objectives they intend to accomplish during the next year or so. These Office of Management and Budget officials will periodically meet with agency officials to review progress toward the objectives. (An example of an objective is the Department of Health, Education, and Welfare's intention to implement the 1971 amendments to the Work Incentive Program. This is broken down into component parts, such as registration of 1.5 million people for the program.) MBO, like PPBS, seeks to determine whether agencies are meeting their objectives (goals); unlike PPBS, however, it does not attempt to evaluate alternative programs for meeting agency objectives.

Agencies may sometimes be specifically directed by congressional legislation to undertake program evaluation. This was the case with the Office of Economic Opportunity and the Job Corps program under the 1967 Economic Opportunity Act Amendments. The pertinent provisions are worth quoting in their entirety as a good example of an evaluation research design (and also of the fact that Congress at times can legislate in fine detail).

Section 113(a). The Director shall provide for the careful and systematic evaluation of the Job Corps program, directly or by contracting for independent evaluation, with a view to measuring specific benefits, so far as practicable, and providing information to assess the effectiveness of program procedures, policies, and methods of operation. In particular, this evaluation shall seek to determine the costs and benefits resulting from the use of residential as opposed to non-residential facilities, from the use of facilities combining residential and non-residential components, from the use of centers with large as opposed to small enrollments and from the use of different types of program sponsors, including public agencies, institutions of higher education, boards of education, and private corporations. The evaluation shall also include comparisons with proper control groups composed of persons who have not participated in the program. . . . He shall also secure, to the extent feasible, similar information directly from enrollers at appropriate intervals following their completion of the Job Corps program. The results of such evaluation shall be published and shall be summarized in the report required by Section 608.

Other sections of the Amendments called for evaluation of some of its other programs by OEO and also directed the General Accounting Office to do an evaluation of the OEO programs.

Policy evaluation, however, is more than a technical or analytical process; it is also a political process. In the next section, a case study of OEO evaluation of the Head Start program illustrates how political factors may affect the conduct and impact of program evaluations.

THE POLITICS OF EVALUATION: THE CASE OF HEAD START

The Economic Opportunity Act of 1964 contained no provisions specifically concerned with the educational problems of poor children. Advocates of a preschool program for poor children, however, found Sargent Shriver, Director of the Office of Economic Opportunity, sympathetic to the idea. Support for such a program as part of the antipoverty program also came from Congress. In January, 1965, President Johnson announced that a preschool program named Head Start would be created as part of the Community Action Program. Initially, $17 million in CAP funds were to be committed for the summer of 1965, to enable 100,000 children to participate. The announcement of Head Start produced a large volume of requests for funds from many localities. OEO officials decided to meet this demand, with the result that ultimately $103 million was committed to provide places for 560,000 children during the summer of 1965. To say the least, the program was highly popular, undoubtedly because it directed attention to preschool poor children who readily aroused the sympathy of the public.

Late in the summer of 1965, Head Start was made a permanent part of the antipoverty program. According to President Johnson, Head Start had been "battle-tested," and "proven worthy." It was expanded to include a full-year program. In fiscal year 1968, $330 million were allocated to provide places for 473,000 children in summer programs and another 218,000 in full-year programs, making Head Start the largest single component of the Community Action Program. Essentially, Head Start was a multifaceted program for meeting the needs of poor children. More than a traditional nursery school or kindergarten program, it was designed also to provide poor children with physical and mental health services and meals to improve their diet. Further, an effort was made to involve members of the local community in the program.

With this as a background, let us turn to evaluation of the program.[19] OEO was among the leaders in efforts to evaluate social programs. Within the agency the task of evaluating the over-all effectiveness of its programs was assigned to the Office of Research, Plans, Programs and Evaluations (RPP&E). Some early efforts had been made to evaluate the effectiveness of the Head Start program, mostly by Head Start officials and involving particular projects, but, as of the middle of 1967, no good evidence existed regarding over-all program effectiveness. This was becoming a matter of concern to OEO officials, the Bureau of the Budget, and some members of Congress. Consequently, the Evaluation Division of RPP&E, as part of a series of national evaluations of OEO programs, proposed an *ex post facto* study design for Head Start in which Head Start children currently in the first, second, and third grades of school would be given a series of cognitive and affective tests. Their test scores would then be compared with those of a control group. The Evaluation Division believed such a design would yield results more quickly than a longitudinal study that, though more desirable, would take longer to complete. (A longitudinal study examines the impact over time of a program on a given group.)

Within OEO, Head Start officials opposed the proposed study on various grounds, including its design, the test instruments to be used, and the focus on only the educational aspect of the program to the neglect of its health, nutrition, and community involvement goals. RPP&E evaluations acknowledged the multiplicity of Head Start goals but contended that cognitive improvement was its primary goal. They agreed with Head Start officials that there were risks, such as possible misleading negative results, in making a limited study but insisted that the need for evaluative data necessitated taking the risks. Following much internal debate, the OEO Director decided the study should be made, and in June, 1968, a contract was entered into with the Westinghouse Learning Corporation and Ohio University. The study was conducted in relative quiet, but hints of its negative fundings began to surface as it neared completion.

Early in 1969, a White House staff official became aware of the Westinghouse study and requested information on it because the President was preparing an address on the Economic Opportunity Act that would include a discussion of Head Start. OEO officials reported the preliminary negative findings of the study. In his message to Congress on Economic Opportunity on February 19, 1969, President Nixon referred to the study, noting that "the preliminary reports . . . confirm what many have feared: the long term effect of Head Start appears to be extremely weak." He went on to say that "this must not discourage us" and spoke well of the program. Nonetheless, his speech raised substantial doubts about Head Start in the public arena.

The President's speech touched off considerable pressure for the release of the study's findings. OEO officials were reluctant to do so because what had been delivered to them by Westinghouse was the preliminary draft of the final report. It was to be used to decide such matters as what additional statistical tests were needed and what data required reanalysis. From Congress, where hearings were being held on OEO legislation, claims were made that the study was being held back to protect Head Start, and that the report was going to be rewritten. The pressure on the White House became sufficiently great that it directed OEO to make public the study by April 14. A major conclusion of the report was that the full-year Head Start program produced a statistically significant but absolutely slight improvement in participant children.

The release of the report set off a flood of criticism from Head

Start proponents, including many academicians, concerning the methodological and conceptual validity of the report. A sympathetic article in the *New York Times* bore the headline "HEAD START REPORT HELD 'FULL OF HOLES.' " Much of the ensuing controversy focused on the statistical methods of the report and involved a considerable range of claims, charges, rebuttals, and denials. The proponents of Head Start seemed to fear that their program was being victimized by devious design. This fear had several dimensions. One was that persons within OEO who favored Community Action over Head Start wanted a study that would indicate Head Start's deficiencies. Another was that the administration was going to use the findings to justify a major cutback in Head Start. Finally, there was the fear that "enemies of the program" in Congress would use the negative results to attack the program. Although there now appears not to have been much factual basis for these fears, they were "real" to the proponents of Head Start and contributed to the intensity of their attack on the evaluation study.

The methodological issues in the controversy over the study focused on such standard items as the sample size, the validity of the control group, and the appropriateness of the tests given the children. An examination of these issues would be too lengthy and too technical to include here. However, an assessment of the study by Walter Williams can be quoted to advantage.

In terms of its methodological and conceptual base, the study is a *relatively* good one. This in no way denies that many of the criticisms made of the study are valid. However, for the most part, they are the kinds of criticisms that can be made of most pieces of social science research conducted outside the laboratory, in a real-world setting, with all of the logistical and measurement problems that such studies entail. And these methodological flaws open the door to the more political issues. Thus, one needs not only to examine the methodological substance of the criticisms which have been made of the study, but also to understand the social concern which lies behind them as well. Head Start has elicited national sympathy and has had the support and involvement of the educational profession. It is understandable that so many should rush to the defense of such a popular and humane program. But how many of the concerns over the size of the sample, control-group equivalency, and the appropriateness of co-variance analysis, for example, would have been registered if the study had found positive differences in favor of Head Start? . . .

We imagine that this type of positive, but qualified assessment will fit any relatively good evaluation for some time to come. We have never seen a field evaluation of a social-action program that could not be faulted legitimately by good methodologists, and we may never see one.

Interestingly enough, the results of the Westinghouse study were as favorable to Head Start as were the earlier evaluations of particular projects made by Head Start officials. These, too, showed that the program had limited lasting effects on the children. What the Westinghouse study, and the controversy over it, did was to put these findings into the public arena and extend the scope of the conflict over them.

Despite the essentially negative evaluations of its impact, the Westinghouse report recommended that Head Start be preserved and improved, at least partly on the ground that "something must be tried here and now to help the many children of poverty who may never be helped again." Head Start was, and is, a politically popular program. Congress and the executive generally have been favorably disposed toward the program, and it has suffered little of the criticism directed at other aspects of the antipoverty program. In 1970, Head Start was transferred from OEO to the Department of Health, Education, and Welfare. In fiscal year 1974, the program budget exceeded $400 million and it was intended to benefit over 300,000 children in year-long, summer, and special programs. The moral of this tale is that good politics may count for more than a bad systematic evaluation in the life of a program.

WHY POLICIES MAY NOT HAVE THEIR INTENDED IMPACT

Policy evaluation often indicates that policies do not achieve their ostensible goals or have the impact on public problems they were intended to have. A variety of factors may impede the attainment of policy goals.

First, inadequate resources may be devoted to dealing with a problem. The Johnson Administration's war on poverty failed partly because, as many commentators have pointed out, only limited resources were allocated to what was supposed to be an "all-out war." Public-housing programs have never produced the amount of housing projected because Congress has failed to appropriate the required amounts of funds.

Second, policies may be administered in a fashion that lessens their impact. The Federal Power Commission, for example, has never been very enthusiastic about regulating the wellhead price of natural gas. At the local level, county governments have often been hostile or stingy in their administration of the federal food-stamp program.

Third, public problems are often caused by a multitude of factors, while policy may be directed at only one or a few of them. Job-training programs may help those who are unemployed because they lack adequate job skills but do little for those who have chronic ailments or inadequate motivation. Price inflation may be the product of several factors, with the result that efforts to counteract it by monetary policy, which deals with the money supply, are alone inadequate.

Fourth, people may respond or adapt to public policies in such manner as to negate much of their impact. The effectiveness of agricultural production control programs in the 1950's and 1960's was reduced because the programs were based on acreage limitations, and farmers were able, through scientific and technological developments such as improved plant varieties and increased use of chemical fertilizers, to produce higher yields on fewer acres. Consequently, there was little reduction in production, and "surpluses" persisted.

Fifth, policies may have incompatible goals that bring them into conflict with one another. Thus, within the Department of Agriculture, the Agricultural Conservation and Stabilization Service was concerned with limiting the production of some commodities, while the Agricultural Research Service was concerned with trying to increase agricultural productivity. The use of tax benefits and exemptions to encourage various forms of economic activity has lessened the attainment of income equality through the graduated income tax.

Sixth, the solutions for some problems may involve costs that are greater than the problems. "Crime in the streets" could probably be eradicated entirely if we were willing to pay the costs in greatly enhanced police surveillance, individual repression, curfews, and the like. The effect of this on individual freedom would be vast and disastrous, and the lack of individual freedom would then become a problem. The *total* elimination of environmental pollution might be another example.

Seventh, many public problems may not be soluble, or at least completely so. Given human nature and national interests, tension and strife to some degree will undoubtedly continue to exist in the world. Some children simply may not be able to learn much in the public schools, regardless of how many times the curriculum is revised and other changes are made.

Eighth, the nature of the problem at which policy is directed may change while policy is being developed or applied. The farm problem may shift from one of too much to one of too little production, or an oversupply of petroleum may give way to a shortage thereof.

Finally, new problems may arise that distract attention and action from a given problem. The "energy problem" may draw attention from the "environmental pollution problem" just as the war in Vietnam did from the War on Poverty.

If few public problems are entirely resolved by policy action, many are partly solved or ameliorated. Employment problems may still exist, but not to the extent they would have, had there been no job training, area development, unemployment compensation, and other programs. Usually, indeed, policy goals are stated, implicitly or explicitly, in relative rather than absolute terms. The intent is to reduce the prevalence of heart disease, not entirely eliminate it, to lessen movements in price levels, not entirely prevent them.

THE RESPONSE TO POLICY

In this chapter, quite a bit has been said about the systematic evaluation of policy. It has clearly become a more widespread and potentially significant part of the policy process. Up to the present time, however, as various observers have remarked, systematic evaluation does not appear to have had significant effect upon policy decision-making.[20] As was seen in the case of Head Start, an essentially unfavorable evaluation of its impact did not lead to its abandonment nor, we might add, to major change in its substantive form. This should not be taken to mean that systematic evaluation is either useless or unlikely ever to have much impact on policymaking. It is a relatively new activity, and it encounters many problems, as we have noted. As time goes on, and as evaluation techniques and designs become more effective, its impact will undoubtedly increase. After all, few would contend that intelligence does not provide a more sound basis than intuition in determining public policy.

People and groups, citizens and officials alike, do, of course, make many judgments concerning the impact and desirability of existing policies and, on this basis, react to them with support, opposition, or indifference. There is much evaluatory activity of the first two kinds discussed at the beginning of this chapter. Political decision-makers may frequently temper their evaluations of the substantive content or impact of policies with responsiveness to political factors—for example, partisan pressures, emotional appeals, or re-election considerations. Ralph Huitt notes that "political feasibility" is a concern entering into the selection of policy priorities and programs designed to meet them by decision-makers. "Will it 'go' on the Hill? Will the public buy it? Does it have political 'sex appeal'? What 'can't be done' is likely to get low priority."[21]

At this point the concept of feedback can be injected usefully into the discussion. This concept, which was briefly touched upon in the treatment of systems theory in Chapter 1, tells us that past policy decisions and impacts can generate demands for change or support for them. Thus, the enactment and administration of the National Environmental Policy Act of 1969 has given rise to various demands for its repeal, modification, and continuation.[22] The Soil Conservation Act of 1935, and the administering agency, the Soil Conservation Service, gave rise to a pressure group, the National Association of Soil Conservation Districts, that has strongly supported their continuation. As a consequence of feedback to decision-makers, a variety of actions subsequently can be taken concerning policy, including: continuation; legislative amendment to strengthen or weaken the policy; adjustments in its administration, such as strong or lax enforcement of given provisions; increasing, decreasing, or restricting funds to support its administration; challenges to its meaning or constitutionality in the courts (this is more likely to be done by private interested parties than by officials); and repeal of the statute (or permitting it to expire if it has a time limit).

So far as major policies and programs are concerned, repeal or termination of them is unlikely to occur, even when much controversy, and even bitterness, attend their adoption. They soon come to be taken for granted, as a part of the environment, and debate over their propriety, if not their details or impact, soon quiets down. This has been the case with the Social Security Act (1935), the Taft-Hartley Act (1947), the Civil Rights Act (1964), and the Elementary and Secondary Education Act (1965), to cite a few. Few statutes have stirred as much controversy as the Economic Opportunity Act, and yet, although it has been variously amended and control of most of the programs it created has been transferred from the Office of Economic Opportunity to other agencies, this Act remains in existence. As a general proposition, it can be suggested that the longer a policy, program, or agency remains in existence, the less likely it is to be terminated. Over time, accommodations are made and support developed that enable them to survive. Exceptions are those policies, programs, or agencies established to deal with emergency problems such as relief during the Depression of the 1930's (e.g., Works Progress Administration) and price controls and rationing as well as production allocation during World War II (e.g., Office of Price Administration, War Production Board).

The revision, or demands for revision, of existing policies will depend upon such factors as the extent to which they are held to "solve" the problem at which they are directed or their perceived impact, the skill with which they are administered, defects or shortcomings that may be revealed during implementation, and the political power and awareness of concerned or affected groups. In addition, the manner in which the costs and benefits of a policy are distributed will have important consequences for its future.

The costs and benefits of public policies may be either broadly or narrowly distributed. In the case of social security, both benefits and costs are broadly distributed; a statute regulating relationships between automobile manufacturers and dealers involves a narrow distribution of costs and benefits. Narrow costs—broad benefits and broad costs—narrow benefits are other possible patterns. The costs and benefits of policies, it will be recalled, can be either material or symbolic. The proposition here advanced is that the response to *existing* policies, and demands for changes thereon, will be affected by the way benefits and costs are distributed.[23]

Broad Benefits and Broad Costs. Policies that involve a broad distribution of costs and benefits, such as social security, highway construction, police and fire protection, public education, and national defense, tend to become readily accepted, institutionalized, and beyond major challenge. Controversy may focus on such particular features as the location of highways, whether to provide sex education, or the acquisition of a weapons system, but the continuation of the programs as a whole is not in question. It is easy to propose and difficult to resist increases in the benefits of a program like social security because of the many specific beneficiaries. National defense provides a collective good (all benefit from it, although the amount of benefit cannot be precisely measured or defined) related to the important value of national security and survival. (Note the defensive position you tend to find yourself in when you argue that something proposed is not really necessary for national defense.) Radical changes in most policies in this category are unlikely.

Some policies, however, that fall in this category may never really gain wide and continued acceptance, as with the War on Poverty. It had many potential beneficiaries, but most of them were poor, and the poor in our society have long lacked political power and, consequently, effective ability to secure and support policies benefiting them. Many changes have been made in the poverty program since 1964.

Occasionally, the costs of a program may come to be seen as exceeding its benefits. This has been true in recent years with the public-assistance programs that provide aid to various needy groups, such as the aged, blind, and families with dependent children. Controversy has been especially intense over aid to families with dependent children. Much has been spoken and written about the "welfare mess," "welfare crisis," and so on. Many proposals for change, including elimination of the programs, have been made, and some have been adopted. A major change proposed by the Nixon Administration, the Family Assistance Plan, failed of enactment in the early 1970's. After much furor, the public-assistance programs remain much the same as they were a few years ago, except that some are now totally funded by the national government. The groups supporting public assistance are sufficiently strong to maintain them, if not to bring about basic reform. The critics are sufficiently strong to prevent major reform while perhaps securing some restrictive changes that, in all, little reduce the scope or impact of the programs. Public education is another policy area in which this kind of conflict, promising much but delivering little, may develop.

Broad Benefits and Narrow Costs. Some policies seem to provide benefits for large numbers of people, while their costs fall primarily upon fairly distinct, identifiable groups in society. Illustrative are environmental pollution control, automobile safety, food and meat inspection, public utility regulation, and industrial and coal mine safety policies. Coal mine companies have felt that they are being asked to bear the burden of safety regulation, and that many specific requirements are unnecessary. They have complained of the unfairness of the regulatory program and have sought both legislative and administrative amelioration of its impact upon them. Just so, many industries have protested having to meet the costs and inconveniences of pollution-control programs. Of course, they may be able to pass the financial costs of them on to consumers as part of the final price of their product. The efforts of the automobile industry to delay the deadline for some auto emission standards is familiar history.

The enactment of policies falling within this category is usually achieved through the actions of a loose coalition of interests, perhaps in response to a crisis of some sort. Once the legislation is enacted, the supporting coalition tends to lose interest in the matter, assuming that with the enactment of legislation the problem is adequately cared for. The groups that opposed the law and perceive themselves as bearing the brunt of it remain concerned and active, as in the cases of the automobile manufacturers and safety legislation and, earlier, the railroads and rate regulation. Much more is heard from them by the enforcing agencies and the legislature concerning the undesirable effects of the legislation. The result may be administrative action and legislative changes tempering the original legislation.[24] Conversely, it may become very difficult for supporters of the original legislation to get together again to secure amendments to strengthen the law. For instance, a loophole was created in the antimerger provision of the Clayton Act in the early 1920's by judicial interpretation. Not until 1950 were the supporters of antitrust able to secure corrective legislation in the form of the Celler Antimerger Act. Again, automobile manufacturers have been unremitting in their opposition to emission control standards for cars since their adoption a few years ago and have succeeded in delaying implementation of some standards.

Narrow Benefits and Broad Costs. Some policies and programs are of benefit to readily identifiable interest groups, while their costs do not appear to fall upon any particular groups. Veteran's benefits, agricultural subsidies, hospital construction grants, rivers and harbors projects, and special tax provisions (for example, the oil depletion allowance) fall within this category. The costs of these policies are usually in the form of higher taxes or prices that affect people generally. Those who benefit from these policies have a clear incentive to organize and act to maintain them. As Wilson notes, policies of this variety encourage the formation of pressure groups to support their continuation, often in close relationship with the administering agency. Good examples are the National Rivers and Harbors Congress and the Corps of Army Engineers, the National Rural Electrification Cooperative Association and the Rural Electrification Administration, and veterans' groups and the Veterans Administration.

Those who are critical of such policies find it difficult to mobilize sufficient interest and political support to bring about changes. Presidents Johnson and Nixon have both urged Congress to reduce greatly the funds for the Rural Environmental Assistance Program, which provides financial grants to farmers for soil-conserving activities, on the grounds that such costs can and should properly be borne by farmers. They did not have much success, because those who benefit from the program work actively for its continuation at present levels, and Congress has been responsive to them. The cost is paid by the fabled John Q. Taxpayer, who is little aware of either the program or the way in which it affects his tax bill. Sometimes, though, policies in this category may arouse sufficient opposition, both among citizens and officials, as to lead to their alteration. An example is the oil-depletion allowance, which has become a symbol of privilege for the oil industry, and which in 1969 was reduced from 27.5 per cent to 22 per cent. The energy crisis has since helped bring the depletion allowance under further attack.

Narrow Benefits and Narrow Costs. Policies that provide benefits to a well-defined group but at the cost of another distinct group tend to be productive of continuing organized conflict among the groups and their partisans. In point here are the conflicts between organized labor and management over the Wagner and Taft-Hartley Acts, oil importers and domestic producers over oil-import quotas (up to the current energy crisis, at least), and railroads and motor carriers over freight regulation by the Interstate Commerce Commission. Conflict repeatedly and continually develops over amendments to, and interpretations of, the original policy. Efforts may also be made to secure its repeal. Top-level appointments to the administering agency are another item of contention. The National Labor Relations Board has alternated between prolabor and promanagement treatments of the labor laws, as Democratic administrations have appointed prolabor people to the board and Republican administrations have reciprocated with promanagement people when the opportunity has arisen.[25] In situations where the costs and benefits of policy are concentrated on active, organized groups, major policy changes tend to result either from shifts in the balance of power among them, such as that leading to the Taft-Hartley Act, or from negotiated settlements, such as that which lead to mandatory oil-import quotas in the late 1950's.

These four policy categories based on the allocation of costs and benefits are only approximate. All policies will not fit neatly and exclusively into one or another of them. The reader may want to refine and develop them further, which he is encouraged to do. The categories are put forward here as being useful in gaining insight into why the responses to policies vary and in estimating what the feedback responses will be to policy actions. Moreover, the categories should also be helpful in analyzing the struggles that attend the adoption of policy, as, to some extent, the kind of policy proposed will help shape the enactment process.

NOTES

1. Quoted in Joseph S. Wholey, *et al.*, *Federal Evaluation Policy* (Washington, D.C.: The Urban Institute, 1970), p. 62.
2. Thomas R. Dye, *Understanding Public Policy* (Englewood Cliffs, N.J.: Prentice-Hall, 1972), pp. 291–95.
3. A useful discussion of externalities in public policy can be found in Larry L. Wade, *The Elements of Public Policy* (Columbus, Ohio: Merrill, 1972), chap. 3.
4. Gabriel A. Almond and G. Bingham Powell, *Comparative Politics: A Developmental Approach* (Boston: Little, Brown, 1966), p. 199.
5. Carol H. Weiss, "The Politics of Impact Measurement," *Policy Studies Journal*, I (Spring, 1973), pp. 180–81.
6. Robert A. Levine, *The Poor Ye Need Not Have With You* (Cambridge, Mass.: MIT Press, 1970), pp. 91–92.
7. Solomon Kalirin and Steven G. Lubeck, "Problems in the Evaluation of Crime Control Policy." Paper presented at the 1973 annual meeting of the American Political Science Association, p. 29.
8. 384 U.S. 436 (1966).
9. President's Commission on Law Enforcement and the Administration of Justice, *The Challenge of Crime in a Free Society* (Washington, D.C.: Government Printing Office, 1967), p. 305.
10. Jeremy A. Lifsey, "Politics, Evaluations and Manpower Programs." Paper presented at the 1973 annual meeting of the American Political Science Association.

11. This discussion draws on Elmer B. Staats, "General Accounting Office Support of Committee Oversight," in *Committee Organization in the House*, panel discussion before the House Select Committee on Committees, 93d Cong., 1st Sess. (1973), II, pp. 692–700. Staats is the head of the General Accounting Office.
12. *Ibid.*, p. 696.
13. *Poverty Amid Plenty: The American Paradox*, report of the President's Commission on Income Maintenance Programs (Washington, D.C.: Government Printing Office, 1969). The quotation is on page 2.
14. An excellent account of this policy episode is Daniel P. Moynihan, *The Politics of a Guaranteed Income* (New York: Random House, 1973).
15. Charles O. Jones, *An Introduction to the Study of Public Policy* (Belmont, Calif.: Wadsworth, 1970), p. 118. Insight into the operation of a commission set up in 1966 to appraise legislation regulating the political activities of public employees can be gained from Charles O. Jones, "Reevaluating the Hatch Act: A Report on the Commission on Political Activity of Government Employees," *Public Administration Review*, XXIX (May–June, 1969), pp. 249–54.
16. Quoted in Allen Shick, "A Death in the Bureaucracy: The Demise of Federal PPB," *Public Administration Review*, XXXIII (March–April, 1975), p. 146.
17. Robert H. Haveman, "Public Expenditure and Policy Analysis: An Overview," in Robert H. Haveman and Julius Margolis (eds.), *Public Expenditure and Policy Analysis* (Chicago: Markham, 1970), pp. 14–15. Several selections in this volume are useful for gaining an understanding of PPBS.
18. Joel Havemann, "Administration Report: OMB Begins Major Program to Identify and Attain Presidential Goals," *National Journal*, V (June 2, 1973), pp. 783–93.
19. This account draws upon Walter Williams, *Social Policy Research and Analysis* (New York: American Elsevier, 1971), and Walter Williams and John W. Evans, "The Politics of Evaluation: The Case of Head Start," *Annals of the American Academy of Political and Social Sciences*, CCCLXXXV (September, 1969), pp. 118–32.
20. E.g., Wholey, *op. cit.*, pp. 46–51; Sar A. Levitan, *The Great Society's Poor Law* (Baltimore: Johns Hopkins Press, 1969), pp. 310–11; Jonathan Spivack, "Rating Federal Projects a Tricky Task," *Wall Street Journal*, May 29, 1969, p. 12.
21. Ralph K. Huitt, "Political Feasibility," in Austin Ranney (ed.), *Political Science and Public Policy* (Chicago: Markham, 1968), p. 266.
22. Walter A. Rosenbaum, *The Politics of Environmental Concern* (New York: Praeger, 1973), pp. 265–72.
23. This discussion leans heavily upon James Q. Wilson, *Political Organizations* (New York: Basic Books, 1973), chap. 16. The student of policy formation cannot afford to ignore this book.
24. In some instances, the regulated group may succeed, at least for a time, in "capturing" the administering agency. A classic case study is Samuel P. Huntington, "The Marasmus of the ICC: The Commission, the Railroads, and the Public Interest," *Yale Law Journal* LXII (December, 1952), pp. 171–225.
25. Cf. Seymour Scher, "Regulatory Agency Control Through Appointment: The Case of the Eisenhower Administration and the NLRB," *Journal of Politics*, XXIII (November, 1961), pp. 667–88.

6. Policy Study and the Public Interest

In the preceding chapters, I have sought to present a general scheme for the analysis of public policy-making, along with a discussion that focuses primarily on policy-making in the United States. One conclusion that should emerge is that the process of policy-making on most problems—certainly those of any magnitude—is continuous. A policy is officially adopted and implemented, evaluation and feedback occur, changes or adjustments are made, more implementation follows, evaluation and feedback again take place, and so on. Somewhere along the line the problem at which policy is directed may be redefined, as when the "farm problem" moves from surplus production to insufficient production. When this happens, the result may be a substantial change in the thrust and content of policy.

A second conclusion is that, in modern, pluralistic political systems, public policy-making is usually a very complex process. Many participants may be involved, and many factors may affect its outcome. Those who provide easy, quick answers to why a particular policy was adopted or rejected are often guilty of gross oversimplifications. While one should indeed try to be parsimonious in explaining political phenomena, all relevant factors should be taken into account. The scheme presented here should not be taken as a complete theory of the policy process (obviously, it is not) but as one means for organizing and directing one's inquiry into that process.

A third conclusion is that the analysis of public policy-making can provide much information and insight into the nature and operation of the political system and political processes generally. It helps shift our attention from a narrow concern with micropolitical phenomena (voting behavior, political attitudes, political socialization, and so on) to their role in the broad governmental process. I do not wish to argue that we should not be concerned, for example, with how individuals acquire political attitudes. This can be an interesting activity and can yield much information on learning behavior and the process of socialization, among other things. We should, however, also be concerned with the "So what?" question. What difference does it make, for example, so far as governance and public policy are concerned, how people acquire certain political values and beliefs, and when? The focus on policy-making can perform an integrating and unifying function in political inquiry, as well as providing a criterion of relevance to use in determining what political phenomena to analyze. It is a highly useful approach to the study of policy that can yield knowledge that has both scientific and immediate practical value.

A fourth conclusion is that much remains unknown or unexplained concerning how political decisions and public policies are made, although our knowledge here has expanded significantly in the last couple of decades. The field of policy study is open and challenging. It should be especially attractive to those who wish to be "relevant," to engage in research and discovery that has some immediate social utility. Policy study provides ample room for those who are more traditional or more behavioral, more quantitative or nonquantitative, more analytical or more inclined to advocacy, to exercise their talents and pursue their interests. All can contribute through careful scholarship to our knowledge and understanding of public policy and the policy process. Eclecticism in approach helps ensure that fruitful avenues of inquiry will not be closed off by narrow or particular theoretical concerns.

The remainder of this chapter will be devoted to brief consideration of some methodological problems in policy analysis and of the concept of the public interest.

METHODOLOGICAL PROBLEMS

Methodological problems exist for all research, and policy research is not without its share, especially given the complexity of its subject matter.[1] These problems may impede or limit policy research, they may make it frustrating at times, but they do not prevent it. An awareness of some of these problems will help prevent needless errors, wasted efforts, and unsound conclusions.

Solid evidence, facts, or data, as one prefers, on the values and motives of decision-makers, the nature of public problems, the impact of policy, and other facets of the policy process are often hard to acquire or simply not available. The urge to treat assumptions or speculations about what happened as facts must be resisted, as must the often self-serving explanations or statements of political officials and other participants in the policy process. Sometimes quantitative measures of political phenomena such as policy impact are used more because of their availability than anything else. The acquisition of hard facts regarding who did what, why, and with what effects must be the goal of research. We need to be able to say with reasonable confidence that congressmen respond to constituency interests on certain policy matters, for example.

In the explanation of behavior in the policy process empirical evidence is needed that will permit the demonstration or inference of cause-and-effect relationships. Once one gets involved in data-based analysis, it is important to resist the notion that the collection of empirical data is of prime importance, and that the more data one has, the more one can explain. One can drown in a sea of data as well as thirst for a lack thereof. To explain or account for behavior, theory is necessary to guide analysis in potentially fruitful directions. Hypotheses about cause-effect relationships need to be developed and tested on the basis of available evidence.

So, too, one must resist the notion that policy analysis must always involve the manipulation of quantitative data (what some would call "hard data") through the use of high-powered statistical techniques. At this point, some policy areas and problems have not proved amenable to rigorous quantitative measurement and analysis, although this is not to contend that such analysis will never be possible. Many aspects of economic regulatory policy currently fall into this category. How, for example, does one measure the comparative impact of pressure groups, agency values, and economic criteria on railroad rate-making? Yet, it must be emphasized, quantitative measurement, explicit theory, and careful, rigorous analysis have not been as frequently employed in policy study as would be either possible or desirable.

Many valuable and perceptive studies of policy formation exist that employ little or no statistical analysis.[2] The quality of analysis and the use of solid evidence is more important than whether and to what extent quantitative analysis is employed when it comes to determining the value of a study. Those who use quantitative statistical techniques have been known to quarrel with enthusiasm over the reliability of their techniques and the validity of their findings.[3] On the other hand, one must avoid developing a phobia for quantitative or statistical analysis, as many did during the 1950's and early 1960's in reaction to the behavioral movement in political science.

Data derived through interviews and questionnaires administered to public officials and others involved in the policy process is often invaluable and may not otherwise be available to the researcher. Care, however, is required in the use of such techniques and the data acquired. Questions must be properly framed to elicit the needed information. Questions that are "loaded" or are so general as to create strong doubt concerning their intent must be avoided. The data or information so acquired should not be blindly accepted. Officials may not always respond fully or candidly to questions. Self-serving rather than accurate responses may be made. Care must be taken to recognize these and to treat them accordingly.

In conducting research or inquiry, one should avoid a too narrow frame of reference that unduly restricts investigation or predetermines the outcome. If one fervently believes that U.S. policy in Southeast Asia is based on imperialism, and conducts this inquiry accordingly, it will not be surprising if one's findings support one's preconception. A more open-minded inquiry might have found that racism, anticommunism, errors in judgment by public officials, Presidential egoism, or yet other factors may also have been contributory. Of course, any research efforts begin with some premises or assumptions about the value of the event being studied, who was involved, and so forth. This is necessary to focus one's efforts on avoiding a grab-bag approach. They should not be so narrow or rigid as to bias the results.

Case studies of policy-making have come in for much criticism because, in concentrating particular policy event, they do not permit generalization. "What is a case study a case of?" is a familiar jibe. Preferred are studies that deal either with all the cases in a given universe or with a meaningful sample thereof, such as a study of welfare policy in all the American states or a sample of Supreme Court "decisions" involving free speech. Case studies, however, have a variety of uses. They can be employed to test existing theories, to provide detailed analysis of particular events, to analyze deviant cases that run counter to our generalizations, and to help provide an "intuitive feel" for the subtleties and nuances of the policy process and the practice of politics. Both case studies and more broadly conceived studies are needed in policy analysis.

Finally, the preceding chapters should have indicated the invalidity of the assumption that all policy formation occurs within the framework of formal governmental institutions. Much, of course, does, but a lot of policy activity occurs elsewhere, and this also must receive the attention of the policy analyst. We have seen, for example, that in some instances legislatures may simply ratify agreements reached by private groups, or that enacted policies either may not be carried out or not have the intended impact because of successful counterpressures from outside sources. Research efforts should be pragmatic and flexible, shaped by what is useful to describe and explain satisfactorily the topic being studied, and not bound or limited by conformity to such categories as institutional or noninstitutional, formal or informal, traditional or behavioral.

THE PUBLIC INTEREST

The task of government, it is often proclaimed, is to serve or promote the public interest. Statutes sometimes include the public interest as a guideline for the actions of public officials. In this section, we will briefly discuss this rather elusive normative concept.

Most readers, I am certain, if asked whether public policy should be in accord with the public interest or with private interests (the latter could further be described as narrow, selfish, greedy, and the like, but I see no need to overload the argument), would opt for the public interest. Difficulty arises, however, when one is asked to define the public interest. Is it the interest of the majority? If so, how do we determine what the majority really wants in policy? Is it the interest of consumers, who are a rather large group? Is it what people would want if they "thought clearly and acted rationally"? How do you, the reader, define the public interest?

Many people, including most political scientists, would say that it is not possible to provide a universally accepted or objective definition of the concept, especially in substantive terms.[4] Some would contend that whatever results from the political struggle over policy issues is the public interest. If all groups and persons had an equal chance to engage in that struggle, which in fact they do not, that notion of the public interest might be more appealing. I, for one, do not care to define a multitude of tax loopholes or inaction that permits the wanton destruction of natural resources as in the public interest. (By making that statement I indicate a normative bias, which will be especially disturbing to those who hold that "one man's opinion is as good as another's.") Sometimes the public interest is depicted as a myth by which policy, however particularistic, can be rationalized as being in the general interest and hence made more publicly accepted. This, of course, is attempted or done with regularity (just as scoundrels sometimes wrap themselves in the flag to justify their predations). Beyond that, however, I think that the concept can be given enough content to render it a useful general standard for the evaluation of public policy. When evaluating policy, we need to be able to state not only whether the policy is accomplishing its asserted objectives but also whether the objectives are worthy of accomplishment. In this latter regard, a standard of more noble quality than "it is (or is not) in *my* interest" seems needed.

The question now arises of how one can seek to determine the nature of the public interest. Emmette Redford has suggested three approaches to this task.[5] One is to look at policy areas where there is much conflict among group interests, as in agriculture, labor relations, energy, and transportation. In some instances, the direct interests of one or another group may prevail and become accepted as the public interest. There is no reason to assume that private interests and the public interest must always be antithetical. If it is in the private interest of medical doctors to prevent the practice of medicine by various "quacks," so it is in the public interest not to have unqualified people practicing medicine. (It would seem difficult to argue the contrary position reasonably.) However, in the struggle among private group interests, it may become apparent that others are indirectly involved and have interests that should be considered in policy-making. These "public interests," while not represented by organized groups, may be responded to by decision-makers and thus influence the outcome. In the conflict between labor and management over the terms and conditions of employment, it becomes apparent that the public has an interest in maintaining industrial peace, preventing oversevere disruptions of the flow of goods and services, and the like. The result has been the development of various procedures for the settlement of labor disputes. In a particular dispute, such as in the railroad interest, a public interest may clearly emerge along with those of the railroad companies and brotherhoods.

A second approach is to search for widely and continuously shared interests that, because of this characteristic, can be called public interests. Illustrative are the interests of people in such matters as world peace, education, clean air, the avoidance of severe inflation, and an adequate traffic control system. Here the public interest appears as public needs. Clearly, especially in large cities, there is a public interest in having a traffic control system to facilitate the safe, orderly, convenient movement of pedestrians and vehicles. The fact that there are various alternatives for meeting this need can be taken to mean that more than one way exists to meet the public interest; it does not negate its existence. Nor does the concept, to be meaningful, need to be so precise as to indicate whether the traffic flow on a given street should be one-way or two-way.

There is nothing very mystical in talking about the public interest as a widely shared interest. We speak of the shared-interest of wheat farmers in higher wheat prices or of sport fishermen in an adequate fish-stocking program and attribute much reality to such interests. The public interest differs only in its wider scope. There is no way to determine precisely at what point an interest is sufficiently widely shared as to become a public interest. Few interests, indeed, would be shared by everyone. The survival of the nation-state may be opposed by the advocate of world government; even at old-time western rustler lynchings there was at least one dissenter. Qualitative judgments are obviously called for in determining the existence of a public interest, as in many areas of political life and academic activity. They should be made with as much care and rigor as possible.

A third approach to the public interest is to look at the need for organization and procedure to represent and balance interests, to resolve issues, to effect compromise in policy formation, and to carry public policy into effect. There is, in short, a public interest in fair, orderly, and effective government. The focus here is on process rather than policy content. As Walter Lippmann once wrote:

The public is interested in law, not in the laws; in the method of law, not in the substance; in the sanctity of contract, not in a particular contract; in understanding based on custom, not in this custom or that. It is concerned in these things to the end that men in their active affairs shall find a *modus vivendi;* its interest is in the workable rule which will define and predict the behavior of men so that they can make their adjustments.[6]

Although the public is obviously interested in particular laws as well as *the* law, Lippmann's statement well points up the concern with adequate process. How things are done, moreover, often affects the attitudes of the public concerning their acceptability.

The public interest is thus diverse in nature and must be searched for in various ways. While it probably cannot be converted into a precise set of guidelines to inform the action of decision-makers, neither can it fairly be described as merely a myth. It directs our attention beyond the more immediate toward broader, more universal interests. It directs our attention toward unorganized and unarticulated interests that otherwise may be ignored in both the development and evaluation of policy. As policy analysts and citizens we cannot afford to ignore the concept, especially in the evaluation of policy content and impact.

NOTES

1. The lead volume of this series presents an able introductory statement of methodological concerns. See William A. Welsh, *Studying Politics* (New York: Praeger, 1973).
2. E.g., Raymond A. Bauer, Ithiel de Sola Pool, and Lewis Anthony Dexter, *American Business and Public Policy* (New York: Atherton Press, 1963); Mark V. Nadel, *The Politics of Consumer Protection* (Indianapolis, Ind.: Bobbs-Merrill, 1971); and Graham T. Allison, *Essence of Decision: Explaining the Cuban Missile Crisis* (Boston: Little, Brown, 1971).
3. Various controversies of this sort are manifested in recent issues of the *American Political Science Review.*
4. Cf. Frank J. Sorauf, "The Public Interest Reconsidered," *Journal of Politics,* XIX (November, 1957), pp. 616–39.
5. Emmette S. Redford, *Ideal and Practice in Public Administration* (Tuscaloosa: University of Alabama Press, 1958), chap. 5.
6. Walter Lippmann, *The Phantom Public* (New York: Harcourt, Brace, 1925), p. 105.

Annotated Bibliography

ALLISON, GRAHAM T., *Essence of Decision: Explaining the Cuban Missile Crisis* (Boston: Little, Brown, 1971). Examines decision-making on the Cuban missile crisis from the rational actor, organizational process, and governmental politics perspectives.

ART, ROBERT J., *The TFX Decision: McNamara and the Military* (Boston: Little, Brown, 1968). A case study of the controversy over the decision to select a multipurpose aircraft for the military, contrary to its wishes. Insightful on the decision process in the bureaucracy.

BAILEY, STEPHEN K., *Congress Makes a Law* (New York: Columbia University Press, 1950). A classic case study of the legislative process, showing how ideas, interests, individuals, and institutions contributed to the adoption of the Employment Act of 1946.

BAUER, RAYMOND A., and KENNETH J. GERGEN (eds.), *The Study of Policy Formation* (New York: Free Press, 1968). A series of original essays dealing with theoretical and methodological concerns in the study of public policy.

BERNSTEIN, MARUER H., *Regulating Business by Independent Commission* (Princeton, N.J.: Princeton University Press, 1955). A dated but still useful treatment of independent regulatory commissions as policy formulators and implementors.

BOEK, EDWIN A. (ed.), *Government Regulation of Business: A Casebook* (Englewood Cliffs, N.J.: Prentice-Hall, 1965). Case studies of administrative agencies in regulatory policy formation and implementation.

COBB, ROGER W., and CHARLES D. ELDER, *Participation in American Politics: The Dynamics of Agenda-Building* (Boston: Allyn and Bacon, 1972). Highly useful treatment of how problems get on the systemic and policy agendas in American society.

DAHL, ROBERT A., and CHARLES E. LINDBLOM, *Politics, Economics, and Welfare* (New York: Harper & Row, 1953). Comparison of policy-making by polyarchy, hierarchy, bargaining, and the market system. A classic work.

DAVIES, J. CLARENCE, *The Politics of Pollution* (Indianapolis: Bobbs-Merrill, 1970). On the formation and implementation of pollution control legislation. Especially good on the administrative aspects thereof.

DAVIS, KENNETH C., *Discretionary Justice* (Baton Rouge: Louisiana State University Press, 1970). On the nature, use, and abuse of discretion in policy-making and implementation by administrative agencies and officials. Analytical and disturbing.

DROR, YEHEZKEL, *Public Policymaking Reexamined* (Scranton, Pa.: Chandler, 1968). A comparative treatment of policy-making procedures with suggestions for reform. Tough reading and general in approach but useful.

DYE, THOMAS R., *Politics, Economics, and the Public: Policy Outcomes in the American States* (Chicago: Rand-McNally, 1966). A leading study that compares the effects of political and socio-economic variables on state policies. Conclusion: Socio-economic variables are more important.

————, *Understanding Public Policy* (Englewood Cliffs, N.J.: Prentice-Hall, 1972). Discusses a number of models of policy analysis, illustrates them with case studies, and compares their utility for policy analysis.

ENGLER, ROBERT, *The Politics of Oil* (New York: Macmillan, 1961). An analysis of the impact of the petroleum industry on pertinent public policies. Good background reading for the current "energy crisis."

FREEMAN, J. LEIPER, *The Political Process*, 2d ed. (New York: Random House, 1965). A brief analysis of the role of executive bureau–congressional committee–interest group subsystems in policy formation.

FROMAN, LEWIS A., JR., *The Congressional Process* (Boston: Little, Brown, 1967). How congressional procedures can shape policy outputs is one of the concerns of this volume.

HALPERIN, MORTON H., *Bureaucratic Politics and Foreign Policy* (Washington, D.C.: Brookings Institution, 1974). Analysis of bureaucratic participation and decision-making in American foreign policy in the post–World War II era.

HARDIN, CHARLES M., *Food and Fiber in the Nations Politics* (Washington, D.C.: Government Printing Office, 1967). An insightful survey of the politics of agricultural policy formation and administration.

JACOB, HERBERT, and KENNETH N. VINES (eds.), *Politics in the Amer-*

ican States, 2d ed. (Boston: Little, Brown, 1971). Comparative treatment of policy-making and public policies in the American states.

JONES, CHARLES O., *An Introduction to the Study of Public Policy* (Belmont, Calif.: Wadsworth, 1970). Jones presents a sequential approach to policy analysis, replete with short case studies, in straightforward fashion.

KINGDON, JOHN W., *Congressmen's Voting Decisions* (New York: Harper & Row, 1973). A very valuable empirical study of how members of the House of Representatives make decisions and the factors influencing them.

KOHLMEIER, LOUIS J., *The Regulators* (New York: Harper & Row, 1969). A journalist's account of the policy actions of federal administrative agencies.

Lindblom, Charles E., *The Intelligence of Democracy* (New York: Free Press, 1965). An examination of bargaining and other forms of mutual adjustment in policy formation.

LOWI, THEODORE J., "American Business, Public Policy, Case Studies, and Political Theory," *World Politics*, XVI (July, 1964), 667–715. An influential essay that seeks to develop a new framework for policy study. He suggests that the kind of policy (distributive, regulatory, or redistributive) involved in a situation shapes the nature of the policy-making process.

————, *The End of Liberalism* (New York: Norton, 1969). Lowi argues that American public policies no longer are responsive to public needs because they conform to an out-worn philosophy, that is, interest-group liberalism.

MAASS, ARTHUR, *Muddy Waters* (Cambridge, Mass.: Harvard University Press, 1951). A good but dated account of the Corps of Army Engineers's role in water policy formation.

McCONNELL, GRANT, *Private Power and American Democracy* (New York: Knopf, 1966). An examination of the role of private groups in policy formation and how pluralism and decentralization have often made them the dominant force. A highly insightful study.

MOYNIHAN, DANIEL P., *The Politics of a Guaranteed Income* (New York: Random House, 1973). A rambling account by an "insider" of the development of a proposal by the Nixon Administration for a guaranteed annual income and its rejection by Congress.

NADEL, MARK V., *The Politics of Consumer Protection* (Indianapolis: Bobbs-Merrill, 1971). Good analysis of the formation and adoption of consumer protection legislation.

NEUSTADT, RICHARD, *Presidential Power* (New York: Wiley, 1960). A study of Presidential power and leadership in the policy process. A minor classic.

PEABODY, ROBERT L., *et al.*, *To Enact a Law: Congress and Campaign Financing* (New York: Praeger, 1972). Case study of congressional adoption and Presidential veto of the Political Broadcast Act of 1970.

PIERCE, LAWRENCE C., *The Politics of Fiscal Policy Formation* (Pacific Palisades, Calif.: Goodyear, 1971). A political scientist's analyzes the process and politics of fiscal policy formation. Especially strong in its treatment of the development of policy proposals by fiscal agencies.

PIVEN, FRANCES FOX, and RICHARD A. CLOWARD, *Regulating the Poor* (New York: Pantheon Books, 1971). A normative evaluation of welfare policies that finds them to be more a means for controlling the poor than for meeting their substantive needs.

RANNEY, AUSTIN (ed.), *Political Science and Public Policy* (Chicago: Markham, 1968). An uneven collection of essays on issues, problems, and theoretical concerns in the analysis of policy and policy outcomes.

REDFORD, EMMETTE S., *Democracy in the Administrative State* (New York: Oxford University Press, 1969). An insightful examination of the role of administration in the policy process, together with concern for democratic control of administration.

————, *The Regulatory Process* (Austin: University of Texas Press, 1969). An analysis of the economic regulatory process, with emphasis on administrative agencies and commercial aviation regulation.

ROGERS, HARRELL R., JR., and CHARLES S. BULLOCK III, *Law and Social Change* (New York: McGraw-Hill, 1972). An evaluation of the impact of the civil rights legislation of the 1960's.

ROSENBAUM, WALTER A., *The Politics of Environmental Concern* (New York: Praeger, 1973). Concerned with the formation and implementation of national policies affecting the environment.

ROURKE, FRANCIS E., *Bureaucracy, Politics, and Public Policy* (Boston: Little, Brown, 1969). Focused on the role of administrative agencies in the formation of public policy.

SCHATTSCHNEIDER, E. E., *The Semi-Sovereign People* (New York: Holt, Rinehart, and Winston, 1960). A critique of group theory and a discussion of the impact of conflict on political decision-making.

SCHNEIER, EDWARD V. (ed.), *Policy-Making in American Government* (New York: Basic Books, 1969). An anthology organized under the headings of policy formulation, articulation, mobilization, codification, application, and redefinition.

SHAPIRO, MARTIN, *Law and Politics in the Supreme Court* (New York: Free Press, 1964). Discusses the impact of the Supreme Court on such areas of public policy as labor relations, antitrust, and taxation.

SORENSEN, THEODORE C., *Decision-Making in the White House* (New York: Columbia University Press, 1963). Short analysis of Presidential decision-making by the former counsel to President John Kennedy.

STEINER, GILBERT Y., *Social Insecurity: The Politics of Welfare* (Washington, D.C.: Brookings Institution, 1966). An analysis of welfare policy-making that illustrates the relationship between the nature of the policy process and the substance of policy.

STEVENSON, GORDON MCKAY, JR., *The Politics of Airport Noise* (North Scituate, Mass.: Duxbury Press, 1972). Systematic analysis of the participants in, and process of, the development of noise abatement policies. Good on the details of policy action.

STRAAYER, JOHN A., and ROBERT D. WRINKLE, *American Government, Policy, and Non-Decision* (Columbus, Ohio: Merrill, 1972). Short analysis of the policy process and a number of areas of public policy.

SUNDQUIST, JAMES L., *Politics and Policy: The Eisenhower, Kennedy and Johnson Years* (Washington, D.C.: Brookings Institution, 1968). Highly informative case studies of several major areas of domestic policy are combined with a general explanatory analysis.

TRUMAN, DAVID B., *The Governmental Process* (New York: Knopf, 1951). A classic treatment of the role of interest groups in the American political process. Indispensable for an understanding of group theory.

WADE, L. L., and R. L. CURRY, JR., *A Logic of Public Policy* (Belmont, Calif.: Wadsworth, 1970). An examination of American public policy from the "new political economy," or public choice, perspective.

WADE, LARRY L., *The Elements of Public Policy* (Columbus, Ohio: Merrill, 1972). An introduction to policy analysis, focusing especially on decision-making and policy costs and benefits.

WASBY, STEPHEN L., *The Impact of the United States Supreme Court* (Homewood, Ill.: Dorsey, 1970). Nonquantitative analysis of the Court's impact on public policy. Attempts to develop a theory of impact.

WHOLEY, JOSEPH S., *et al.*, *Federal Evaluation Policy* (Washington, D.C.: Urban Institute, 1970). Survey and assessment of the extent and quality of social policy evaluation by federal administrative agencies.

WILLIAM, WALTER L., *Social Policy Analyses and Research* (New York: American Elsevier, 1971). Solid introduction to the systematic evaluation of social policies.

WOLMAN, HAROLD, *Politics of Federal Housing* (New York: Dodd, Mead, 1971). Succinct analysis of the formation and implementation of public housing policies.

Index

stellt ist, nicht zuletzt aus Gründen einer die Dinge schärfer benennenden Diktion und des damals vorhandenen Wortschatzes[58]).

Es ließen sich nun akribistisch gewisse Topoi Wilhelms — mit mehr oder weniger Glück! — mit solchen Wolframs zusammenstellen. Damit aber wäre weder ein ‚Einfluß' statuiert noch wäre das Verständnis hinsichtlich des ‚Parzival' gefördert. Hingegen mag eine die Sprechart Wilhelms wie Wolframs übernehmende, kurze Synthese hinsichtlich des ‚Letzten' Parzivals das Gesagte zusammenfassen.

Parzivals erzählerischer Weg ist nach dem bisher Gesagten der Weg eines *tumben* zum Demütigen, der sich frei den Anforderungen Gottes in der Welt fügt, so daß ihm beides, Welt- und Gotteshuld, gnadenhaft (als gratia gratis data) gewährt wird. Der Weg selbst verläuft jedoch nicht gnostisch von einer stultitia zu einer sapientia, die diese schlechthin transzendiert, sondern jener, der *traeclîche wîs*, d. h. immer wieder von seiner stultitia superba übermächtigt, seinen Weg geht, darf letztlich einsehen, daß seine ‚simple' stultitia und *tumpheit* letztlich die imbecillitas des *dienstes* an Gott und *diemuot* ist, die jeden *zwîvel*, jede duplicitas, in die simplicitas überführt, die eine heilige, sancta, simplicitas ist[59]). Damit

---

[58]) Das schließt die Möglichkeit nicht aus, Wolframs ‚Parzival' unter die Signatur der *einvalt* zu stellen, wie es R. Gruenter (Parzivals ‚einvalt', Euph. 52 [1958] 297—302) im Anschluß an ein paar Verse des mittelalterlichen Wolfram-imitatoren und -nachfolger Albrecht von Scharfenberg schön gezeigt hat. Die Verse stammen aus dem ‚Jüngeren Titurel' (Ausg. W. Wolf, DTM 45, Berlin 1955, Str. 328) und lauten:

Wie dem palas waere zem gral und der gezierde,
des habt ir vor daz maere wie man da Parcifalen condiwierde
durch fragen bi dem trurigen wirte,
des in zuhtrich einvalte me danne unbescheidenheit verirrte.

Parzivals *unbescheidenheit* oder *tumpheit* oder ignorantia wird hier zugunsten einer *zuhtrich einvalte* eigentlich aufgehoben, so daß schon hier — bei Parzivals großem Fehltritt — das ‚Positive' der *tumpheit* herausspringt: einvalte „ist Parzivals Wesen und verursacht ebenso seine lebensgefährlichen Irrtümer, wie sie ihn zur *saelde* führt" (a. a. O. 300).

[59]) Parzival könnte Wilhelms Ausspruch: ‚Sit magna gloria tua quod in servitio tuo subsistet imbecillitas mea' (zitiert bei Déchanet, G. de S. T. 57) am Ende seines Wegs schließlich als eine eigene Einsicht aussprechen, sosehr führte seine *tumpheit* bruchlos in die *diemüete* hinein. Zurückzuverweisen wäre in diesem Zusammenhang auf die Erwähnung der *tumben* und *wîsen* im Prolog (vgl. oben S. 54 f.), wo die *tumben* gar nicht schlecht wegkommen, so wenig schlecht, daß G. Weber zur Illustration gar den heiligen Paulus mit Recht bemühte (1 Kor 1, 19—25; Eph 5, 9—17: Parzival, Ringen und Vollendung 203). Die Positivität der stultitia spricht schließlich Wilhelm theoretisch ganz allgemein aus, wenn er sagt: Est autem omnis superbia stulta, quamvis non omnis

der Weg dahin führt, ist immer wieder stufenhaft sich artikulierende Einsicht (bis zur letzten Stufe der *bîhte verte*) in die stultitia superba notwendig; nur so wird *tumpheit sleht* und schließlich in der Apotheose einer letzten *linge* gerechtfertigt, so, daß der eine, einfache Mensch (homo simplex) in sich vereint, was sonst unheilvoll auseinander bliebe: Welthuld und Gotteshuld[60]).

Insofern in Parzivals Leben und Weg eine ,innere' Erfahrung und eine ,geistliche' *lêre* mit ,äußerer' Erfahrung und ,weltlicher' *lêre* verschmilzt, und insofern als die ,geistliche' Transformation des Protagonisten exemplarisch für dessen ,weltliche' *linge* werden kann, darf mit Fug Wilhelms scheinbar rein geistliche Diktion im Sinne eines (beinahe zeitgenössischen) Synonyms zur Erklärung von Parzivals Weg herangezogen werden. In letzter Analyse demonstriert Wolfram, der ,simplex laicus', — getragen von einer sozialen Bewegung, die sich bewußt oder unbewußt die Integration der niederen Ministerialen in den grundbesitzenden Hochadel vorgenommen hatte, und von einer geistlichen Bewegung, der es um die apostolica vita, um die abstrichlose Nachfolge in Armut und Torheit, ging —, wie solches in sich Widerständiges (,reine' Weltlichkeit — ,reine' Geistlichkeit) vermittelt und in einer neuen, überraschenden Totalität eines ganzheitlichen Lebens glaubwürdig gemacht werden kann: als *linge* weltlichen Herrscherglücks unter geistlichen Vorzeichen. Daß dabei ein weltlich Dummer arriviert, ist möglich nur aufgrund einer erzählerischen Exaltation des Toren, zuerst als eines ungesitteten Toren (aus Waldeseinsamkeit und Menschenferne), dann als eines Toren in sancta et sana insania, als eines Toren in simplicitas sancta, in untadeligem Lebenswandel, in törichter Weisheit (stulta sapientia), in humilitas. Dem ge-

---

stultitia superba. Stultitia enim sine superbia, nonnunquam simplicitas invenitur; quae si ignorat, forsitan est docibilis; si nequit doceri, forsitan est tractabilis (Ep. aurea, Ed. Davy 63). Diese Worte umschreiben haargenau Parzivals Weg, der von einer nie recht eindeutigen superbia stulta zur simplicitas führt, die ja nur Kern dieser stultitia selber schon ist.

60) Es wäre vielleicht erlaubt, Parzivals Weg enger mit Wilhelms ,mystischer' Aufstiegslehre zu parallelisieren: vom Psychiker zum Gnostiker zum Pneumatiker, vom animalis zum rationalis zum spiritualis, vom Menschen der Anima zum Menschen des Animus zum Menschen des Spiritus (als ,Aufstieg' von der fides nuda zur intelligentia zum amor). Dieser Weg, vorgezeichnet in der Epistola aurea, wäre wohl vergleichbar, müßte aber im selben Maße von Parzivals Weg, der ein Weg in die Welt hinein ist, als ein Weg monastischer Anleitung abgehoben werden. Der Vergleich sei daher nur visiert, nicht ausgeführt.

demütigten Toren ist (als dem insanus anagogicus) jenes Licht, jene Caritas, jene suavitas bereitet, die in der humiliata divinitas für jeden Menschen ansichtig werden mußte. Parzival kehrt humiliato capite dort ein, wo ihm *der sêle ruowe* verheißen ist[61]).

3. Ebenfalls von diesem ‚Letzten‘ der gedemütigten Torheit Parzivals her drängt sich noch ein hinweisendes Wort über die Konstanz dieses von Chrétien und Wolfram geschaffenen Torenbildes im geistigen Haushalt der Weltliteratur auf. Der Tor ist von nun an gültige Gestalt in der Satire oder im Drama des deutschen Spätmittelalters[62]), er ist immer wieder Vorwurf des spanischen Romans im 16. Jahrhundert und in dessen deutschen Ablegern: als lächerlich gewordener Ritter (im ‚Don Quijote‘ des Cervantes), als Schelm (im spanischen und später im deutschen Schelmenroman)[63]). Er ist gegenwärtig im deutschen Volksbuch (als ‚Till Eulenspiegel‘, erstmals 1515) und wieder beinahe im ganzen Barock (‚Der abenteuerliche Simplicissimus‘ des Christoffel Grimmelshausen)[64]). Die deutsche Romantik mit ihren Gestaltungen verhaltener oder offenbarer Narrheit wäre geradenwegs an Hamanns ‚Torheit um Christi willen‘ anzuschließen (unter Ausschluß beinahe der ganzen Goethezeit): bei Eichendorff findet sich solche Narrheit, dann wieder, nach dem Exodus des Romantischen, bei Stifter, bei Keller: *ein* Strom untergründigen Narrentums bis in unsere Zeit, bis zum ‚Narr in Christo Emanuel Quint‘ Gerhart Hauptmanns.

Besonders aber ist zu nennen der ‚Don Quijote‘ des Cervantes, der „zwielichtig in der Wende zwischen Mittelalter und Neuzeit" steht[65]), ein Roman, in dem der irrende Ritter nochmals seltsame Urständ feiert. Ein Ritter, auferstanden aus fiebriger Lektüre kitschiger Ritterromane, wird zum Symbol des Ritterlichen schlechthin: Don Quijote, ein ritterlicher Narr, rettet das Beste des Mittelalters in die Neuzeit hinüber, den Donquijotismus als ‚nacktes Christentum‘ (wie Unamuno[66]) solches Rittertum interpretiert). „In der Wende vom ritterlichen Mittelalter zur bourgeoisen

---

[61]) In der Mystik schließlich wird diese *ruowe* in einer stulta mors erkauft: vgl. M. Bindschedler, Der lat. Kommentar zum Granum Sinapis, Basel 1949, 120, 246.

[62]) H. Wyss, Der Narr im schweizerischen Drama des 16. Jahrhunderts, Bern 1959.

[63]) W. Beck, Die Anfänge des deutschen Schelmenromans, Diss. Zürich 1957.

[64]) P. Gutzwiller, Der Narr bei Grimmelshausen, Bern 1959.

[65]) E. Przywara, In und Gegen 158.

[66]) Unamuno, Don Quijote, München 1926.

Neuzeit wird das Rittertum ‚christlich gemacht‘, indem es ‚lächerlich gemacht‘ wird“[67]). Und — möchte man nun hinzufügen — was im ‚Perceval/Parzival‘ als christliche Ideologie geretteter, weil verdemütigter Torheit vorgestellt wurde, ist im ‚Don Quijote‘ letztes Skandalon der Narrheit geworden. Wiederum ist das Geistliche auch für den ‚Don Quijote‘ bedeutsam, wiederum taucht, kaum ein Lebensalter vor Cervantes, jene bedeutsame, für den Roman unabsehbare Formel der ‚sancta insania‘ auf, vermutlich in direkter Abkunft von Wilhelms Theologie heiliger Torheit; es ist der ignatianische Ausdruck der *locura santa,* der ‚heiligen Torheit‘, die man öffentlich (wie ist diese ‚Öffentlichkeit‘ bedeutsam!) begeht, um sich mit Christus verspotten zu lassen, der der ‚Eine Narr‘ als ‚Narr Christus‘ war[68]). In diesem Sinn ist nach Unamuno Cervantes' Werk eine ‚liturgische Komödie‘, in welcher Christi Torheit weltlich-öffentlich durchexerziert wird (man denke an Ignatius' ‚Exerzitien‘).

Von ‚Don Quijote‘ fällt ein Licht auch auf den ‚Parzival‘. Denn dieser größte spanische Roman, in dem die Totalität einer auseinanderberstenden Welt nochmals im restlosen Scheitern erfahren wird, präsentiert letztlich nichts anderes denn das Selbstverständnis des Ritters, wie er sich auch zu Wolframs Zeiten verstanden hat: als total Irrender, der total auch heimfindet, durch alle Verdemütigungen hindurch zur Demut des Grals selbst, die eben letzte *linge* bedeutet.

4. Das Letzte der *tumpheit* Parzivals ist daher — um es nochmals und etwas abgeändert zu sagen — die kaum abmeßbare Tatsache, daß der Mensch, und zwar der Mensch schlechthin, das Schauspiel der Welt und Gottes (oder: die Komödie, in der beide, Gott und der Mensch, engagiert sind) nicht als ein unbeteiligter Zuschauer betrachten kann, sondern „daß er vielmehr — wie Parzival von den Wundern der Gralsburg — mit seinem ganzen Sein von dem Geschauten eingefordert ist“[69]); ja schon als Unerfahrener, als *tumber* Tor ist er derart mit diesem Schauspiel verhängt und darin gefangen, daß er diese seine Torheit nur demütig annehmen kann, indem er sie der wunderlichen Synästhesie der christlichen Tugenden zugesellt und so in *triuwe, kiusche, mâze, staete, dienst, einvalt* und *tumpheit* total disponibel ist für die hohe *linge,* die ihm gerade im Roman bildhaft geschehen darf. Geradeso aber ist im ‚Parzival‘ Wolframs von Eschenbach der Menschenweg gezeichnet: als ‚Geschichte‘, in welcher der Tor

[67]) Przywara a. a. O.

[68]) Vgl. Karrer/Rahner, Ignatius von Loyola: Geistliche Briefe, Einsiedeln 1942, 126 f.

[69]) E. Biser, Erkenne Dich in Mir, Einsiedeln 1955, 89.

über ‚Wissen' in tieferes ‚Nichtwissen' geführt wird, in Sünde, in die Verdemütigung in der Beichte und schließlich in die ‚Gefolgschaft' und Nachfolge Christi. Gerade das germanische, allzu natürliche Gefolgschaftsethos wird hier ins Christliche aufgesprengt, so daß die Abständigkeit, welche christliche Nachfolge von bloß ritterlicher trennt, durch alle Nähe zum naturhaften Nachfolgen hindurchblitzt. Gerade in der *tumpheit* aber ist jenes ‚Natürliche' angelegt (als dichterisches und erzählerisches Arrangement), das die ‚Vollendung' des Über-natürlichen anzieht und anfordert, so daß schließlich „in den Episoden des Parzival ... Nähe und Abstand in allen Stellungen beobachtet werden"[70]), also natürliche Gefolgschaftstreue und übernatürliche Ver-dienstung als ‚Narrheit in Christo' evident werden können.

Diese ritterliche Narrheit schillert nun allerdings nicht in jener gespenstischen Facettierung, wie sie bei Cervantes aufgrellt. Bei Wolfram kehrt mit Parzival selbst die ganze heile Welt in den Gottesfrieden ein: Schöpfung und Schöpfer finden sich in der Aufforderung der Schlußverse einträchtig zueinander:

> swes leben sich sô verendet,
> daz got niht wirt gepfendet
> der sêle durch des lîbes schulde,
> und der doch der werlde hulde
> behalten kan mit werdekeit,
> daz ist ein nütziu arbeit.   (827, 19—24)

Und so kehrt Parzival, der Tor, in *tumbem* Kindessinn wieder in die Schöpfung zurück, in der er das *nütziu arbeit* der Ineinssetzung von Gottes- und Welthuld vorbildlich für alle Menschen tätigt. Und es gilt Schwieterings Wort: „Ausstrahlung des Glücksgefühls aus der Nähe zur Schöpfung des väterlichen Gottes ist eine der überzeitlichen Erfahrungen an Wolframscher Dichtung"[71]).

---

[70]) Balthasar, Sponsa Verbi, Einsiedeln 1960, 135.
[71]) Natur und *art* 137.

ANHANG

Die Vorprägung von Parzivals *tumpheit* durch Percevals *niceté* in Chrétiens ‚Contes del Graal‘

Als eindeutig faßbare Quelle des Wolframschen ‚Parzival‘ ist bis jetzt immer noch der unvollendete Roman Chrétiens von Troyes anzusehen: Li Contes del Graal[1]). So differenziert Wolfram und Chrétien ihre eigenen künstlerischen Wege gehen, so sehr sind sie Kinder beinahe derselben Zeit und derselben Kultur. Die „tiefer gegründete, durch die Zeiten wirkende überpersönlich deutsche Art (Wolframs) gegenüber der französischen Erzählkunst Chrestiens"[2]), d. h. einfach die *andere* Art Wolframs, dürfte heute anders und vorsichtiger ausgedrückt werden, als Bodo Mergell es 1943 noch allzusehr dem Zeitgeist verpflichtet sagen konnte. Die Kriterien der Beurteilung müssen auch anderswo liegen als in allzu schnell berufenen, nationalen Kategorien, in denen sich leicht Selbstdünkel und Stolz einnisten.

Ist die Mächtigkeit eines Dichters durch das Zeugnis seiner Ruhmesgeschichte und die Strahlkraft seines Werks besiegelt — und wer möchte

---

[1]) Chrétiens ‚Perceval‘ wird im Folgenden nach der altfranz. Ausgabe W. Roachs: Chrétien de Troyes, Le Roman de Perceval, publié d'après le ms. fr. 12 576 de la Bibliothèque Nationale, Genève/Lille 1956; und nach der deutschen Übersetzung K. Sandkühlers: Chrétien de Troyes, Perceval oder die Geschichte vom Gral, aus dem Altfranz. übersetzt, Stuttgart 1957 (zitiert: Sandkühler und Seitenzahl) zitiert.
Zum Vergleich wurden herangezogen: Der Percevalroman (Li Contes del Graal) von Christian von Troyes, unter Benutzung des von Gottfried Baist nachgelassenen handschriftlichen Materials herausgegeben von Alfons Hilka, Halle/S. 1932. Und: Christian von Troyes, Der Percevalroman (Li Contes del Graal), in Auswahl herausgegeben von Alfons Hilka, Halle/S. 1935. Dazu die ausgezeichnete Übersetzung ins Neufranzösische von Lucien Foulet: Chrétien de Troyes, Perceval le Gallois ou Le Conte du Graal, préface de Mario Roques, Paris 1947. Die Ausgaben von Potvin und Baist waren für diese eng gestellte Aufgabe entbehrlich.

[2]) Bodo Mergell, Wolfram von Eschenbach und seine französischen Quellen, II. Teil: Wolframs Parzival, Münster/Westf. 1943, 354.

das bei Chrétien von Troyes im geringsten in Zweifel ziehen? —, dann geht es nur noch um den Versuch des Verstehens, nicht mehr um die Gewaltkur der Klassifizierung, des Verdikts oder der gnädigen Akzeption. Die Sprache der Interpretation hat sich des schnellen Werturteils zu enthalten und nur dem Lauf der Dinge zu folgen, die ihm die Dichtung darbietet.

Gefragt ist also nach einer Vorprägung der Torheit Parzivals im ‚Perceval' Chrétiens von Troyes. Nur schon ein flüchtiges Lesen des französischen Gralromans überzeugt von der Tatsache, daß es das zweifellos gibt. Denn Perceval tritt gleich eingangs als jener wallisische Märchendümmling auf, der später in allen möglichen Variationen literarisch Furore machen wird[3]).

1. Gleich nach dem zwischen unverhohlener Geldforderung und evangelischer Caritas schwankenden Prolog[4]), der eine devote Widmung an den Grafen Philipp von Flandern darstellt, setzt die Romanhandlung stummfilmhaft ein[5]):

> Ce fu au tans qu'arbre foillissent,
> Que glai et bois et pre verdissent,
> Et cil oisel en lor latin
> Cantent doucement au matin
> Et tote riens de joie aflamme,
> Que li fix a la veve fame
> De la gaste forest soutaine
> Se leva, ...   (69—76)[6])

Gleichsam von außen her, aus dem Frühlingsglanz und der flammenden Freude der Natur (*et tote riens de joie aflamme*) und der sich verjüngenden Gegenwart, tritt man an den vorerst noch namenlosen Perceval[7]), *li fix a la veve fame*, heran. Aber nicht um zu verweilen. Denn dieser sattelt schon sein Pferd und ist mit seiner Ausrüstung beschäftigt. Und:

---

[3]) S. C. Strucks, Der junge Parzival, Diss. Münster 1910; W. Golther, Parzival und der Gral in der Dichtung des Mittelalters und der Neuzeit, Stuttgart 1925; ders., Parzival in der deutschen Literatur, Berlin 1929.

[4]) Für den Prolog vgl. J. Frappier, Le roman breton: Perceval ou le Conte de Graal, Les Cours de la Sorbonne, Paris 1959, 20 ff.

[5]) a. a. O. 29: „L'attaque du récit nous met *in medias res.*"

[6]) „Es war zur Zeit, da alle Bäume blühen, die Wälder sich belauben, die Wiesen in frischem Grün prangen, und die Vögel in ihrem Latein am Morgen süß singen, und jedes Ding vor Freude flammt, da erhob sich der Sohn der Witwe im öden, einsamen Walde ..." (Sandkühler 9).

[7]) Vgl. Frappier, a. a. O. 29.

Ensi en la forest s'en entre (85), d. h. schon ist er untergetaucht und ein-
gegangen in den Frühlingsmorgen, so daß sich sein Herz im Leibe freut
ob des schönen Wetters und des Vogelgesangs. Und wiederum: schon beginnt der Sohn der Witwe mit Wurfspießen (*gabilos*) um sich zu werfen,
nach rückwärts, nach vorwärts, hinauf, hinunter. Es ist eine in Natur und
Körperkraft verzweckte Alltäglichkeit, in die wir geraten sind. Freude
am Gegenwärtigen und seiner Lust ist es, die diesen jungen Menschen einhüllt und ihn befähigt, die Lust, die täglich neu in der Natur ihr Auge
aufschlägt, als eine Eigenschaft vorauszunehmen. Die überstürzende Eile,
mit der Tag, Held und Natur in den Fluß des Geschehens tauchen, markiert Anfang überhaupt. Anfängliches scheint zu b e g i n n e n. Die Frische,
mit der Perceval sein Pferd sattelt, um sein im Grund doch unnützes
Werk des Speerwerfens auszuüben, antwortet einem Instinkt der Natur,
die ihrerseits ja immer auf ihre Mächtigkeit bedacht zu sein scheint. Anders gesagt: die Einheit von Perceval und Umwelt ist bruchlos. Das eine
erschöpft sich darin, Echo des anderen zu sein[8]).

Gleich aber wird der Akzent gesetzt, der diese Einheit ironisiert, in Frage
stellt und als Mangel klassifiziert. Perceval treibt nämlich sein Spiel genau
so lange,

> tant qu'il oi parmi le gaut
> venir cinc chevaliers armez,
> De totes armes adoubez.   (100—102)[9])

Nach dem Waffengetöse der fünf eintreffenden Ritter schließt Perceval
zunächst in schnell fertiger Überlegung auf Teufel, *les plus laides choses
del mont* (116). Er greift nach seinem Spieß, denn jene Art der Verteidi-
gung, die ihm seine Mutter beigebracht hat, nämlich gegen die Teufel ein
Kreuz zu schlagen, verwirft er stolz und verläßt sich lieber auf die eigene
Kraft. Wie er aber der farbigen Montur der Ritter ansichtig wird, ver-
kehrt sich sein vordem noch grimmiges Wesen in Wohlgefallen und Freude.
In sich übersteigernder Verzückung glaubt er zuerst Engel und dann Gott
den Herrn selbst zu erblicken. Er wirft sich auf den Boden, spricht sein
Glaubensbekenntnis und alle Gebete, die er von seiner Mutter gelernt hat.

---

[8]) Wie sehr dieses „Vorwärtstreibende, siegreich Strahlende und Zukunfts-
erfüllte des jungen Burschen" mit tiefem Ernst verbunden ist, macht E. Auerbach (Literatursprache ... 163/164) anschaulich: „wir wissen überdies, daß es
sich um die Exposition zur Graalsuche handelt, daß also der junge Bursche der
Erwählte ist, durch den das Abenteuer des bretonischen Romans in den Dienst
der Eschatologie und des Erlösungsdramas tritt."

[9]) „... bis er durch den Wald fünf bewaffnete, in volle Rüstung gekleidete
Ritter kommen hörte" (Sandkühler 9).

Ja, im Zwiegespräch mit dem erstaunten Ritter verliert er sich soweit, daß er sagt: *Mais vos estes plus biax que Diex.* Und dann gleich der Wunsch: *Cor fuisse je ore autretiex, Ausi luisanz et ausi fais* (179—181)[10]. Nichts kann nun seine Neugierde zurückhalten: wissen will er, was es mit den Rittern für eine Bewandtnis hat. Die Ungeduld des Ritters, der seinerseits nichts als eine exakte Auskunft über den Durchritt von fünf anderen Rittern und drei Jungfrauen haben möchte, kann Percevals Beharrlichkeit und Wißbegierde nicht brechen. Lanze, Schild, Panzerhemd und zuletzt die Art, wie man ein Ritter wird, werden nacheinander die naiv und hartnäckig umfragten Objekte dieser seltsamsten aller Einführungen ins Rittertum. Denn ein Tor ist's, ein Dummkopf, der hier so zäh über alles, was einen Ritter betrifft, Auskunft heischt. *Vallet, tu iez toz sos ...* Junker, du bist ja dumm! muß er sich gefallen lassen. Die anderen Ritter, die bis jetzt beiseite standen, sprengen hinzu und fragen: „Herr, was sagt euch dieser Walliser?" — „Er weiß gar nichts von unseren Gesetzen", sprach der Herr, „so Gott mir helfe; denn auf keine meiner Fragen antwortet er richtig, sondern er fragt bei allem, was er sieht, wie es heiße und was man damit mache" (234—241; Sandkühler 11). Den anderen Rittern wird es darauf ganz einfach zu dumm, denn die Nervenprobe dieser ländlichen Fragestunde ist ihnen zuviel. Vorwurfsvoll und mit leisem Erstaunen fragen sie ihren Führer, der sich so intensiv mit dem Dummkopf abgibt:

> „Sire, sachiez tot entresait
> Que Galois sont tot par nature
> Plus fol que bestes en pasture;
> Cist est ausi come une beste.
> Fols est qui dalez lui s'areste,
> S'a la muse ne velt muser
> Et le tans en folie user." (242—248)[11]

Das ist eine klare Sprache und erklärt den, der sich mit dem Verrückten abgibt, selbst zum Narren. Der vergeudet seine Zeit mit Torheit, der sich mit diesem Menschen befaßt, der dümmer als ein Vieh auf der Weide ist (schon rein durch seine geographische Abstammung!). Der angerempelte

---

10) „Niemals kannte ich einen Ritter, sprach der Junker, niemals sah ich einen noch hörte von einem sprechen. Ihr aber seid schöner als Gott; o wäre ich doch ebenso glänzend und so gestaltet!" (Sandkühler 10).

11) „Herr, Ihr wißt doch sicherlich, daß die Walliser alle ihrer Natur nach dümmer sind als die Tiere auf der Weide. Der ist auch wie ein Tier; ein Narr, wer sich bei ihm aufhält, wenn er nicht ganz und gar seine Zeit verdudeln oder mit Torheit vergeuden will" (Sandkühler 11).

Ritter antwortet weder mit Zorn noch beleidigtem Stolz. Er setzt solcher gewaltsamen Rede ein bedeutsames ‚Je ne sais quoi' entgegen (*Ne sai* ... 249). Etwas scheint ihm an diesem so direkten und dummen Toren bedeutsam; etwas Unbestimmtes, aber doch deutlich Fühlbares hält ihn vor vorschnellem Urteilen zurück. Er will, ‚so wahr ihm Gott hilft', diesen Toren erst anhören, ihm alles erklären und sagen, was er fragen will ... Ein Vorwissen und ein Vorverständnis um die kommende Größe und hohe Bestimmung dieses so ganz in Natur versponnenen und ständig sich auf die Worte der Mutter berufenden Menschen lassen den völlig in ritterlicher Gesittung verhafteten Sire zögern. „Er (Perceval) verhält sich ganz formlos und wird dennoch in all seinen Begegnungen mit der Ritterwelt ahnungsweise erkannt und geduldig unterrichtet"[12]). Ja, es hat tatsächlich den Anschein, als hätte die Ritterwelt vom terminus a quo ihrer verklausulierten Standesethik her den terminus ad quem ihres eigenen Überstiegs in diesem albernen und töricht sich gebärdenden Junker gefunden. Von nun an wird es so sein, daß sich gleichsam der ganze ritterliche Stand vor Perceval immer neu auszudeuten und zu erklären hat.

Der Höhepunkt von Percevals alberner Fragerei steht noch bevor. Nachdem er entsetzt und erfreut eingesehen hat, daß die Hirsche und Hirschkühe zum Glück keine Panzerhemden tragen — wie wollte er sie sonst erlegen? — fragt er unüberbietbar naiv, ob man als Ritter gleich mit Schild, Panzerhemd und Spieß auf die Welt komme. Die Stelle lautet:

> Et cil qui petit fu senez
> Li dist: „Fustes vos ensi nez?"   (281/282)

Der Dichter selbst muß erklärend beifügen: *cil qui petit fu senez*, ‚und der Junker, der von geringem Verstande war'. Das scheint eine endgültige Klarstellung: der Jüngling i s t von geringem Verstand. Da ist nichts mehr zu machen. — Und doch ist gerade diese Frage vielleicht die beste und notwendigste, die Perceval stellen konnte. Denn da er gleichsam in Hautnähe zu Natur und Waldeseinsamkeit lebt, begegnet ihm nichts, das sich einhüllt, verbirgt oder tarnt und maskiert. Alles begegnet ihm so, wie es ist, d. h. so, wie es zur Welt gekommen und geboren worden ist. Die Tiere, die Pflanzen und sicher auch die ihn umhegenden Menschen stehen in einem direkten Bezug zu ihm, der sich nicht in Masken äußert. Alles tritt eben und einfach an ihn heran. Die damalige Zivilisation mag, soweit sie Ritterliches betraf, vollständig außerhalb seines Blickfeldes gelegen haben.

---

[12]) Sandkühler a. a. O. 197 (Nachwort). Vgl. dazu Frappier a. a. O. 32 und ausführlicher: 39.

Die Sorge und Vorsicht der Mutter achtete wohl zu genau und behutsam darauf, als daß irgendwelche ‚Zivilisation‘ ins behütete Leben Percevals hätte eindringen können. Daher ist Perceval naiv, albern. Aber im Maß als er von geringerem Verstand ist, ist sein Denken unverstellt. Seine Direktheit im Fragen und in der Begegnung mit seiner Umwelt sichert ihm in hohem Maß einen klaren Blick für geöffnete oder geschlossene Verhältnisse. Das abgemacht Konventionelle des Rittertums macht ihn vor Freude selig. Gleichzeitig deckt er aber mit seiner Frage den Grund des Ritterlichen überhaupt auf: d.h. das Gesellschaftliche, Uniformierte an ihm. Indem Perceval ein Gesellschaftliches erstmals in den Blick bekommt, geht er quer durch dessen Ambiance hindurch und zwingt den in die Gesellschaft Eingeführten zum Bekenntnis:

> „Naie, vallet, ce ne puet estre
> Qu'ensi peüst ja nus hom nestre." (283/284)

(„O nein, Junker, das kann nicht sein, daß ein Wesen so geboren würde“, Sandkühler 12).
Damit aber hat Perceval das, was ihm als göttlich erschienen, auf die Ebene menschenmöglicher Erreichbarkeit gezwungen: das Rittertum steht ihm nach dieser entscheidenden Frage offen. Alles gerät nun auf einmal in Fluß: der Junker, der vom Nullpunkt menschlichen Daseins ausgegangen zu sein scheint, bekommt plötzlich und unverhofft Kenntnis von einer ihm bislang unbekannten Existenzweise, der des Ritters. Der bloß ‚lieber Sohn‘, ‚lieber Bruder‘ und ‚lieber Herr‘ genannte Junker empfängt in dem Moment, da er erfährt, daß es ein gewisser König Artus ist, der seinen Vasallen Rüstungen verleiht und den Ritterschlag erteilt, eine Richtung und ein Ziel in sein Leben. Der Fluß der Geschichte nimmt ihn auf und wird ihm ein persönliches Geschick zuerteilen.
Vorerst ist aber noch eine Überlegung einzuschalten: es stellt sich nämlich die Frage schon hier, ob Percevals *niceté*, seine Dummheit, die klinisch feststellbare Oligophrenie eines Kretinen sei, ob sie sich darin erschöpfe. Diese Frage stellen, heißt sie verneinen. Denn Percevals albernes Gebaren vor den Rittern ist wohlverstanden nicht die Dummheit eines in seine engen Verhältnisse gebundenen Bauern (man kennt die Verachtung, welche die Ritter damals den Bauern erwiesen!). Es handelt sich bei Perceval also nicht um eine innere Dummheit, sondern um eine künstliche, von einer aufmerksamen Mutter *kultivierte* und gleichsam anerzogene Dummheit. Eine Dummheit als Resultat einer übersteigerten Mutterliebe. Ein Simpel von Natur, ein integraler Dummkopf wäre Chrétien offenbar ungelegen und unpassend erschienen. Um Perceval richtig zu sehen, muß man sich

die Tatsache vor Augen halten, daß er ein Dummer durch Erziehung, daß er im Glashaus der unberührten Natur ‚dumm‘ *geworden* ist. Seine Furchtlosigkeit und sein Mut, überhaupt sein strahlender Eintritt in eine strahlende Natur und in eine mit allen erzählerischen Finessen ausgespielte Geschichte suggerieren aber auch die Gestalt eines Menschen, der durch die Schale einer kultivierten Albernheit hindurch das große Erbe einer nobeln Gesinnung und einer glanzvollen Bestimmung sichtbar zu machen versteht. Die Kunst Chrétiens, Perceval in dieser glücklichen Ambiguität darzustellen, verfolgt daher ein ganz bestimmtes Ziel. Indem er scheinbar einen künftigen Ritter komisch und lächerlich vorstellt, spricht er indirekt das Lob einer Ritterschaft aus, deren Ruf unausrottbar ist. So wird Chrétiens Gedicht zur Hymne und zum Loblied auf die Berufung zur Ritterschaft. Das machtvoll darzustellen ist ein großes Ziel von Chrétiens Dichtung.

2. Die Geschichte von Percevals *niceté* aber geht weiter: wie er vor seiner zu Tode erschrockenen Mutter von den Rittern zu erzählen beginnt, fällt diese in Ohnmacht, beginnt aber, nachdem sie wieder zu sich gekommen ist, Perceval vom Tode seines Vaters und seiner zwei Brüder im Waffengange zu erzählen. Perceval reagiert auf den Schmerz seiner Mutter überhaupt nicht; brutal und grobianisch meint er:

> „A mengier, fait il, me donez;
> Ne sai de coi m'araisonnez.
> Molt m'en iroie volentiers
> Au roi qui fait les chevaliers,
> Et je irai, cui qu'il em poist." (491—495)[13]

Der grobe Ton, in dem er zu seiner Mutter spricht, scheint nun schon wieder eher Ausdruck einer unüberholbaren Dummheit. Daher bekommt er auch zu tragen, was ihm geziemt: die Mutter kleidet ihn in ein derbes Hanfhemd, eine wallisische Hose (an der Hosen und Strümpfe zusammengewirkt sind) und in einen Kittel mit einer ringsum geschlossenen Hirschledermütze. Ein Bauernkleid also, das seine Torheit geradezu ständisch markiert!

---

[13] „Laßt mir zu essen geben", sprach er, „ich weiß nicht, was ihr mir da vorredet; aber gerne würde ich zu dem König gehen, der die Ritter macht, und ich werde auch gehen, wen es auch quäle!" (Sandkühler 15/16). Man beachte die in den letzten Worten deutlich ausgesprochene Absicht, selbst dann zum König zu gehen, wenn es auch jemanden quälen sollte. Percevals ‚Dummheit‘ ist hier also schon sündhafter Stolz und Eigenwille. Der böse Gedanke impliziert hier die böse Tat, die ihr daher unausweichlich auch folgt.

Die Räte, die ihm die Mutter hierauf mit auf den Weg gibt, werden im gleichen Maß, als sie eine Sitte anvisieren, an die sich Perceval hinfort halten soll, zum Kennzeichen der Dummheit und Bewußt-losigkeit, in der Perceval schon als Kind geübt wurde. Für die Ohren eines Ritters der Zeit muß das alles possierlich und komisch getönt haben, für Perceval war es erster Aufschluß über die Welt und ihre bestimmende Gesellschaft und nicht zuletzt auch über Gott und seine Institution in der Welt: die Kirche. Es sind gleichsam die ritterlich-ständischen Konstanten: Frauendienst, ritterliche Gesittung der Edelleute und Dienst an Gott (Messe und Morgenandacht, Liturgie als opus dei in Münster und Kirchen), die in dieser unnachahmlichen und gepreßten Einführung ins Rittertum abgehandelt werden.

Der Abschied, den die Mutter durch ihre hilflos-geniale Anleitung zu ritterlichem Leben mehr gefördert als gehindert hat, ist unwiderruflich. Noch einmal wird Perceval vom Dichter in einer Momentaufnahme vorgestellt: bäurisch, nach Art der Walliser gekleidet, mit drei Spießen in der Hand (die Mutter läßt ihm zwei davon wegnehmen, „weil er zu sehr wie ein Walliser aussah", Sandkühler 17). Besser läßt sich die Mischung von Welterfahrenheit, kindischem Stolz und wagemutiger Torheit kaum mehr festhalten, zumal diese Kennzeichnung Mutter u n d Sohn treffen muß (denn Percevals Mutter ist die kurzsichtige Erzieherin zur ‚Dummheit').

Percevals Weg ist in ein paar Versen prägnant geschildert: die Mutter wünscht ihrem scheidenden Sohn noch Freude zu, da ist er schon fort:

> Quant li vallés fu eslongiez
> Le get d'une pierre menue,
> Si se regarde et voit cheüe
> Sa mere al pié del pont arriere,
> Et jut pasmee en tel maniere
> Com s'ele fust cheüe morte.
> Et cil cingle de le roorte
> Son chaceor parmi la croupe,
> Et il s'en va . . .   (620—628)[14]

Chrétien schildert Percevals Schuld als letzte Entfremdung von der Mutter, als Herzenshärte: er schaut noch zurück, sieht seine Mutter hinfallen,

---

[14] „Als der Junker einen kleinen Steinwurf entfernt war, wandte er sich um und sah seine Mutter am Brückenkopf hinter ihm hinstürzen; und sie lag ohnmächtig, wie wenn sie tot hingefallen wäre. Er aber schlägt mit der Gerte sein Jagdroß über das Kreuz; es trabt fort . . ." (Sandkühler 18).

aber schon schlägt er seinem Pferd übers Kreuz und reitet schnellstens in den *grant forest oscure* (630). Seine Dummheit äußert sich hier als kaum mehr tragbare Mitleidlosigkeit, als seltsam entfremdete Haltung gegen die Liebe zum Nächsten, d. h. zu seiner Mutter. Als wie von einem Dämon getrieben wird Perceval geschildert. Ein Fremdes haftet ihm an. Konnte er sich noch kurz vorher an der flammenden Freude der Natur mit-freuen, hier fehlt jede Spur davon. Die Folge der Abenteuer, in die er sich nun treiben läßt, hat etwas Zufälliges, Freudloses.

Eine dumpfe Objektivität bekommt im Munde des Dichters — da die Anteilnahme nach dieser Schuld fehlen m u ß — als eine Form des Berichts die Oberhand. Der Junker schläft, der Junker erhebt sich beim Gesang der Vögel, der Junker erblickt ein Zelt . . . Da die Umwelt um Perceval durch den Entschluß zum Auszug und durch den vollzogenen Ausritt ein-mal gestört ist, ist in Perceval die bare Freudlosigkeit eingetreten. Seine *niceté*, sein linkisches Ungestüm, seine Torheit, zuerst als Un-kenntnis der Welt, als Un-bewußtheit ihm von seiner Mutter anerzogen, ist böse ge-worden. Naivität ist einer dumpfen Beharrlichkeit und sturen Einfalt gewichen. Und es wird nun alles darauf ankommen, ob ihm eine neue Innerlichkeit und Beseelung aus der Folge der Abenteuer zuwachsen wird.

3. Das Abenteuer Percevals mit dem im Zelte schlafenden Fräulein be-stätigt jedenfalls seine *niceté*: gleich doppelt wird er als *niches*[15]) und *fols* bezeichnet, einmal vom Dichter (681), einmal vom erschreckt aus dem Schlafe fahrenden Fräulein beim stolpernden Eintritt des Junkers (688). Ja, das Fräulein bezieht diese Feststellung der *folie* Percevals gar auf sich selber und macht sich den Vorwurf der Verrücktheit, da sie sich von einem solchen Menschen allein und einsam finden lassen habe (689/690). Die Szene, die sich nun abspielt, ist grotesk. Perceval umarmt das Fräulein, küßt sie (*Si l'embracha molt nichement* 701; „er umarmte sie gar linkisch", Sandkühler 19), raubt ihr den Smaragdring, den sie von ihrem Freund bekommen hat, und tut sich hierauf noch am Wein und an den Reh-pasteten gütlich, die er im Zelte bereit zum Mahle findet. Mit einem „*Diex vos salt, . . . bele amie*" (767) verabschiedet er sich von ihr, die er in tiefem Unglück zurückläßt (der Freund des Fräuleins glaubt nicht an ihre Unschuld und straft sie hierauf brutal und unmenschlich). Auf die Frage des Ritters nach Percevals seltsamem Besuch antwortet die so schmählich behandelte *pucele*, daß ein wallisischer Junker da gewesen sei: „der war zudringlich und grob und dumm" (Sandkühler 20; *anieus et vilain et sot*

---

[15]) = niais, simple. Vgl. Roach, a. a. O. Glossaire 350.

792). Ein Fluch auf diesen selbstsicheren, grausamen, verdrießlichen, ge-
meinen und dummen Junker schließt das Abenteuer, das durch seine gra-
ziöse Ambiance entzückt und durch die Begegnung von ritterlicher Zivilisation mit dem Toren Perceval ergötzt. Und doch — Percevals Unschuld
bestätigt sich hier nur in ihrer negativen Seite als Weltfremdheit, Kurzsichtigkeit, Verfremdung und Schuld.

Auffallend ist bei diesem Abenteuer eine eigenartige Absenz einer nur im
geringsten psychologisch gearteten Vermittlung. Das Geschehen passiert
im Vorfeld dessen, was Kausalität genannt werden könnte. Die Torheit
Percevals gebärdet sich derart selbständig, daß nicht mehr auszumachen
ist, wo ihre Wurzeln liegen. Wüßte der Leser nicht, daß Perceval aus
Waldeseinsamkeit und Abgeschiedenheit kommt, so müßte ihm dies Benehmen vorsintflutlich, marionettenhaft und schemenhaft erscheinen. Mit
anderen Worten: die Vermittlung liegt allein in den gebebereiten Händen
einer autonomen Dichtung. Die Vorstellung eines Kausalzusammenhangs
zwischen Geschehenem und Geschehendem hat souverän die *Dichtung*
übernommen. Die Torheit Percevals ist darum in erster Linie ein dichterisches Stigma, das sich einzig in der dichterischen Konstruktion bezeugt.
Noch ihr krudester Eigenschaftscharakter am Helden spricht etwas aus
über die ursprüngliche Absicht, mit der sie ihm zugesprochen wurde. Und
zwar dichterisch, nicht psychologisch[16]). Die Art, wie Perceval ins Zelt
dieses einsamen Fräuleins bricht: roh und brutal, muß daher i n n e r h a l b
der Dichtung etwas zu tun haben.

---

[16]) Die Schuld Percevals, die er sich mit seinem stolzen und mitleidlosen
Denken, Reden und Handeln aufgeladen hat, ist dichterisch nicht so kenntlich
gemacht, daß Perceval nun im *Bewußtsein* seiner Schuld weiter agiert. Im Gegenteil, jeder Anschein einer psychologischen Innerlichkeit, in der solches Bewußtsein Platz hätte, ist im Rahmen des Erzählten peinlichst vermieden. Perceval erscheint in rein epischer, unreflektierter Gegenwärtigkeit. Diese bloße
Gegenwärtigkeit der dichterisch, d. h. in der Erzählung vermittelten Gestalt,
ohne Doppelbödigkeit, Hintergrund und Schlupfwinkel für eine sich in Schuld
quälende Seele, bekommt dadurch, und nur dadurch, Zeichencharakter und
Symbolhaftigkeit. Man kann es geradezu als ein Gesetz dichter Dichtung formulieren: Bei Chrétien scheint nicht die existenzielle Persontiefe dichterisch
von Belang, sondern die existenzielle Oberfläche, das ,Naturell', Gehaben und
äußere Sichgeben eines Menschen. Im Maße als das dichterisch verwirklicht ist,
wächst den Gestalten Sinnhaftigkeit, Symbolwertigkeit und gleichsam eine
konstruktiv erreichte (d. h. durch die Techniken der Typik usw. komponierte)
Tiefe zu. Die Komposition vieler in ihrer Oberfläche genau umrissener Gestalten suggeriert Tiefe, Hintergründigkeit, selbst Rätselhaftigkeit. Davon lebt
nicht zuletzt der moderne Symbolismus z. B. eines Julien Gracq.

Ganz allgemein darf man sagen, daß die *aventure* einen „Versuch zur ‚In-Eins-Setzung' von Innen und Außen"[17]) darstellt. Die Suche nach dem Abenteuer, die Perceval ihm selbst unbewußt nun eben begonnen hat, ist der Art nach freischweifend, unbestimmt und offen, ihrer metaphysischen Bestimmung nach aber gerichtet, aufs Ende der Geschichte und aufs vollendete Geschehen hin tendierend. Jedes erlebte und durchlebte Abenteuer hat daher teil an der Gesamtvollendung und am Gesamtende der Erzählung. Was der Held hier am einzelnen, zufälligen Abenteuer ‚fertig gemacht' und zu Ende gebracht hat, hat er an sich selber vollendet. Ein Stück Weltsinn sollte ihm zugefallen sein, wenn er — und das ist in der Könnerschaft weniger Dichter begründet — alles *richtig* gemacht hat. Indem Perceval diese Abenteuer im Zelt besteht, demonstriert er eine Möglichkeit der In-Eins-Setzung von Außen und Innen oder vielmehr einen V e r s u c h dazu. Denn wäre es eine *gültige* Möglichkeit, so wäre es zugleich ihre Erfüllung. Das Versuchshafte daran garantiert aber erst die Geschichtlichkeit des eben Vergehenden und registriert sie, indem sie die ‚Vollendung' verunmöglicht. Die Geschichte Percevals ist im Entstehen, weil es eine falsche Möglichkeit der Übereinstimmung von Individuum (Perceval) und Gemeinschaft (Fräulein im Zelt in ihrer ritterlichen Umgebung) ist, die hier ad absurdum geführt wird.

4. Nach dem Abenteuer mit dem Fräulein im Zelt setzt der Junker seinen Weg fort. Er trifft einen Köhler, den er verächtlich mit „*Vilains*"[18]) (Ed. Hilka 817; nach Ed. Roach aber „*Preudom*") anredet und von dem er den Weg nach Carduel zum Hof des Königs Artus erfragt. Die Auskunft dieses Mannes über die Trauer und die Freude des Königs Artus ist

---

[17]) E. Köhler, Ideal und Wirklichkeit in der höfischen Epik, Studien zur Form der frühen Artus- und Graldichtung, Tübingen 1956, 82.

[18]) Man beachte, wie diese Szene, da Perceval einen Köhler mit *vilains* anredet, jener entspricht, da er selber von einem Ritter als *vilain* bezeichnet worden ist (Vers 792). Die *niceté*, die ihn damals noch vor den ihm begegnenden Rittern in die Knie zwang, scheint hier einem dünkelhaften, aber fürs damalige Rittertum bezeichnenden Standesstolz gewichen zu sein. Die ritterliche Standesideologie, die den niedrig Geborenen, den *vilain* zu gebührender Hochachtung zwingt, wird bei Chrétien in derselben Gestalt, in Perceval, von zwei Seiten gezeigt. Indem Perceval nämlich selbst als *vilain* die engelgleiche Art des Rittertums bezeugt, formuliert er sich seine eigene ständisch abgeschirmte Auserwählung. Aber in beiden Situationen ist er der *sot*. Indem Perceval daher dem Rittertum sowohl vom Gegensätzlichen wie vom Ebenbürtig-Gleichen her absolute Schönheit zugesteht, verifiziert und kompromittiert er (da er in beiden Situationen ein *sot* ist) die ständische Ideologie.

ihm keinen „roten Heller" wert (Sandkühler 21), obwohl er die Richtung einschlägt, die jener ihm gewiesen.

Auch der *Rote Ritter*, der eben in Auflehnung und offenem Widerstand gegen König Artus den Hof verläßt, vermag wenig Eindruck auf den Junker zu machen. Es sei denn, die guten Waffen und die schöne rote Rüstung, die haben es ihm angetan, und er will sie daher von König Artus für sich verlangen. Die Fehdeansage an König Artus, die der rote Ritter ihm als Botschaft mitgibt, schert ihn wiederum wenig. Ja er hat sie überhaupt nicht gehört: „Nun kann er sich einen anderen suchen, der diese Botschaft ausrichtet, denn der Junker hat kein Wort davon vernommen" (Sandkühler 22).

Perceval scheint mit jeder mitmenschlichen Begegnung die Variationsbreite seiner ihm eigenen, in der Erziehung mitgegebenen Torheit zu erweitern. War er erst naiv und wurde er am Tode der Mutter durch Mangel an Mitleid und durch Grobheit und zynisches Verhalten am Schicksal des Fräuleins im Zelt schuldig, so zeigt er sich nun als habitueller Frechling und habgieriger, verblendeter Mensch, der Mein und Dein nicht mehr zu unterscheiden vermag und den Mitmenschen überhaupt nicht achtet.

Als vollendeter Tor hält er Einzug am Hof des Königs Artus. Sackgrob fragt er nach dem König, reißt energisch sein Pferd herum und will wieder gehen, da der König nicht sofort antwortet und in tiefes Sinnen versunken ist; dabei streift er ihm den Hut vom Kopf, ganz wie einer, „der schlecht bei Sinnen ist" (Sandkühler 23; *Au guise d'ome mal sené* 934). Mit höfisch-entwaffnender Freundlichkeit antwortet der aufgeschreckte König und heißt den Junker mit der Anrede *„Biax frere, bien veigniez!"* willkommen (941). Ja er entschuldigt sich gar, da er auf seinen Gruß hin geschwiegen habe. Aber er sei eben noch voll Zorn über die Bosheit des *Roten Ritters,* der seine Gemahlin geschmäht habe, indem er einen Becher voll Wein über sie goß. Dieselbe Reaktion beim Junker wie schon vorher bei der Begegnung mit dem Köhler und dem *Roten Ritter*: „Den Junker kümmerte keinen Deut, was der König ihm da sagte und erzählte, und nichts lag ihm an seiner Trauer noch an der Schande der Königin: ,Herr König', sprach er, ,macht mich zum Ritter, denn ich will wieder gehen'" (Sandkühler 23). Ein schärferer Kontrast als das Verhalten dieser beiden Gesprächspartner läßt sich für eine höfisch gebildete und gesittete Zuhörerschaft gar nicht mehr denken. Aber seltsam, wie der Dichter weiterfährt:

> Cler et riant furent li oeil
> En la teste au vallet salvage.
> Nus qui le voit nel tient a sage,

Mais trestot cil qui le veoient,
Por bel et por gent le tenoient.   (974—978)[19]

Chrétien macht seinen Lesern den Gefallen nicht, Perceval in einem Ge-
samtportrait vorzustellen; dafür liefert er einige gut placierte Züge,
gleichsam punktuelle Durchblicke auf eine lebendige Gegenwärtigkeit des
Helden. Und da alles Lebendige nicht aufzurechnen und in sich vieldeutig
ist, löst der Anblick Percevals auch einen zwiespältigen Eindruck aus: für
weise kann man ihn offensichtlich nicht halten, aber schön und edel ist er.
Perceval zwingt seinem Partner eine Dialektik auf, die vorläufig unruhig
zwischen Phäno- und Genotyp zündet. Dumm ist er, aber schön! Diese
auch heute noch geläufige Redensart ist hier nicht platt und eben hinzu-
nehmen. Das ‚gent‘ ist das Dynamit, das diese kurze Widersprüchlichkeit
sprengt. Es heißt: gentil, noble, agréable (nach Ed. Roach, Glossaire 340).
Auch hier also wieder das schon früher angetönte ‚Je ne sais quoi‘, das den
höfischen Menschen hellsichtig abhält, ein vorschnelles Urteil über diesen
offensichtlichen Dummkopf zu fällen. Einzig der Seneschall Keu, eine
zwischen Torheit und Tabuhaftigkeit seltsam schwankende Gestalt, wagt
es, die Torheit Percevals auszunützen, indem er ihn heißt, doch selbst die
Waffen des *Roten Ritters* zu holen. Ironisch meint er zu Perceval: „Ihr
habt nicht als Tor gehandelt, wenn ihr deshalb hierhergekommen seid"
(Sandkühler 24). Artus aber gibt darauf eine bedenkenswerte und schlüs-
selhafte Antwort: „Wenn auch dieser Junker einfältig (*niches*) ist, so ist er
doch, hoffe ich, ein rechter Edelmann (*gentix hom*), und wenn er es bisher
so gelernt hat, da er bei einem schlechten Meister war, so kann er doch
noch tüchtig und weise werden" (Sandkühler 24). Mit König Artus' Replik auf Keus Frechheiten triumphiert das gemerkige und wohlgesittete,
aber auch (gemäß der mittelalterlichen discretio) unterscheidungstüchtige
Rittertum über seine um vieles simpler und auf magischen Vorstellungen
beruhenden Ursprünge, für die man die Gestalt Keus wohl als ein Relikt
nehmen darf.
Bezeichnenderweise ist es nun in den beiden folgenden Szenen auch wieder
Keu, der als ungefüger Dämon des ritterlichen Daseins auftritt. Eine
Jungfrau, die mehr als sechs Jahre nicht mehr gelacht hatte, beginnt bei
Percevals Gruß hellauf zu lachen und nennt ihn den besten Ritter auf der
ganzen Welt. Chrétien berichtet kommentarlos von der Tatsache, daß
diese Jungfrau nicht mehr gelacht hatte. Magisch und märchenhaft er-

---

[19] „Hell und lachend waren die Augen im Kopfe des wilden Junkers. Keiner,
der ihn sieht, hält ihn für klug, doch alle, die ihn sahen, hielten ihn für schön
und edel" (Sandkühler 23).

scheint das heute. In zwangshafter und ungeklärter Kausalität dazu ärgert sich Keu über die Worte der Jungfrau und gibt ihr dafür eine gewaltige Maulschelle, „daß er sie der Länge nach zu Boden warf" (Sandkühler 25)[20]. Diese seltsame Kausalität weitet sich aber gleich um die Dimension einer Person, des Narren nämlich, den Keu sich umwendend auf dem Kamine stehen sieht. Er stößt ihn brutal mit dem Fuß ins brennende Feuer, „weil der Narr immerfort zu sagen pflegte: ‚Diese Jungfrau wird nicht lachen, bis sie den sehen wird, der den höchsten Preis aller Ritterschaft erlangen soll‘ " (Sandkühler 25). Selbst diese unerquickliche Szene läßt den torenhaften Junker offenbar kühl. Stumm (mit Stummheit und verdumpftem, eigensinnigem, geschlossenem Gemüt hat er bisher alles ihn Ansprechende und ihn als menschliche Person Anfordernde beantwortet!), ohne ein Wort zu verlieren, macht er sich davon und kehrt zum *Roten Ritter* zurück.

Gerade in dieser Szene mit Keu findet eine Konfrontation zweier typischer Vertreter des Rittertums statt: Keu und Perceval. Keu ist der ‚Reaktionär‘, der Mann, der, in den keltisch-mythologischen Hintergrund verfilzt, deutlich archaische Züge trägt: Gewaltanwendung ist ihm eine Anlage, der er nur zu leicht entspricht, Unberührbarkeit ist ihm innerhalb des Artushofes ein schützendes Tabu; niemand wagt es, seine Schandtaten im Moment, da sie begangen werden, zu rächen. Ein anderer Ritter hätte solches nicht ungestraft begangen. Mitten in der ritterlichen Gesellschaft lebt er als handgreifliche Sanktion, die über alles ihr Verdikt spricht, was archaische Zauber lösen möchte. Der eigentlich Dumme, d. h. der unüberholbar und unbelehrbar Beschränkte ist Keu. Perceval dagegen gewinnt im Maße, als seine Berufung in dieser Konfrontation mit einer immer noch bedrohlichen Vergangenheit ‚schöne‘ und ‚edle‘ Gestalt gewinnt, sein Eigenes, seine Bestimmung (die Erzählung manövriert ihn vom Grund seiner *niceté* her in die Rolle des Erwählten, des Erlösers). Die Bestimmung ist da, bevor sie Perceval erkennt, ein Resultat seiner ‚Torheit‘.

Nach dem Mord am *Roten Ritter*, den Perceval nur dank seiner nun sich bewußt am Leben vergreifenden Torheit und Brutalität erfolgreich zu-

---

[20]) Frappier sagt dazu: „Annonce d'un destin exceptionel, et ce n'est pas, dans le *Conte du Graal*, le seul trait qui infléchisse Perceval vers la figure d'*un héros prédestiné* (von uns kursiv), bien que ce caractère de prédestination ne soit jamais clairement énoncé et qu'il reste latent, impliqué dans certaines aventures, et aussi dans le lignage du fils de la ‚veuve dame‘ et du cousin du Roi Pêcheur" (a. a. O. 42 f.).

stande bringt, konstatiert Chrétien angesichts Percevals, der sich weigert, die Torenkleider mit der ritterlichen Rüstung zu tauschen, sententiös: *Molt grief chose est de fol aprendre* (1173), „gar schwer ist es, einen Toren zu belehren" (Sandkühler 27). Yonet hilft, den Untauglichen ritterlich auszustaffieren, und berichtet dann von dem Ereignis bei Hofe. Nochmals fällt dabei ein ernst gemeinter Tadel für Keu ab. Indem Artus Keu tadelt, umschreibt er auch die epische ‚Stufe', auf welcher Perceval, der inzwischen ziellos davongeritten ist, steht: „Weh, weh! Keu, wie habt ihr mich heute erzürnt! Wenn einer den Junker in den Waffen abgerichtet und gelehrt hätte, so daß er sich ihrer bedienen könnte, sowohl des Schildes als der Lanze, dann würde er ohne Zweifel ein guter Ritter werden; aber er versteht gar nichts von den Waffen noch von anderen Dingen, so daß er nicht einmal das Schwert ziehen könnte, wenn er seiner bedürfte. Nun sitzt er bewaffnet auf seinem Roß, und wenn ihm irgendein Vasall begegnet, mag dieser ihn, um sein Pferd zu gewinnen, ohne Zweifel schlimm zurichten: er wird ihn rasch getötet oder verstümmelt haben, denn der Junker wird sich nicht verteidigen können, so töricht und dumm wie er ist (*Tant est niches et bestiax* 1299). Sein Neider wird darum leichtes Spiel mit ihm haben" (Sandkühler 28). Hier umgreift schon ein eindeutiger Konditionalis Percevals Torheit, die in ihrem letzten Sinn eben behebbar und ablegbar ist: „Wenn Perceval gelernt hätte . . ." Im Zeitpunkt, da er das vorerst einzige Ziel seines Aufbruchs aus der Waldeinsamkeit vollständig erreicht hat (wenigstens äußerlich!) und stolz in der über die Torenkleider gestülpten Montur des *Roten Ritters* einherreitet, ist auch seine Torheit am offensichtlichsten. Sie ist noch leeres, unerfülltes Versprechen, besonders da sie mit der doppelten Schuld (Schuld am Tod der Mutter und Schuld an der Tötung des *Roten Ritters*) im Wesen verbunden und gekoppelt ist. Es ist schuldhafte Torheit, aber auch — weil völlig unpsychologisch anerzogen und zum Habitus der Unerfahrenheit geworden — Torheit der Auserwählung, handgreifliche aufs Ziel schießende Beschränkung. Einschränkung des Blicks, die anlagemäßig in stets neuen Anläufen das Eine Notwendige anspringt. Kurz, eine Torheit, die nur episch durch die stets neu einfordernde Gewalt der *aventure* ihr Ziel einer In-Eins-Setzung von Innen und Außen zustandebringen wird, in einem Abenteuer, das als endgültig geglücktes diese Synthese erfüllt. Aber vorerst — wie könnte einer anders geartet sein als Perceval, der einem höheren epischen Gesetz (ganz schlicht dem Gesetz des Erzählens, dem die Notwendigkeit des Geschehnisses, der Episode innerlich ist) zu gehorchen hat? Mit anderen Worten: Percevals Torheit hat epische Funktion, ist ein

Anreiz des Erzählens, der Reihung von Episoden; nicht um eine Entwicklung zu demonstrieren, sondern um eine Welt zu ‚flicken', einen Menschen vor-zu-stellen und in ihm Weltgegensätze zu versöhnen. Die ‚Entwicklung' ist mittelalterlich uninteressant, weil das Ziel, der Endpunkt interessanter ist als die Kausalität des Weges, der zu ihm führt, vor allem wenn der Weg psychologisch determiniert sein soll. Das Künstlerische, d. h. die dichterische und kompositionelle Bewältigung dieses Ziels ist wichtiger als die psychologische, vermutlich auch, weil unterhaltsamer und spannender.

5. Die folgende Szene, da Perceval ohne besonderes Wollen, aber darum um so sicherer zum Schloß des Edelmannes Gornemant von Goort gelangt, kann nur noch in Abbreviatur bestätigen, was Artus deutlich ausgeführt hatte. Nur wird bei ihm der Konditionalis aufgelöst und die Montur Percevals mit ihrem Inhalt gefüllt: Perceval lernt bei Gornemant das Ritter-Handwerk. An der naiven Berufung auf die Lehren seiner Mutter erkennt der Edelmann Perceval gleich „als einfältig und dumm" (Sandkühler 30; *niche et sot* 1365). Das köstliche Gespräch zwischen den beiden, wo Gornemant Perceval in höfischer Manier diskret und erfahren zugleich aushorcht, bringt die Unerfahrenheit Percevals, aber auch seine noch völlig modulierbare und zu gestaltende Seele zutage. Er will nach der Lehre seiner Mutter von den Edlen beraten werden und Nutzen haben. Gleich aber, nachdem man ihn entwaffnet und seines ritterlichen Überzugs entledigt hat, steht er lächerlich in seiner *roube sote* (1423), in seinem einfältigen Gewand da. In Gornemant aber erweist sich von neuem die Diskretion und der höfische Anstand, den das Rittertum bis anhin vor Perceval immer an den Tag gelegt hat. Nichts von Schaulust und schnöder Neugier! Gornemant beginnt gleich mit den Waffenübungen, die Perceval bitter not tun. Wo das Rittertum Mangel statuiert, reicht es sofort die helfende Hand, wenn der Mangel brachliegende Begabung ist. Die Handhabung von Schild, Lanze und Pferd werden eingeübt, bis der Jüngling es so gut kann, wie wenn er es sein ganzes Leben so gehalten hätte. Interessant ist hier ein Doppeltes: die erzählerisch und psychologisch unvermittelte Art und die schnelle Weise, in der Perceval das Ritterhandwerk lernt. Es sehen und können ist eines (*car il li venoit de nature* 1480).

Nach der Mahlzeit, die Perceval mit seinem neuen Lehrer einnimmt (man beachte die grenzenlose, geradezu wieder *ungeschickte* Autoritätshörigkeit Percevals, ein Zug, der von nun an bis zur abstrusen, aber in sich konsequenten Gestalt Eulenspiegels sich literarisch manifestieren wird), geschieht etwas, das erstmals völlig unerwartet Percevals bisheriges Benehmen in Frage stellt und sich als ein Anzeichen von Mitleid und christlicher Caritas an ihm äußert: dem ritterlichen Gornemant, der seinen jugendlichen Gast zu längerem Bleiben einladen möchte, antwortet Perceval mit leisem Ahnen: „Herr, ich weiß nicht, ob ich nahe bei dem Schlosse bin, wo meine Mutter wohnt, aber ich bitte Gott, er möge mich hinführen, damit ich sie noch einmal sehen könne; denn ohnmächtig sah ich sie am Brückenkopf vor dem Tore fallen, und ich weiß nicht, ob sie lebt oder tot ist. Aus Schmerz über mich, da ich sie verließ, fiel sie ohnmächtig zu Boden, *das weiß ich wohl*, und deshalb könnte es sein, daß ich lange verweile, ehe ich nicht ihren Zustand kenne; also werde ich morgen bei Tag aufbrechen" (Sandkühler 33). Wie von weit her scheint Perceval seine Er-innerung wiedergegeben. Das *bien le sai* (1588) scheint dem wohlwollenden *ne sai* (ich-weiß-nicht) des ersten ihm begegnenden Ritters seltsam zu entsprechen. Die Verheißung, die in der Gestalt Percevals dem Rittertum widerfährt, wird hier erstmals in einer zarten und fast scheuen Weise bestätigt. Dazwischen aber liegt die vollbrachte Schuld.

Mühelos läßt sich Perceval hierauf seine Torenkleider mit feinerem und ritterlichem Gewand vertauschen. Seine Erscheinung geht nun vollends im Ritterlichen auf. Er gibt sein mütterliches Erbe (die Torenkleider) preis, jetzt, da er sein erstes Ahnen und seinen ersten Schmerz über den Verlust der Mutter verspürt. Das heißt: er gibt eine Hülle seiner Torheit, ihr äußeres Kennzeichen im anschaulichen Kleid auf, im Moment, da seine Torheit ihm innerlich als Schmerz widerfährt. Dieses Geschehen ist psychologisch wiederum unvermittelt, hingegen *kompositionell*. Das Faktum, daß Perceval nun seine Torenkleider preisgibt, ist eine Antwort auf das ebenso unpsychologisch und unkausal hingestellte Faktum der Verleihung der Kleider durch die Mutter. Inneres und Äußeres sind bei Chrétien Momente der dichterischen Komposition: ihre Setzung oder Nicht-Setzung bedeutet immer je eine neue Antwort auf das Gegenstück. Was so geschieht, ist episches Geschehen, wobei sich wohl Seele äußert, aber keine Psychologie.

Danach reicht Gornemant Perceval mit bedeutungsschweren Worten das Schwert und sagt,

> que donee li a
> Le plus haute ordene avec l'espee
> Que Diex ait faite et comandee:

C'est l'ordre de chevalerie,
Qui doit estre sanz vilonnie. (1634—1637)[21]

Mit dieser technischen Einführung ins Waffenhandwerk des Rittertums gibt sich Gornemant jedoch nicht zufrieden. Was sich im Kleidertausch symbolisch vorgezeichnet hat, wird nun in eindeutigen, sittlich-moralischen Prinzipien, die das Wesen der ritterlichen Existenz formulieren, an die Adresse Percevals übermittelt. Drei Räte[22]) oder besser Prinzipien sind es, die Perceval von seinem ritterlichen Freund erhält: der erste betrifft die höfisch-ritterliche Generosität, nämlich keinen besiegten Feind, der um Erbarmen fleht, zu töten; der zweite die höfische Diskretion, nämlich nicht zuviel zu sprechen und nicht neugierig zu sein (mit einem biblischen Hinweis auf die Proverbia 10, 19: *Car li sages dit et retrait: ,Qui trop parole, il se mesfait'* 1653/54). Dieser Rat entspricht auf seltsame Weise dem Verhalten, das Perceval bisher beachtet oder einfach instinktiv beobachtet hat: sein ichbezogenes, nur auf sein Ziel bedachtes *Stummsein*[23]). Was er bisher aus Egoismus äußerlich so gehalten hat, wird ihm nun als ein Gebot der Nächstenliebe hingestellt, als ein Gebot der gegenseitigen, kommunikativen Rücksichtnahme. Natürlich handelt es sich hier nicht um zwei schlechthin gleiche Verhaltensweisen, sondern bloß um äußerlich Gleiches, inhaltlich aber Verschiedenes. Sowohl bei der Begegnung mit dem Köhler als auch mit dem *Roten Ritter* mangelte es Perceval an innerer Bereitschaft, auf den ihm als ein Nächster begegnenden Menschen überhaupt zu hören und ihn als einen Gesprächspartner anzuerkennen. Jetzt, da er innerlich bereitet wäre für solches Begegnen, wird ihm auch gleich ein Riegel vorgeschoben. Das liegt wiederum in der Konzeption des ,Gedichtes' beschlossen. Indem Chrétien nämlich die psychologische Folgerichtig-

---

[21] „... daß er ihm nun mit dem Schwert den höchsten Orden verliehen habe, den Gott gestiftet und anbefohlen habe: das ist der Orden der Ritterschaft, der keine Unehre leiden darf" (Sandkühler 34). Zu beachten ist hier, daß Gornemant seine Unterweisung im Ritterhandwerk nicht mit bloßem technischem Erlernen der ritterlichen Leibesübungen ein Bewenden haben läßt. Die Initiation dieses auserwählten Junkers ins Rittertum ist doppelt: das Faktische hat nur Sinn vor dem Hintergrund seiner geistigen Bedeutung.

[22] Frappier a. a. O. 45: „le prud'homme cherche aussi à lui inculquer les principes moraux qui font l'essence de la chevalerie ...".

[23] Percevals Stummsein erschöpft sich in dieser Szene nicht. Ihre stärkste Auswirkung steht noch bevor. Vgl. Jean Frappier, Chrétien de Troyes, Paris 1957, 174: „Un rapport étroit unit le silence de Perceval chez le Roi Pêcheur à sa ,niceté' (naiveté), due à l'éducation qu'a voulue pour lui une mère aimante et timorée."

keit ausklammert, erreicht er die Vorbildlichkeit seiner Dichtung, das eben Exemplarisches und nicht psychologische Einheitlichkeit will. Und all diese Züge Percevals (angefangen bei seiner *niceté*) und das Faktum seines Weges sind Formen und Bildwirklichkeiten des Dichterischen, nicht einer irgendwie gearteten Zuhandenheit, die man nachträglich nach modernen wissenschaftlichen Kriterien der Dichtung ‚entnehmen‘ könnte. — Der letzte Rat Gornemants betrifft die höfische Gesittung: Perceval soll sich hüten, sich überall auf die Ratschläge seiner Mutter zu berufen; und auf die naive Frage Percevals, auf wen denn sonst, fügt Gornemant hinzu: „Der Vasall, könnt Ihr sagen, der Euch den Sporen anlegte, lehrte es Euch und beriet Euch" (Sandkühler 35). Denn würde er sich weiterhin auf seine Mutter berufen, *a folie le tenroit l'en* (1683), man würde es ihm als Torheit auslegen.

6. Anstatt auf der Suche nach seiner Mutter an ein Ziel zu gelangen, trifft Perceval in einer stattlichen Burg *Blanchefleur*, die von einem gewalttätigen Freier (König Clamadeu) stark bedrängt ist. Im getäfelten und reich hergerichteten Gemach, wo Perceval höfisch empfangen wird, spielt sich eine amüsante Szene ab. Perceval, noch ganz unter dem Eindruck von Gornemants Lehren, wagt nicht, sein Wort an das Burgfräulein zu richten. Die anwesenden Ritter halten ihn für stumm (ob wohl dieser Ritter stumm [*muiaus* 1863] ist?). „Gar stattlich sitzt er neben unserer Herrin und unsere Herrin ebenso neben ihm, wenn sie nur nicht beide stumm wären! So schön ist er, so schön ist sie, daß niemals Ritter oder Jungfrauen zusammenkamen, die so gut wie diese beiden zusammenpaßten. Scheint es doch als ob Gott sie beide füreinander geschaffen habe, da er sie zusammenführte" (Sandkühler 38). Percevals *niceté* hat hier einen amüsanten, eher unschuldigen Aspekt. Blanchefleur, deren Namen man erst spät erfährt (übrigens auch den Percevals!)[24], eröffnet eine Unterhaltung auf das Risiko hin, unhöflich zu erscheinen. Leicht und mit höfischem Anstand spricht sie über Gornemant von Goort, ihren Onkel, und über den Mangel an Lebensmitteln, der ihr und der Burgstadt unheilvoll auflastet. — Völlig unbefangen gibt sich dann Perceval: nichts vermag ihm den Schlaf zu rauben, dem er sich nach dem Mahl in einem kostbaren und angenehmen Bett hingibt. Etwas maliziös und als Kenner höfi-

---

[24] Über die späte Namengebung in Chrétiens Roman und deren Tragweite siehe die trefflichen Erläuterungen in: Reto R. Bezzola, Le sens de l'aventure et de l'amour (Chrétien de Troyes), Paris 1947, 33—62 (nun auch deutsch: Liebe und Abenteuer im höfischen Roman, rde Bd. 117/118 Hamburg 1961, 39—66).

scher Bettsitten fügt Chrétien hinzu: „Alle Bequemlichkeit und Freude, die man für ein Bett ersinnen kann, bekam der Ritter diese Nacht, außer der Wonne an einer Jungfrau oder einer edlen Frau, wenn es ihm gefiele oder erlaubt wäre. Jedoch wußte er davon nichts, und er dachte nicht im geringsten daran, sondern er schlief kurze Zeit danach ein ohne Sorge und Kummer" (Sandkühler 39). Der spielerische Ton dieser Stelle darf nicht über die ernste Aussage, die sie enthält, hinwegtäuschen. Denn Perceval ist in dieser so leichthin gesagten Bemerkung als ein unberührter und durch die „amor fine‘ noch nicht befleckter Ritter gekennzeichnet. Seine *niceté*, so sehr sie durch Schuld belastet scheint, schließt immer noch eine im Kern unberührte Unschuld des Lebens und Daseins in sich (auch die Szene mit dem Fräulein im Zelt hat in dieser Hinsicht nichts Anrüchiges).

Auch das durch die Belagerung verängstigte Fräulein, das nur mit Hemd und scharlachrotem Seidenmantel bekleidet in der Nacht vor sein Bett kniet und den Helden umarmt und ihm ihr Leid klagt, vermag nichts Unzeitiges im Helden zu wecken. Tröstend meint er zu ihr: „ ‚Liebe Freundin, seid diese Nacht guten Mutes, tröstet Euch und weint nicht länger. Kommt hier herauf an meine Seite und trocknet die Tränen von Euren Augen. Wenn es Gott gefällt, wird er Euch morgen ein besseres Leben bescheren als Ihr mir eben erzählt habt. Legt Euch neben mich in dieses Bett, es ist breit genug für uns beide; heute sollt Ihr mich nicht mehr verlassen.‘ Und sie sprach: ‚Wenn es Euch gefällt, so will ich es tun.‘ Und er küßte sie und hielt sie in seinen Armen; er bettete sie ganz sanft und bequem unter die Decke; und sie duldete, daß er sie küßte, und ich glaube nicht, daß es ihr leid tat. So lagen sie die ganze Nacht Seite an Seite, Mund an Mund, bis zum Morgen, da der Tag anbrach" (Sandkühler 41). Die zweifelnde Frage Jean Frappiers: „Serait-il par hasard devenu soudain moins ‚nice‘ qu'on aurait pu le croire?" darf ruhig mit Frappiers eigener, brillanter Darstellung verneint werden. Die Streitfrage der französischen und amerikanischen Chrétien-Forschung um Percevals bewahrte Keuschheit (in dieser Nacht) scheint mit den Ausführungen von Amalia Klenke und Jean Frappier endgültig gelöst[25]). Jean Frappier: „c'est exactement le

25) Vgl. dazu Jean Frappier, Le roman breton . . ., a. a. O. 48—50. Noch eindringlicher: M. Amelia Klenke, The Blancheflor-Perceval Question, Romance Philology 6 (1952/53) 173—178. Klenke unterstreicht energisch, „that the conte del Graal is profoundly liturgical in its poetic preoccupations" (173) und kommt nach einer gründlichen Untersuchung der einschlägigen Textstellen (Verse 1983—1988; 2040—2045; 1935—1942) zum Schluß, daß „the accent has always been on chastity" (177). Ein Hinweis auf Wolframs Parzival-Condwiramurs-Episode kann diesen Eindruck nur noch verstärken. Klenke nimmt diese Argumente, mit

même degré de plaisir (wie es Perceval in der Umarmung mit dem Fräulein im Zelt gefunden hat), et rien de plus, qu'il demande à Blanchefleur, et sa nouvelle expérience, si elle est plus délicieuse que les précédentes, n'est pas une initiation où il perdrait toute sa ‚niceté' — cette ‚niceté' *encore indispensable à la suite du roman*[26]) —, mais, par un transfer ingénieux sur le plan psychologique et sentimental, elle fait naître en son coeur un émoi encore inconnu qui est la tendresse, mêlée à la pitié pour la ‚pucelle desconseillée', et c'est là un prélude au raffinement courtois d'une pensée d'amour." Die *niceté* also bleibt Perceval. Vielleicht darf man in dieser Szene gar ihre schönste Frucht erblicken; ihre dem Unschuldigen verschwisterte und verwandte Seite tritt nirgends klarer und eindeutiger hervor. Was höfisch in einer solchen Szene zur Pikanterie und raffinierten Erotik Anlaß gegeben hätte, biegt Chrétien ins Idyll einer der ‚Sünde' und höfischer *fine amor* noch un-bewußten und daher schuldlosen Natur. Wenn Unschuld in der Literatur je Reiz und schöne Gestalt gewonnen hat, dann hier.

Es muß dem Leser nunmehr folgerichtig erscheinen, daß Perceval den hochmütigen Seneschall Anguingueron besiegt und sich furchtlos dem König Clamadeu im Zweikampf zu stellen wagt. Obwohl alle Männer und Frauen der Burg — Blanchefleur an erster Stelle — Perceval inständig bitten, doch ja vom Zweikampf mit Clamadeu abzulassen, weigert sich der junge Ritter beharrlich, auf dieses in seinen Augen beschämende Anerbieten seiner Freunde einzugehen. Im Gegenteil, er schlägt einen neuen und harten Ton an: „‚Ihr Herren, nun schweiget nur!' spricht der Junker,

---

anderen verstärkt, in einem neuen Aufsatz: The spiritual ascent of Perceval, Studies in Philology, 53 (1956) 1—21 wieder auf; hier, indem sie sich vor allem gegenüber Helaine Newstead (The Blancheflor-Perceval Question Again, Romance Philology 7 [1953] 171—175), R. S. Loomis und Raphael Levy (Quest for Biographical Evidence in Perceval, Medievalia et Humanistica 6 [1950] 82, Anm. 29) wirkungsvoll verteidigt. Tatsächlich ist es der Begriff der *drüerie*, der alles klärt (2104) (drüerie = amitié, amour: Roach Glossar 330). *Mais se je l'ochi et conquier, / Vostre drüerie vos quier*, sagt Perceval („Wenn ich ihn [Anguingueron] jedoch töte und besiege, so erbitte ich Eure Minne als Pfand" Sandkühler 41 f.); er bestimmt damit eindeutig die Liebe und Vereinigung in Liebe als ein Späteres, das als Vollendung der Begegnung zwischen ihm und Blanchefleur erst zu erwarten ist. Frappier a.a.O. 50: „Le terme de druerie éclaire le sens de l'épisode . . .". Zuletzt darüber: Edward B. Ham, The Blancheflor-Perceval idyll and Arthurian polemic, in: Kentucky Foreign Lang. Quart. 6 (1959) 155—162.

[26]) Von uns kursiv.

‚dann handelt ihr gut, denn ich möchte es (den Kampf mit Clamadeu)
um keines Menschen der Welt willen unterlassen' " (Sandkühler 50). Wenn
man bedenkt, daß sich Perceval erst seit vier, fünf Tagen im Ritterhandwerk versucht (man achte auf die gesamtmenschliche, einzig dichterisch
möglich gemachte Unmöglichkeit solchen ‚Fortschrittes'!), dann erscheint es
völlig klar, daß hier etwas Neues, aber ganz innerhalb der epischen Folge
des Gedichts, passiert: Perceval setzt sich ein erstes Mal ausdrücklich und
willentlich gegen die Sozietät ab. Davon ist die Gemeinschaft der Liebe
(die *druerie*) mit Blanchefleur, die ja eben erst als überschwengliches Versprechen begonnen hat, nicht ausgeschlossen. Perceval gewinnt Sinn für
notwendige Autonomie, oder besser: er findet sich plötzlich in deren Be-
sitz, völlig unvermittelt; allerdings indem er eindeutig d e r bleibt, der er
werden soll. So ist er in der Lage, Blanchefleur — nicht mehr durch die
Un-anständigkeit seines unhöfischen Gehabens, aber durch eine innere,
ihm plötzlich selbstverständliche Kraft der Selbstüberwindung und Selbst-
verfügung — gegen sie selbst zu verteidigen. Ihre liebevolle Angst um
ihren eben erst erworbenen Geliebten — von der höfischen Umgebung
akzeptiert und mitgefühlt — kann diesen nicht hindern, die erkannte
Pflicht der ritterlichen Hilfeleistung zu erfüllen. Diese Autonomie, in sich
ja schon verlängert in eine weiter als der hilfebedürftige Nächste blickende
Liebe zum Nächsten, erweist sich aber noch um eine Dimension reicher.
Denn Perceval, von den ihm begegnenden Rittern in dieser Eigenschaft
längst ahnungsweise bestätigt, zeigt sich hier erstmals in einer die höfische
Gesittung nicht verletzenden Weise als Held *einer vollen Disponibilität*[27]).
Er handelt in einem Auftrag, der ihn wesensgemäß übersteigt und sich
ihm gleichsam nur in zu erfüllenden Weisungen des Augenblicks als solcher
anzeigt. Von daher gesehen, ist der Kampf mit Clamadeu letztlich sym-
bolischer Ausdruck dessen, was Perceval an der ganzen Menschheit in
Ordnung bringen wird (gerade indem er die höfisch-ritterliche Gesellschaft
in ihren Ansprüchen an den Einzelnen übersteigt). Die Disponibilität
gegenüber dem ihn einfordernden Auftrag gewinnt im Zweikampf mit
Clamadeu eine den Weg weisende Vorbildlichkeit und einen in sich
schlüssigen Bildcharakter.

7. Nach der Begegnung mit dem Fischerkönig, der Perceval von seinem
Schiffchen aus den Weg zum Gralsschloß weist, tut Perceval seinen seltsam ungeduldigen und überstürzten Ausspruch. Er ist nach der Weisung
des Fischerkönigs auf den Gipfel eines Berges geritten, von wo er im Tal

---

[27]) Frappier a. a. O. 53: „il doit rester le héros de la disponibilité".

eine Burg (*une maison* 3033) erblicken sollte. Im ersten Moment aber erblickt er nur Himmel und Erde, von einem Haus keine Spur. Da bricht er los: „Was bin ich gekommen, hier zu suchen? *Dummheit und Narrenspiel* (*Le musardie et le bricoigne* 3041)! Gott gebe dem heute Scham und Schande, der mich hierhergewiesen hat. Schön hat er mich auf den Weg gebracht, als er mir sagte, ich würde ein Haus finden, wenn ich hier heraufkäme! O Fischer, der mir dies sagte, du hast ein zu großes Unrecht getan, wenn du es mir im Bösen gesagt hast!" (Sandkühler 57). Dieser Text weist insgemein in die Zukunft. Der Junker, der in das Gehaben und Tun eines Ritters nun vollends eingeführt scheint, äußert sich im selben stolzen und daher immer verfrühten Ton, den er beim Köhler, bei Artus usw. schon angeschlagen hat. Scheinbar mit Recht. Ist er doch jetzt tatsächlich ein Eingeführter, der um Ritterliches Wissende und ein selbstbewußter Ritter. Das läßt sich sagen, solange man das Perceval innerliche Gleichgewicht entweder von Stolz und Demütigung (die immer ein Korrektiv darstellt) oder von Demut und Erhöhung (die nicht Korrektiv, aber Vollendung besagt) verkennt. Hier spielt die Dialektik eindeutig noch im ersten Gegensatzpaar: Perceval, der seinem größten Wohltäter (den er nicht als solchen erkennt) in überstürzter Empörung ‚Scham' und Schande wünscht, zwingt durch solches Gebaren seine eigene Schande und Demütigung herbei. Die ‚Dummheit und das Narrenspiel', im Innersten angelegt zu seinem und vieler anderer Heil, ist für seinen kurzen Verstand eben von zu weit her beabsichtigt, als daß er es durchschauen könnte. Er kann daher nur mit eiserner Konsequenz die Schande, die er in Kurzsichtigkeit seinem Retter wünschen möchte, auf sein eigenes Haupt laden. Da er aber Erwählter und Auserkorener *ist*, der per definitionem nicht nur sich erlöst, sondern die ganze Umwelt dazu, erfüllt sich dieser negative Wunsch auch wörtlich: er fügt auch dem Fischerkönig Unheil und Schande zu. Die Wahrheit dieses im Zorne ausgesprochenen Wunsches ist daher doppelt in der Zukunft des Geschehens verkoppelt: einerseits beschwört er in innerer Antithese zur wörtlichen Eindeutigkeit Percevals eigene Schande, andererseits verursacht er mit die Schande des Fischerkönigs und verhindert oder vertagt dessen Erlösung.

Percevals Verhalten beim Fischerkönig vor dem Graal ist letztlich nicht mehr bloßes Resultat seiner *niceté*, sondern auch Sündenfolge. Während das Schwertgeschenk noch seine Auserwähltheit und sein besonderes Schicksal zu symbolisieren scheint, sind die blutende Lanze und der Graal schon ziemlich ausgesprochen Zeichen von Percevals Versagen, d. h. sie werden es, da sie innerlich als Bewährungspunkte im Geschehen angelegt sind.

„Das Wort des weisen Edelmannes" (Sandkühler 60), das sein Herz und seinen Mund zu einer Frage, „wen man mit dem Graal bediene" (Sandkühler 61), untüchtig macht, ist allerdings Ausdruck einer üblen Autoritätshörigkeit. Zwar hätte er „von Herzen gern" gewußt, wen man damit bediene. Chrétien macht diesen inneren Zwiespalt in einem dreimaligen Anstoß mit derselben Wendung anschaulich (*cui l'an an sert* 3244/45; 3292/93; 3300/02). Von Mal zu Mal kommt aber Perceval die Mahnung Gornemants von Goort in den Sinn, und so verhält er seine Neugier. Man könnte eine Streitfrage daraus konstruieren, ob dieses in seinen Folgen so törichte Schweigen eine Folge der *niceté* oder eine Folge der an seiner Mutter begangenen Sünde sei. Am besten aber scheint es, alles in der Schwebe von Fragen-Wollen und tatsächlichem Nicht-fragen zu belassen und einen Akzent auf die begangene ‚Sünde' zu setzen. Denn Chrétien spricht sich selbst noch nicht eindeutig darüber aus.

Erst am kommenden Morgen, da Perceval mit seinem Pferd unter Lebensgefahr die Zugbrücke überschritten hat und nun von irgendeinem unsichtbaren Knappen Auskunft über das seltsame Geschehen im Graalsschloß heischt, erhält der Leser von Chrétien dafür einen Tip. Perceval ruft: „‚He da! . . . du, der die Brücke aufgezogen hat, sprich nun mit mir! Wo bist du, da ich dich nicht sehe? Tritt hervor, damit ich dich sehe und dich frage nach etwas, das ich wissen möchte.' So müht er sich *mit dummen Worten* . . ." (Sandkühler 62/63). Percevals Rede ist nicht dumm, weil er etwa bloß zu spät mit seinem Anliegen kommt, sondern weil sich in seinen Worten die alte Stumpfheit des Empfindens und die Verschlossenheit des innerlichen Hörens und Sehens auf den Mitmenschen ausdrückt. Jetzt, nachdem er gut genährt und ausgeschlafen ist, möchte er noch so schnell unter der Hand Auskunft haben über die seltsamen Geschehnisse vom vergangenen Abend. Während des Mahls jedoch kümmerte er sich kaum je um seinen kranken und offensichtlich leidenden Gastgeber, er begnügte sich lediglich mit einem mageren und wohleinstudierten höfischen Anstand. Diese Dummheit ist erworbene Dummheit und entspringt einem verstellten und unter Verschluß gehaltenen Herzen.

8. Bei der Begegnung mit seiner Cousine, die er unter einer Eiche weinend und schluchzend mit dem erschlagenen Geliebten auf dem Schoße antrifft, erhält Percevals *niceté* eine neue, in sich doppelwertige Bestimmung: die der Unwissenheit. Nachdem Perceval der Leidenden in einer etwas groben Objektivität sein Erlebnis im Graalsschloß erzählt hat, fragt diese ihn: „‚Wie heißet ihr mit Namen Freund?' Und der Junker, der seinen Namen nicht wußte, rät und spricht, er heiße Perceval der Walliser;

er weiß nicht, ob er die Wahrheit spricht oder nicht, jedoch spricht er wahr und weiß es nicht" (Sandkühler 65). Diese Stelle verträgt keinen Zusatz: Chrétien selbst erläutert in dem in sich verschlungenen Wortspiel von den-Namen-nicht-wissen und die-Wahrheit-sprechen und es-nicht-wissen vollkommen die Sachlage. Die solide Torheit Percevals bekommt in dieser ihm gleichsam angeworfenen Ahnung seines Namens einen Zusatz von gänzlicher Unwissenheit, die nur noch umschlagen kann in ein im Höheren versichertes und aufgehobenes Wissen. Eine Erklärung[28]), die dieses Ahnen als eine plötzliche Bewußtseinserleuchtung und Ausschaltung der *niceté* ausdeuten möchte, trifft etwas Richtiges; es ist aber beizufügen, daß die *niceté* die Bedingung der Möglichkeit solchen Erahnens ist. Die Möglichkeit einer Erleuchtung ist identisch mit dem positiven Moment der *niceté*, die in Ansätzen schon einmal festgestellt werden konnte[29]). Denn erst gleichsam entschlackte *niceté*, das heißt nur ein totales Tor-werden und Nicht-wissen vermag — paradoxerweise — die Namens-findung zu begründen. Sonst verliert sie ihr Überraschungsmoment und ihren Kairos. Es wäre falsch, vergäße man hier den mittelalterlichen, kompositorischen Grundsatz[30]), wonach der Dichter typologisch nach Ähnlichkeit oder Gegensatz das Dichterische erreicht. Fierz-Monniers Interpretation der Namensfindung als Persönlichkeitsfindung scheint, so sehr sie Richtiges anvisiert, dieses Gesetz zu übergehen[31]). Im Moment, da

[28]) Frappier a. a. O. 60: „Sa surprise est grande quand il entend les reproches, et presque les malédictions de la pucelle; il reçoit un choc, bientôt suivi d'un autre — la nouvelle que sa mère est morte par sa faute —, et sous l'effet de ce choc un voile semble se déchirer en lui; on dirait qu'il entrevoit comme dans un éclair de conscience son être véritable, et cette brusque découverte d'un moi que jusqu'alors ignorait le *nice*, docile aux conseils et cependant rempli de confiance en lui-même, s'accompagne du sentiment douloureux d'une indignité et d'une faillite." Im Grunde aber hat sich das gesamte bisherige Dasein des *nice* in solchen Bewußtseinserleuchtungen abgespielt: er hörte nie zu, wenn ihm jemand etwas mitteilte, tat aber dennoch in einer ‚oberflächlichen', abstrakten und tiefenlosen Helle des Bewußtseins das Richtige!

[29]) Vgl. die zuvorkommende und ahnungsvolle Art, in der der Perceval zuerst begegnende Ritter den wallisischen Dummkopf anhört, oder die Begegnung Percevals mit Artus, das Verhalten des Narren und des ernsten Fräuleins, das bei seinem Anblick hell auflacht.

[30]) de Lubac, Der geistige Sinn der Schrift, Einsiedeln 1952, 34 Anm. 11.

[31]) Antoinette Fierz-Monnier, Initiation und Wandlung, Zur Geschichte des altfranzösischen Romans im zwölften Jahrhundert von Chrétien de Troyes zu Renaut de Beaujeu, Bern 1951, 66. Bezzolas Interpretation der Namensfindung vermag künstlerisch-kompositionelle mit psychologischen Gesichtspunkten glücklich zu vereinen (Le sens de l'aventure . . . 47 ff.).

Perceval über das Schicksal seiner Mutter, d. h. über ihren Tod aus Leid[32]),
über die Verhältnisse, unter denen der Reiche Fischerkönig krankt, und
über sein eigenes Versagen am Graalsschloß aufgeklärt wird, ist diese
völlig überraschende Art der Namensfindung die einzig richtige Replik,
soll beides ausgedrückt werden: nämlich Percevals gründliches Versagen
(seine Cousine nennt ihn *Perchevax li chaitis* 3582) u n d seine Auserwählung. Man müßte Augustins Formel über Gott, der sich in der Schrift
offenbart, als Erläuterung herbeiziehen: „mehr bedeutet als gedeutet"
(magis significatus quam demonstratus)[33]). Denn das Signum, das *Zeichen-
hafte* ist hier stärker als das Demonstratum, das Bezeichnete, das innerlich
und kausal Abgeleitete. Chrétien steht als Dichter in der Situation, in der
Sinn nicht anders mehr entstehen könnte, ohne daß ein Neues sich gebiert,
das auf nichts Früheres zurückzuführen ist. Das Neue ist die Namensfindung.
Daß Perceval nicht bis in seine seelischen Abgründe hinein durchleuchtet und
erhellt ist, beweist sein forsches Weiterreden, das in engem Zusammenhang
mit seiner schon oft und nachdrücklich festgehaltenen *niceté* zu denken ist.
Auch das weist auf den vornehmlich kompositorisch-typologischen Gehalt
dieser Namensfindung. Denn wie wollte man sonst die saloppe, dem
Volksmund abgehorchte Redewendung „Die Toten den Toten, die Lebenden den Lebenden", womit Perceval die Leiche des erschlagenen Ritters und das Andenken an seine tote Mutter im Herzen so leichthin über-
geht, in Zusammenhang bringen mit jener in die Seelenabgründe reichenden Persönlichkeitsfindung, die wohl eher einem modernen Empfinden
abgehandelt ist. Ein sicheres Kennzeichen, daß Perceval noch tief in seiner
niceté verstrickt ist, ist seine Bemerkung zu seiner Cousine: „Mir scheint
es eine große Torheit von Euch zu sein, daß Ihr hier so einsam diesen
Toten bewacht" (Sandkühler 66). Es ist beinahe ein Indiz für Percevals
eigene ‚*folie*', wenn er sie andern glaubt zusprechen zu müssen. Hingegen
hat die Namensfindung sehr wohl etwas zu tun mit Symbolismus[34]). So,

---

32) Die Erklärung Jean Marx' (La légende Arthurienne et le Graal, Paris 1952,
207 und 318 Anm. 1) zu dieser Stelle, wonach es eine Absurdität Chrétiens sei,
den Tod der Mutter durch Percevals Seelenhärte zu erklären, da er ja mit ihrer
vollen Zustimmung die Waldeseinsamkeit verlasse, entbehrt der Grundlage.
Vgl. dazu Frappier a. a. O. 60 Anm. 1.

33) Augustin, C. Maxim. arian. 2, 10; PL 42, 811. Zitiert bei de Lubac a. a. O. 45
Anm. 36.

34) „Les noms étaient eux aussi, pour les philosophes, des signes efficaces des
réalités qu'ils désignaient" (M.-D. Chenu, La théologie au douzième siècle,
Paris 1957, 164). Was für den Philosophen galt, war noch viel mehr gültig für
die Dichter. Man denke an Alanus von Lille.

daß Perceval durch seinen Namen ,Perceval der Walliser' zum erstenmal den „Urgrund seiner Persönlichkeit" (Bezzola) ahnt, aber auch so, daß er als ein situierter Mikrokosmos in den gewaltigen Makrokosmos eingefügt und so ein Zeichen im großen Systemzusammenhang aller Bezeichneten wird. Persönlichkeitsfindung wäre ein Loten in die Tiefe der menschlichen Person, eine Initiation in die seelischen Tiefengründe, mithin eine Gegebenheit der Vertikale. Was aber mit Perceval geschieht, ist eher eine Erstreckung im Horizontalen und Ebenen des epischen Verlaufs. Die Zeit reicht eigentlich gar nicht hin, die Tiefe seiner Person ans Licht der Erzählung zu heben. Chrétien erzählt echt mittelalterlich der Oberfläche nach (nicht im modernen Sinn!), d. h. im Sinn eines Zeichenteppichs, in dem jedes Zeichen einen Eigenwert nur dadurch hat, daß es zur Gestalt des Ganzen seine Genauigkeit beiträgt. Die Genauigkeit dieser Namensfindung liegt hier in der inneren Dialektik von positiver, bis zur unbewußten Denomination an sich selber reichenden Unwissenheit und negativer, in die Sünde sich erstreckender Torheit. Diese Denkart ist in einem hohen Sinn einfach, aber doch komplex genug, daß sie einem modernen Bewußtsein entgehen kann.

9. In der Begegnung mit dem Fräulein vom Zelt und Orilus von der Heide findet Perceval eine geradezu bewegte Sprache, in der er das so offensichtliche Leid des Fräuleins beklagt und seine Hilfe anbietet. Man darf diese Szene daher in antitypischen Gegensatz zur eben geschilderten stellen. Klang dort Percevals Rede noch hart und einigermaßen salopp, so findet er hier ein sprachlich vermitteltes Mitgefühl zu seinem Nächsten. Und wer kann ihm im Momente näher stehen als dieses Fräulein, dessen Unglück s e i n Vergehen mitbewirkte? Die ruchlose und in sich fragwürdige Art, wie Orilus seine Eifersucht gegenüber Perceval begründet (daß nämlich eine Frau überall siegen will, außer im Liebeskampf, wo sie sich gern mit Gewalt nehmen lasse), gipfelt in dem selbstgerechten Spruch: „Wer eine Torheit begeht, muß es büßen, damit er sich vor Rückfall hüte" (Sandkühler 70). In charmant kühner Manier antwortet Perceval, daß e r jener sei, der die Jungfrau gegen ihren Willen geküßt und die Pasteten und den Wein zu sich genommen habe, „soviel ich wollte; hierin handelte ich wohl kaum als Tor" (Sandkühler 70). Gab sich Perceval kurz vorher noch als reiner Tor, der seine Unwissenheit derart strapazierte, daß sich ihm auf beinahe magischem Weg sein Name in der Helle des Bewußtseins einstellte, so steht hier ein Perceval, dem die Torheit zur Attitüde und Anlaß zum Scherzen geworden ist. Gerade weil er weiß, daß er damals als

Tor handelte (der Ansatz einer Reflexion äußert sich hier!), kann er das Nebensächliche untertreibend als nicht zu seiner Torheit gehörig bezeichnen. Daß er Pasteten aß und Wein trank, wird nun zum witzgeladenen Gegenstück der ernstzunehmenden Torheit, die er an dem Fräulein im Zelt beging, indem er ihr Ring und Kuß raubte. Der Witz könnte der Szene die Schwere rauben, stünde nicht doch ein Kampf auf Leben und Tod bevor, den Perceval natürlich siegreich beenden wird.

Die epischen Klammern, deren eine sich schon im Kampf mit Orilus geschlossen hat[35]), beginnen sich nun konsequent nach und nach zu schließen. Denn wie sich Orilus am Hofe Artus' als Gefangener stellt, ist es der Narr, diese auffällige Kommentar- und Schlüsselfigur auf dem Wege Percevals, der mit der Jungfrau zusammen, die der Seneschall Keu geschlagen hatte, Percevals ritterliche Legitimität als Rächer immer neu dokumentiert und Percevals Kommen gleichsam innerweltlich für den Artushof eschatologisch anzeigt: „Herr Keu, so Gott mich segne, dies werdet Ihr wahrhaftig büßen, und es wird in Bälde sein" (Sandkühler 76).

10. In der Blutstropfenszene[36]) darf man vielleicht die schönste und stärkste Auswirkung von Percevals *niceté* sehen. Eine am Hals von einem Falken verwundete Gans hat drei Blutstropfen in den Schnee fallen lassen, die Perceval mit dem unberührten Weiß des Schnees zusammen ans Antlitz seiner Freundin erinnern. Er, der eben noch erstmals die Augen zu einem in sich gültigen Dasein des liebenden Mitgefühls zu seinem Nächsten aufgeschlagen hat (im Kampf und im Streitgespräch mit Orilus), versinkt nun in eine schlafähnliche Verzückung, in der er nur noch seiner Geliebten gedenkt. *Si pense tant que il s'oblie* (4202): das Denken strömt mit einer unerklärlichen Gewalt in ihn ein. Eine im Mittelalter nicht unverständliche geistige Vertauschung und Konkretisierung der Phantasmata vollzieht sich, da Perceval vom abstrakten Rot-Weiß der Blutstropfen im Schnee her einkehrt in die Innerlichkeit seines Seelenraumes, wo die Geliebte in voll erblühter Gestalt wohnt. Die conversio

---

35) Würde Perceval Orilus von der Heide nicht begegnen und ihn im Kampf nicht besiegen, dann wäre die Szene mit dem Fräulein im Zelt episch ungesichert, d. h. hätte keinen Sinngehalt im erzählerischen Ablauf. Nur indem Perceval in dieser zweiten Begegnung die Möglichkeit geboten ist, seine frühere Torheit durch ritterliche Tat aufzuheben, ratifiziert er seine Unschuld und damit den Fortgang der Erzählung.

36) Zur Blutstropfenszene vgl. auch R. R. Bezzola, Le sens de l'aventure et de l'amour, 19—32. Neuerdings auch: E. Köhler, Die drei Blutstropfen im Schnee, Bemerkungen zu einem neuen Deutungsversuch, GRM 9 (1959) 421—425.

ad phantasmata, sonst gern als eine Wendung ins Äußerliche der Umwelt gedeutet, wird hier dichterisch dialektisch eingebogen in eine Wesensschau, in der das Abstrakte erst innerlich zur Gestalt zusammenwächst und sich im innerlich geschauten Leib konkretisiert. Man muß die Stelle hören, um ihren Schmelz zu verstehen: „Als Perceval den Schnee aufgewühlt sah, auf dem die Gans lag und das Blut erblickte, das da erschien, stützte er sich auf seine Lanze, um dieses Bild zu betrachten; denn das Blut und der Schnee zusammen gleicht der frischen Farbe, die im Antlitz seiner Freundin war. Er träumt so tief, daß er sich ganz vergißt; denn ebenso lag in ihrem Antlitz das Rote auf dem Weißen, wie diese drei Blutstropfen auf dem weißen Schnee erschienen. Im Anschauen gefiel es ihm so sehr, daß ihm war, als sähe er die frische Farbe auf dem Antlitz seiner schönen Freundin selbst.

Perceval träumt über den Blutstropfen und bringt den ganzen Morgen dabei zu, bis die Knappen aus den Zelten kamen und ihn da träumen sahen. Sie dachten, er schliefe" (4194—4215; Sandkühler 78/79).

Chrétien bedient sich des Stilmittels der Wiederholung, die, indem sie dasselbe immer wieder angeht, den Ausdruck des Ganzen leistet. Denken, sich Vergessen, Träumen, Zeit verlieren (*muser*) und Schlafen sind die Worte, die das Geschehnis einkreisen und die Gestalt des versunkenen Perceval schließlich als einen dichterischen Ertrag hinstellen. Die *niceté* scheint aufgehoben in ihrer besseren, der Beschauung geneigten Bestimmung. Sagremor und Keu fallen notwendigerweise als Störenfriede, als zu Recht Verwundete aus dem Idyll aus (Chrétien meint triumphierend: „Wahr ist nun die Prophezeiung des Narren" Sandkühler 80). Es braucht schon einen in den letzten Raffinessen der höfischen Ambiance geübten Ritter, nämlich Gauvain, um den versunkenen Perceval mit höfischen Worten zum König Artus zu bitten. Auf Percevals Vorwurf, daß es gar nicht edel gewesen sei, ihn aus seinem Sinnen so brutal reißen zu wollen, meint Gauvain entschuldigend: „Wahrlich dieses Träumen war keineswegs unedel (*vilains*), sondern es war gar höfisch und süß (*cortois et dols*); und der war ein grober Narr (*fel et estols*), der Euer Herz davon ablenkte" (4457—4461; Sandkühler 82). Dieses Gespräch spielt auf der höchsten Ebene höfischen Anstandes und höfischer Repräsentation: Perceval steht Gauvain in nichts nach, im Gegenteil, er ist es, der solche Repräsentanz als einzig mögliche Form der Intersubjektivität überhaupt herausfordert. Indem Perceval sich ihr unterzieht, gibt er sich als ihr Meister und darf sie daher als eine petitio principii an seinen Mitmenschen delegieren, den er ebendadurch in den Rang eines Gesprächspartners erhebt. Die *acointance* (4490; amitié, familiarité, Roach Glossar, 311) ist deshalb als eine Verbrüderung unter Rittern zu verstehen, die sich auf der Höhe gesellschaftlichen Verständigt- und Vertrautseins gleichsam als kostbarste Frucht einer durch Anstand vermittelten Diskretion und Freundschaft ergibt. Ritterlich ist an Perceval mithin nichts mehr zu bekritteln. Nachdem er in Sagremor den durch Zorn überforderten Mut und in Keu den unritterlichen Neid und die falsche Mißgunst im Kampfe besiegt hat, bleibt nur noch die Begegnung mit Gauvain als positive Bestätigung dieses Siegs von Belang. Frappiers Feststellung läßt sich voll unterschreiben: „Il (Perceval) est devenu désormais l'égal du modèle de la chevalerie et de la courtoisie, il est comparable à un Gauvain" (a.a.O.71). Und weiter unten: „Un cycle se ferme, semble se fermer; si la déstinée de Perceval était seulement d'égaler un Gauvain, l'histoire pourrait s'arrêter là. Mais il n'en est rien" (a.a.O.). Daß dem nicht so ist, beweist der epische Ort dieser Szene. Schließlich ist nicht zu vergessen, daß Perceval von der Erzählung her eigentlich gar nicht vorbereitet und innerlich ausgewiesen ist für eine derart in die letzten Spitzen der höfischen *fine amor* und *amor de lonh* (amour de loin, Jaufré Rudel, chanson V; siehe Frappier, a.a.O. 70) reichende Exaltation des liebenden Gefühls. Eine der regulae amoris des Andreas Cappellanus erfüllt sich in Percevals Verhalten geradezu vorbildlich: Verus amans assidua sine intermissione coamantis imaginatione detinetur (zitiert bei Frappier, a.a.O.). Aber eben — Perceval bringt weder psychologische noch pädagogische Voraussetzungen dazu mit, es sei denn seine *niceté*, die hier als Öffnung und Disponibilität ins Gesellschaftliche und intim Zwischenmenschliche zu verstehen ist.

11. Obwohl Perceval in der Szene mit dem häßlichen Fräulein mit keinem Wort *nice* oder *sot* gescholten wird, geschieht hier etwas höchst Entscheidendes. Percevals Courtoisie ist voll präsent. Die Art, in der er Artus, die Königin und das von Keu gemaßregelte Fräulein begrüßt, beweist es. Artus' Begrüßungsrede beglaubigt Percevals gesellschaftliche Höhe und Vollkommenheit von höchster Warte; offiziell wird Perceval zum Auserwählten der Gesellschaft deklariert.

Die Ankunft des häßlichen Fräuleins erhält durch die höfisch-perfekte Art, in der die höfische Gesellschaft der Artusrunde Perceval aufnimmt, erhöhtes Gewicht. Wie ein Einbruch aus einer anderen Welt, die man als ein magisch und zauberhaft versponnenes Jenseits verstehen muß, wirkt ihr Auftritt. Auch ihre Worte scheinen Zauberworte: „Ach! Perceval. Fortuna ist kahl von hinten und behaart von vorne. Wehe über den, der dich grüßt, und der dir etwas Gutes wünscht und erbittet. Denn du hast Fortuna nicht bei dir gehalten, als du sie trafest! ..." (Sandkühler 85). Zum Märchenhaften gesellt sich die gestelzte Attitüde eines antik undurchschaubaren Schicksals. Perceval ist der Blinde, der sich dem Glück, dem er als Auserwählter begegnete, nicht zu stellen vermochte: er konnte es, obwohl es nahe war, nicht halten. Seine Signatur ist die eines gewaltigen, für viele unheilvollen Versagens. Er, der Auserwählte, der Vorherbestimmte vermochte seine Bestimmung und sein ihm aufgegebenes Schicksal nicht zu halten. Sein Versagen hat die Zauber, die den *Reichen Fischerkönig* umfingen, gefestigt, geradezu versteinert. Er, der dem Leid die Zunge zu lösen vermocht hätte, hat nur dazu beigetragen, sie weiter und stärker zu binden. „O wie unselig ist der, der eine so schöne Zeit sieht, wie sie schöner nicht sein kann, und doch noch wartet, bis eine schönere käme" (Sandkühler 85). Perceval hat den Kairos, seine Zeit verpaßt, er, der doch der Zeit immer zugleich voraus (in der Art wie er sein Handeln in die Zukunft entwarf) und ihr hintenach ist (in seiner ihm durch eine verfehlte, seiner Bestimmung nicht Rechnung tragende Erziehung aufgezwungenen *niceté*). Alle gesellschaftlichen Erfolge, die eben noch in den feierlichsten Formeln des höfischen Anstandes sich in einer totalen Notwendigkeit in den Worten Artus' exemplifizierten, werden durch das häßliche Fräulein wie von Geisterhand weggewischt. Niemand widerspricht ihr. Percevals Verfluchung scheint total. Er ist zwar nicht gesellschaftlich erledigt (niemand diffamiert ihn im Hinblick auf die höfische Gesellschaft, auch das häßliche Fräulein nicht), aber in seiner besten und gewagtesten Aufgabe verhindert. Seine Bestimmung, deren Erfüllung bisher sicher stand, ist ihm versagt, abgesprochen und annulliert. Sein Wesenskern ist Verfehlen, Versagen der ihm mitgegebenen Bestimmung. Daß Frauen ihre Gatten verlieren, Länder verheert werden und Jungfrauen verlassen und verwaist sein werden, ist Percevals Schuld. Wie ein kosmischer Schleier scheint sich Percevals Vergehen als ein Verhängnis über alles Lebendige zu spannen. „All diese Übel werden durch dich eintreffen" (Sandkühler 86); dieser Satz schließt kategorisch die gewaltige Reihung der Wehrufe. Das häßliche Fräulein wendet sich nun direkt und mit einem anderen Thema (die Belagerung der Jungfrau auf dem Berg Montesclaire) an den König und damit an die versammelte Runde der Ritter (damit auch diese in die epische Wende einbezogen werden und eine *Queste* unternehmen). Perceval aber scheint sich nicht lange bei seiner ihm als fruchtlos und verderblich gebrandmarkten *niceté* aufzuhalten: er beantwortet die Klagerede des häßlichen Fräuleins mit einem Schwur:

„er werde nicht zwei Nächte Zeit seines Lebens in derselben Herberge schlafen noch Kunde von seltsamen Wegen erfahren, ohne sie zu befahren, noch von einem Ritter, der besser wäre als ein anderer Ritter oder zwei, ohne mit ihm zu kämpfen, bis er erfahren habe, wen man mit dem Grale bediene, bis er die blutende Lanze gefunden habe und ihm die klare Wahrheit gesagt worden sei, warum sie blute. Keine Mühe will er scheuen und nie davon ablassen!" (Sandkühler 86/87). Dieser Schwur, so verklausuliert und verschroben er erscheinen könnte, ist Zeichen von Percevals Auserwählung („Perceval . . . ruft *etwas ganz anderes: . . .*" sc. als die anderen Ritter, Sandkühler 86) und seines nun auf ein Einziges, Einfaches gerichteten Lebens. Gral und blutende Lanze werden nun Horizont und Ziel seines Suchens, seiner vollen ritterlichen Existenz. Ausgespart ist alles Fremde, das nicht in den Lebensraum dieser Suche gehört. Selbst das Leben am Hofe des Königs Artus, das eben noch so glanzvoll in einem Höhepunkt gefiel, ist als ein Ungehöriges aus Percevals Dasein ausgeklammert.

Hier begegnet uns Percevals *niceté* gleichzeitig von ihrer befremdlichsten wie von ihrer erfreulichsten Seite. Einerseits scheint es klar, daß den vom häßlichen Fräulein vorgetragenen Wehrufen nichts, aber auch gar nichts von seiten Percevals entgegengesetzt werden kann. Die Wehrufe sind absolut, sie lassen keinen Raum für ihre Widerlegung. Das Unheil ist als ein unaufhaltsames, unbedingtes dargestellt. Percevals Schwur ist ein reines Trotzdem, ein Dennoch. Sein Beginnen ist absurd, weil es sich gegen die eindeutigen Enthüllungen des häßlichen Fräuleins richtet. Perceval ist der Dumme, weil er Unmögliches erstrebt; er ist aber andererseits auch der Auserwählte, der seinen Weg über alles Unheil hinweg nimmt. Was wir beim ersten Auszug (aus der Waldeinsamkeit) in Ansätzen feststellen konnten, läßt sich hier mit voller Eindeutigkeit sagen: Percevals *niceté*, so krud und töricht sie unverkennbar ist, hat ihren Grund in einer geheimen Symbiose mit seiner Auserwählung, ja man kann noch weitergehen und sagen: die *niceté* kann sich geradezu als ein Stigma seiner Auserwählung erweisen[37]). Sie ist rein stilistisch schon die Kennzeichnung einer Besonderung, durch die der Held aus dem gleichmäßigen Strom des Epischen emanzipiert und für ein höheres Geschick freigestellt wird.

12. Die Szene, da Perceval den heiligen Einsiedler aufsucht, bietet wiederum ein völlig neues und ungewohntes Bild von Percevals *niceté*. Fünf

---

[37]) E. Köhler, Ideal und Wirklichkeit 190: „Die Simplizität des Helden unterstreicht seine Berufung."

Jahre sind seit dem Auszug der Ritter des Artushofes auf ihre verschiedenen Questen vergangen. Was mit Perceval in dieser Zeit geschehen ist, faßt Chrétien in 20 Versen zusammen (6217—6237). Über Ritterruhm hat er in dieser Zeit wahrlich nicht zu klagen: sechzig ausgezeichnete Ritter schickte er in diesen fünf Jahren als Gefangene an den Hof Artus'. Aber er hat das Gedächtnis so sehr verloren, daß er sich Gottes nicht mehr erinnert (*Ot si perdue la miemoire / Que de Dieu ne li sovient mais* 6218/6219). Er hat kein Münster mehr betreten und Gott und sein Kreuz nicht mehr angebetet. Obwohl er sonst jede schwierige Aufgabe gemeistert hat, hat er Gral und Lanze nicht mehr gefunden. Das bedeutet: im Maß als er sich ritterlichen Ruhm vor der Welt erworben hat, hat er vor Gott und seinen in Gral und Lanze verkörperten Symbolen versagt. In kürzester Zeit (so, daß Chrétien in diesem Fall wiederum für psychologische Motivierungen und Kausalitäten gar keine Zeit mehr findet) hat er sein innerweltliches Ziel hoher Ritterschaft erreicht, damit aber auch das geistliche Rittertum im Sinn einer Militia Christi verfehlt. So hat er auch jeden Sinn für Zeit verloren, denn Zeit ist dem mittelalterlichen Menschen nur verständlich durch die Zeit Christi, die sich in den Rhythmen des Kirchenjahres veranschaulicht. Die Szene des Anfangs, wo der törichte Perceval den fünf Rittern im Wald begegnet, scheint sich nun antitypisch, d. h. mit umgekehrten Vorzeichen und neuem *sen* zu wiederholen. Drei Ritter und zehn Edelfrauen in Bußgewändern und barfuß begegnen Perceval mitten in einer Einöde. Perceval ist hoch zu Roß und voll bewaffnet. Seine Erscheinung ruft bei den Rittern und den Edelfrauen ein gewaltiges Erstaunen hervor: „Lieber guter Herr, glaubt Ihr denn nicht an Jesus Christus, der das Neue Gesetz schrieb und den Christen gab? Wahrlich es ist nicht recht und billig, an dem Tage, da Jesus Christus starb, Waffen zu tragen, sondern es ist ein großes Unrecht" (Sandkühler 112). Mit diesen Worten hat die Szene schon ihr ganzes Gewicht und Abgrenzung gegenüber der Begegnung des jungen Perceval mit den fünf Rittern. Frappier erklärt sehr treffend: „les cinq chevaliers de passage dans la forêt galloise avaient révélé la chevalerie mondaine à Perceval, et, depuis, le *nice* s'était élevé très haut sur le plan humain; mais devant ces pieux chevaliers et ces pieuses dames, qui représentent pour l'heure le divin, il est de nouveau dans un état de *niceté* à peu près totale" (a. a. O. 76). Mit anderen Worten: am Karfreitag, da sich Percevals Rittertum auch in seiner geistlichen Dimension auszuweisen hätte, demonstriert Perceval notwendigerweise und in strenger Angleichung an sein erstes Abenteuer mit Rittern seine *niceté* in einem vollumfänglichen Sinn. Allerdings ist ihm damit auch seine Gabe, in direkter und unverstellter Art seinen Nächsten auszufragen, wieder gegeben. So fragt er sich denn durch zum Geheimnis dieses Tages, „an dem man das Kreuz anbeten und seine Sünden beweinen muß" (Sandkühler 113). Dabei erfährt er auch den Weg zum heiligen Einsiedler, der ihm helfen kann. Die innere Verkrustung ist nun gebrochen, und mit den Tränen strömt auch Percevals Seele hervor:

> Et cil en son chemin s'en entre,
> Qui sozpiroit del cuer del ventre
> Por che que mesfais se sentoit
> Vers Dieu, dont molt se repentoit;
> Plorant s'en va tot le boschage. (6333—6337)

Schuldgefühl und Reue sind hier, wie es christlich nicht anders sein kann, rein aufeinander bezogen und gemischt. In dieser Gesinnung kniet sich Perceval „demütig und weinend" (*simple et plorant* 6351) vor dem Einsiedler hin, umfaßt seine Füße, faltet seine Hände und bittet ihn um Rat.

> „Sire, fait il, bien a cinc ans
> *Que je ne soi ou je me fui,*
> Ne Dieu n'amai ne Dieu ne crui,
> N'onques puis ne fis se mal non." (6364—6367)

Zu diesem globalen Schuldgeständnis fügt er die Erzählung von der Lanze und vom Gral, nach denen er nicht gefragt hat.

Hier ist einzuhalten: die Worte: *simple et plorant* sind für unsere Untersuchung von Gewicht. Perceval kann sich nicht analysieren. Er trägt seine ganze Schuld, d. h. seine ganze schuldhafte Existenz vor den Richter in der Beichte. Nichts läßt er aus. Er ist als ganzer Mensch schuldig vor Gott, weint und bereut als ganzer Mensch, wirft sich als ganzer Mensch in totaler Demut und in totalem Selbstverzicht vor dem Einsiedler nieder. Die Simplizität seines Wesens, die sich bis ins Komische erstreckt, ist nun aber auch diaphan auf das Geheimnis seiner Auserwählung, seiner einzigartigen Möglichkeit, als einziger von allen Rittern der Tafelrunde dem höchsten Anspruch zu genügen und zu entsprechen. Der Ausruf eines himmlischen Ehrenmannes in der ‚Queste del Saint Graal‘[38] über Perceval: „*Ha! Perceval, ... toz jorz seras tu nices!*" hat eine tiefberechtigte Bedeutung. Denn Perceval i s t bis zuletzt der Tor, allerdings ein innerlich (aber nicht aufgrund psychologisch evidenter ‚Entwicklungen‘) gedemütigter und bekehrter Tor. Darum aber nicht minder Tor. Die Bauernschläue,

---

38) Edition Albert Pauphilet (Les classiques français du moyen-âge 33), Paris 1949, 112, 25/26.

das Tolpatschige und allzu rasch Zugriffige seiner *niceté* ist ihm abhanden gekommen; seine Simplizität ist dafür mit Seelenfrische und strahlender Durchsichtigkeit erfüllt. Bestand seine *niceté* einst in einer Taubheit der inneren Sinne, so ist sie nun einfache Durchsichtigkeit, eine einzigartige Sinnhaftigkeit ('Sinn' im alten Wortsinn als 'Weg') fürs Göttliche und seinen Anspruch an den Ritter. Er kann und darf daher gar nichts über seine Sünde im einzelnen ausmachen. Der Einsiedler hingegen kann diese Sünde als ein Heiliger (Einsicht in die Sünde hat christlich eben nur ein Heiliger!), der er ist, dingfest machen und sie sachlich nennen: „Bruder, gar sehr hat dir eine Sünde geschadet, *von der du gar nichts ahnst:* das war der Schmerz, den deine Mutter um dich hatte, als du von ihr fortrittest; denn ohnmächtig fiel sie zu Boden am Brückenkopfe vor dem Tore, und an diesem Schmerze ist sie gestorben. So fügte es sich wegen der Sünde, die du damit auf dich geladen hast, daß du nicht nach der Lanze noch nach dem Grale fragtest, und manch andere Übel sind dadurch über dich gekommen. Du hättest auch nicht solange das Leben ausgehalten, wenn sie nicht bei Gott dem Herrn Fürsprache für dich eingelegt hätte, das wisse wohl! Denn ihr Gebet hatte solche Kraft, daß Gott um ihretwillen dich ansah und vor Tod und Kerker behütete. Die Sünde schnitt dir das Wort auf der Zunge ab, als du die Lanzenspitze, die nie aufhörte zu bluten, vor dir sahst, und du fragtest nicht nach dem Grunde. Als du dich nicht erkundigtest, wen man mit dem Grale bedient, da hattest du ganz irren Sinn (6414: *fol sens eüs*) . . ." (Sandkühler 115). Ein verrückter, irrer Sinn war es damals; nun ist es Demut, die Perceval es möglich macht, all das zu verstehen. Dem Text ist eigentlich nichts beizufügen, er ist klar und verständlich in sich. Die Schuld, die wir noch bei der Gralsszene nur mit Zweifeln seinem Wegzug von der Mutter zuschreiben konnten, ist hier lokalisiert und genauestens bestimmt. Die *niceté* ist in sich eine indifferente Anlage[39]) und läßt sich bei entsprechender Anstrengung mühelos in Demut und christliche simplicitas wandeln, die sich mit völlig ein-fältigen Einsichten zufrieden geben kann. Das Geschehen beim Einsiedler schließt demnach mit einem durchaus schlichten Satz: „So erkannte Perceval wieder, daß Gott am Freitag den Tod er-

---

[39]) Das soll nicht heißen: die *niceté* sei innerhalb des Romans eine bloße Anlage, die sich nicht äußern kann. Im Gegenteil, sie ist indifferente Anlage erst durch die Konkretionen ihrer epischen Erscheinungen. Die Bilder ihrer Erscheinungen evozieren erst so etwas wie ihre Idee. Der epische Verlauf führt daher von den vermischten (d. h. das Letzte nicht anzielenden) Bildwirklichkeiten zur idealen Vollendung, wo *niceté* nichts anderes mehr besagt als reine Disponibilität, reines Verfügenlassen.

litten hatte und gekreuzigt wurde. An Ostern empfing Perceval würdig die heilige Kommunion" (Sandkühler 116). Schlichter läßt sich das Resultat der Begegnung zwischen Ritter und Einsiedler nicht mehr fassen. Das Einfachste ist hier gerade gut genug, das überwältigende Geheimnis von Percevals Anlage und Bestimmung in verborgenere Einheit zu stiften. Ein Forschen über den weiteren Verlauf der Handlung, der uns durch Chrétiens Tod verborgen ist, wäre müßig. Daß die Lanze und der Gral nicht in der leeren Bedeutungslosigkeit eines stumpfen Motivs verblieben wären — hätte Chrétien Zeit und Kraft gefunden, den Roman fertig zu schreiben —, scheint sicher. Das Schicksal Percevals ist zu sehr nach einer letzten Bestimmtheit gerichtet und gezielt. Das Wie aber ist bloß zu erraten.

Außer Frage steht die Notwendigkeit einer christlichen Interpretation des Percevalromans. Die leibliche Verwandtschaft zwischen dem Einsiedler und Perceval steht ganz unter dem Zeichen der im Glauben vereinten Christen und ist zu verstehen durch die nachfolgende Ermahnung zur Gottes- und Nächstenliebe. Auch der Hinweis auf die Messe, der Perceval, wenn immer möglich, beiwohnen soll, darf als Hinweis auf das Liebesmahl der Gemeinschaft, auf die Agape genommen werden. Zum einzelnen, auf Gott in der Liebe durchsichtigen Menschen tritt damit die Gemeinschaft, die als Kirche und Braut in Einfältigkeit durchsichtig zu sein hat auf ihren Bräutigam und Herrn. Hier und anderswo die *niceté* als eine abenteuerliche Zugabe des Dichters ausklammern zu wollen, hieße den *sen* des ganzen Romans verkennen. Die *niceté* gehört zur unübersehbaren Reihe von Punkten im Werke Chrétiens, wo *matière* und *sen* sich zu einer höheren, über das Kunstwerk in seiner Vereinzelung hinauswachsenden Einheit und Vorbildlichkeit treffen. Sie ist, da jede ethische und psychologische Aufrechnung der epischen Momente in ‚Entwicklungen' bei Chrétien fehl geht, ein eminent künstlerisches Merkmal Percevals. Das heißt, die Kunst des Romans geschieht, neben anderen typologischen und in sich dialektischen Merkmalen, zu großen Teilen durch die *niceté*, die gerade durch ihre ein Einfaches anvisierende Bedeutung ein Einfaches in der Hand des Künstlers wird, das sich so oder so, d.h. unter den verschiedensten Bestimmungen dem Helden applizieren läßt.

Zusammenfassung

Bei einer zusammenraffenden Überschau über die *niceté* Percevals gilt es Folgendes zu berücksichtigen: die punktuelle, die einzelnen Stationen aufreihende Überschau darf grundsätzlich nicht mit der Suggestion einer irgendwie gearteten ‚Entwicklung' verwechselt werden; der Begriff der ‚Entwicklung' scheint in diesen Zusammenhängen fehl am Platz und fälscht das Anliegen von einst in eines von heute. Wichtig ist hingegen der Begriff der ‚epischen Station': er läßt der mittelalterlichen Ästhetik mit ihren vorwiegend formalen Kategorien (der typologischen Konstruktion usw.) genügend Entfaltungsraum[40]). Es werden daher immer solche epischen Stationen gemeint sein, wenn im Folgenden die einzelnen Szenen nach der Zählschnur aufgereiht und im Hinblick auf die *niceté* durchleuchtet werden.

1. Percevals *niceté* ist ‚erzieherisch' bewerkstelligt, künstlich geschaffen und künstlich erhalten (indem Perceval von klein auf die gesellschaftliche Welt in ihrer ständischen Stufung durch das Arrangement der Waldeinsamkeit vorenthalten wird). Diese an einem Menschen und mit ihm inszenierte *niceté* hat von daher in der Realität ihrer Erscheinungsweise einen doppelten Aspekt:

a) da sich Perceval seiner künstlich arrangierten Existenzweise nicht bewußt sein kann, i s t er naturverbunden, rustikal und direkt in seinen Äußerungen gegenüber den Mitmenschen. Er trägt die ‚Dummheit' seines durch Vergesellschaftung unverstellten Daseins als zweidimensionale Eigenschaft zur Schau, *positiv* als Naturverbundenheit und intersubjektive Direktheit, *negativ* als totale Unkenntnis der geistigen und realen ‚Umwelt' und als radikaler Mangel an Reflexion über sein eigenes Dasein.

b) Percevals gesellschaftliche, nicht aktuierte Potenz, d. h. seine unbesetzte Stellung im mittelalterlichen Ordogefüge, für die er wesensmäßig angelegt ist, wird zur spürbaren Realität eines Mangels, der durch das providentiell gesicherte Gralskönigtum eine das Geschick Percevals vorwärtstreibende Note erhält. Diese reale und von Anfang auf den Gral hingeordnete Artung Percevals steht als ernst zu nehmende Realität in ironischem Gegensatz zu seinem faktischen Wald- und Jägerdasein, kann sich also nur

---

[40]) Erich Auerbach weist in seiner Schrift: Typologische Motive in der mittelalterlichen Literatur, Krefeld 1953, hin auf die völlig eigenartige ‚Geschehensauffassung' der typologischen Betrachtungsweise: „die typologische Interpretation ... verknüpft zwei zeitlich und kausal weit voneinander entfernte Ereignisse, reißt jedes von ihnen aus dem Zusammenhang, in dem es geschah, heraus und verknüpft sie durch einen beiden gemeinsamen Sinn. Sie gibt also nicht eine kontinuierliche Entwicklung der Geschichte, sondern eine Interpretation derselben" (13). Selbst Auerbachs nun folgende Hinweise aufs Erlösungsdrama im dichterischen Geschehen können im Zusammenhang des Artusromans von Belang sein, besonders für Perceval.

als Form seiner *niceté* äußern. So sehr die ihm begegnenden Ritter ‚merken‘, was es mit Perceval im Letzten für eine Bewandtnis hat (wenigstens einer der Ritter merkt das sehr eindeutig), so sehr finden sie ihn auch ‚dumm‘.

2. Perceval kann sich aus der Schwebe dieser in sich doppelwertigen Situation (arrangiertes, unreflektiertes Walddasein — Gralsbestimmung) nur durch (teilweise bewußte) *Schuld* lösen: er tötet seine Mutter, indem er sie verläßt. Auch die Schuld trägt das Gesicht seiner *niceté*.

3. Bei der ersten Begegnung mit der Welt, beim ersten Versuch einer In-Eins-Setzung von Außen und Innen, d.h. beim ersten Versuch einer Vergesellschaftung seiner selbst, kann Perceval nur als eminent *komischer Naivling* und Tor erscheinen. Das Fräulein im Zelt sieht an ihm mit Erstaunen nur seine Torheit und *niceté*. Da der Tor aber schon schuldig ist, muß er selbst in seiner heitersten Rolle Schuld zeugen.

4. Die Szene am Artushof, der Mord am *Roten Ritter*: Percevals *niceté* ist nun vollends doppelgesichtig und ambivalent. Einerseits identisch mit zügelloser *Frechheit*, Anmaßung und törichtem, unanständigem Gehaben spürt der Hof gerade in seinem obersten Vertreter, in Artus, Percevals geheime, noch unerfüllte *Verheißung*. Die Jungfrau, die sechs Jahre nicht mehr lachte, und der Narr bestätigten das im positiven Sinn, der Seneschall Keu im Negativen durch seinen Neid.
Der Mord am *Roten Ritter* beweist Percevals freches Draufgängertum, aber auch sein Vermögen, dem Rittertum selbst in seinen besten Vertretern beizukommen. Gerade durch seine *niceté*. Dazu kommt wieder *die komische Seite* seiner Torheit: er weigert sich, seine Torenkleider auszuziehen.

5. In der Begegnung mit Gornemant von Goort bindet Perceval einen Zug seiner *niceté* auf den Rat seines älteren und diskreten Freundes an ein Gesellschaftliches. Seine *Stummheit*, bisher als freche und lieblose Antwortlosigkeit gegenüber dem Nächsten öfters geübt, wird verlängert in die Liebe zum Nächsten und zu einem Gebot der Diskretion. Zugleich erinnert sich Perceval seiner Mutter. Das bedeutet erste Einkehr und Abkehr von der Schuld, die dadurch aber weder aufgehoben noch getilgt ist.

6. Percevals *niceté* hat in der Begegnung mit Blanchefleur vornehmlich einen unschuldigen Charakter. Das Präludium seiner Stummheit gegenüber der bedrängten Blanchefleur wirkt amüsant. Das unschuldige Verhalten aber, das Perceval in der Bettszene als selbstverständliche Liebe

zu der ihm Nächsten entfaltet, hat für höfische Ohren gerade in seiner Natürlichkeit etwas Enttäuschendes und dadurch *wunderbar Unschuldiges*; Percevals *niceté* eröffnet ein Herzgeheimnis, indem sie sich der Frucht der Liebe vorerst enthält. Indem Perceval die in die letzte Geschlechtlichkeit reichende Vereinigung in Liebe als ein Zukünftiges ausspart, macht er sich zum Helden einer grenzenlosen Disponibilität. Er wird verfügbar für die weiten Ansprüche zuerst seiner Liebe zu Blanchefleur, dann für die Ansprüche der Gesellschaft, zuletzt (und daher auch zuerst) für die Ansprüche Gottes, der ihm das Gralskönigtum vorbestimmt hat. Das Herzgeheimnis seiner *niceté* ist daher Herzenseinfalt, *Disponibilität*, Demut und Unschuld.

7. Die Szene mit Blanchefleur war erst Lichtblick, noch keine Lichtfülle. Die Schuld hat auf ihre Stunde gewartet. Die gewonnene Disponibilität wird überdeckt von einer üblen *Autoritätshörigkeit*, ein Aspekt der *niceté*, der sich in der ständigen Berufung auf die Lehren der Mutter anzeigte. Perceval schweigt vor dem Gral und fragt nicht, wen man damit bediene. Die ursprüngliche, künstliche Dummheit bricht nochmals durch, nun zwar im Zenit von Percevals Laufbahn. Perceval müßte seine Torheit merken, hätte er sie nicht mit *Schuld* verschwistert.

8. In der Begegnung mit seiner Cousine zeichnet sich in Perceval eine strenge Dialektik von *Nicht-wissen* (das Getane, d. h. das Unterlassene) und *Wissen* (Namensfindung — Wesenserkennung) ab. Wissen und Nicht-Wissen sind Aspekte der einen *niceté*.

9. In der Szene, da Perceval den Kampf mit Orilus von der Heide aufnimmt und gewinnt, wird Vergangenheit bewältigt. Perceval ist der Souveräne, der Gewitzigte, der selbst aus seiner Torheit nun den Nutzen eines Siegs zu schlagen versteht. Das Spielerische darf aber nicht hinwegtäuschen über die ernste Art, in der Perceval seine *niceté* mit *Mitleid* vertauscht und an der Jungfrau vom Zelt gutzumachen sucht, was er einst an ihr verbrach.

10. In der Blutstropfenszene zeitigt das Heile, das in der Begegnung mit Blanchefleur als Blüte begann, die Frucht einer großen Erfüllung. Die *Kontemplation der Geliebten* ist nicht anders möglich als vor dem ambivalenten Hintergrund der *niceté*. Einzig diese *amour fol*, die sich in die Geliebte hinein vergißt und in sie sich vertört, hat diese innere Gewalt, die sie vor der Gesellschaft (wenigstens vor den besten ihrer Vertreter: Gauvain, Artus) als ein Zeichen von Adel legitimiert. Damit erweist sich die

Liebe als die beste Partnerin der *niceté*: sie ist ihr gleich in der Kraft der Selbstaufgabe und Selbstübergabe, der Disponibilität.

11. Der Auftritt des häßlichen Fräuleins schlägt wieder dunklere Töne an. Perceval muß sich die Vorwürfe eines beinahe kosmisch sich auswirkenden *Versagens* und eines unüberholbaren *Versäumens* gefallen lassen: seine nun in schrecklichem Licht erscheinende *niceté* ist das Stigma eines, der zwar nicht das Gesellschaftliche, dafür aber seine vieles umfassende, transzendierende Bestimmung verfehlt hat. Andererseits schafft Perceval mit seinem trotzigen Schwur das fait accompli eines radikalen *Neubeginns*. Er beantwortet eine Torheit mit einer neuen und wird sein Ziel erreichen.

12. Beim Einsiedler ist Perceval in einem Zustand erneuter, beinahe totaler *niceté*. Alles wächst ihm nun zu: seine begangene Sünde, aber auch Reue und Leid; völlige Verlorenheit, aber auch letzte und köstlichste Geborgenheit in der Lossprechung. Nichts kann mehr ausgespart werden, weil sein ganzes Wesen *Durchsichtigkeit, Einfalt* und *Demut*[41]) geworden ist. Seine Simplicitas erweist sich als letzter und einzig gültiger Nenner seiner Torheit, und man ist versucht, diese Torheit als der *matière* tiefsten *sen* zu bezeichnen.

Wollte man schließlich Parzivals *tumpheit* mit Percevals *niceté* vergleichen, so käme man zur Einsicht, daß die Vorprägung des Toren im französischen Roman weit schlüssiger, stimmiger und deutlicher ist als dessen Darstellung durch Wolfram. Was bei Chrétien kausal verknüpft ist (*niceté* und simplicitas aufgrund faßbarer Schuld und Sühne!), ist bei Wolfram Spiel in Analogien und Dialektizismen: Parzivals *tumpheit* ist weniger Eigenschaft des Protagonisten (was bei Chrétien die *niceté* ist) denn dessen undefinierbarer Personkern. Das Kausale des geschichtlichen Ablaufs bei Chrétien schafft Luzidität, während das Atmosphärische, Undefinierbare von Wolframs Analogiewelt den Zuhörer immer im Kern seines Wesens anspricht, ohne doch zum Beispiel den Wandel von Parzivals *tumpheit* zu *diemüete* erzählerisch deutlich zu machen (im Gegenteil, die Zeit, in der sich Parzivals innere Wandlung vorbereitet, bleibt im Dunkeln). Letztlich handelt es sich beim deutschen und französischen Dichter um eine je eigene Stillage, deren nationale Typisierung äußerst fragwürdig, deren Deutlichkeit jedoch nichts zu wünschen übrig läßt. Während Percevals endlich

---

41) Vgl. dazu die schöne Darstellung bei W. Henzen, Die Vorprägung der Demut im Parzival durch Chrestien, PBB 80 (1958) (West) 422—443.

sichtbar gewordene simplicitas mit der Gewalt erzählerischer Notwendig-keit den Leser in seinem Nachvollziehen bestätigt und dadurch ‚erbaut‘, ist Parzivals *diemüete* weit mehr Geschenk, Gnade, die dem Publikum im Bilde gibt, was es insgeheim auch im Alltag für sich als eine Über-raschung erhofft: die Kunst des rechten Lebens vor Gott und Menschen.

Literatur

(Um das Literaturverzeichnis nicht allzusehr zu belasten, sind die meisten bei-
gezogenen *Aufsätze* hier nicht zitiert; sie lassen sich hingegen mühelos anhand
der Anmerkungen verifizieren. Ein paar speziell wichtige Abhandlungen sind
jedoch vermerkt.)

A. Texte und Übersetzungen

Wolfram von Eschenbach, herausgegeben von K. Lachmann, 7. Ausgabe, neu
bearbeitet und mit einem Verzeichnis der Eigennamen und Stammtafeln
versehen von E. Hartl, Band I: Lieder — Parzival und Titurel, Berlin 1952.

Wolfram von Eschenbach, Werke, herausgegeben von K. Lachmann, 6. (voll-
ständige) Ausgabe, bearbeitet von E. Hartl, Berlin 1926.

Wolframs von Eschenbach Parzival und Titurel, herausgegeben und erklärt von
E. Martin, 2 Teile, Halle a. S. 1900/03.

Wolframs von Eschenbach Parzival und Titurel, 4. Auflage, bearbeitet von
M. Marti und K. Bartsch, 3 Teile, Leipzig 1927/32.

Christian von Troyes, Der Percevalroman (Li Contes del Graal), herausgegeben von A. Hilka, Halle a. S. 1932.

Christian von Troyes, Der Percevalroman (Li Contes del Graal), in Auswahl
herausgegeben von A. Hilka, Halle a. S. 1935.

Chrétien de Troyes, Le Roman de Perceval ou Le Conte du Graal, publié par
W. Roach, Genf/Lille 1956.

Chrétien de Troyes, Perceval le Gallois ou Le Conte du Graal, mis en français
moderne par L. Foulet, Paris 1947.

Chrestien de Troyes, Perceval oder Die Geschichte vom Graal, Aus dem Altfranzösischen übersetzt von K. Sandkühler, Stuttgart [2]1957.

Albrecht von Scharfenberg, Jüngerer Titurel, herausgegeben von W. Wolf,
Deutsche Texte des MA's 45, Bd. I, Berlin 1955.

B. Sekundärliteratur

Aarne A., Verzeichnis der Märchentypen, FFC 3, Helsinki 1910.

Adorno Th. W., Noten zur Literatur I, Frankfurt 1958.

Auerbach E., Mimesis, Dargestellte Wirklichkeit in der abendländischen Literatur, Bern [2]1959.

Ders., Neue Dantestudien, Istanbul 1944.

Ders., Typologische Motive in der mittelalterlichen Literatur, Krefeld 1953.

Ders., Literatursprache und Publikum in der lateinischen Spätantike und im MA, Bern 1958.

Bachem R., Dichtung als verborgene Theologie, Bonn 1956.

von Balthasar H. U., Geschichte des eschatologischen Problems in der modernen Literatur, Zürich (Diss.) 1930.

Ders., Apokalypse der deutschen Seele, Studien zu einer Lehre von Letzthaltungen, 3 Bände, Salzburg/Leipzig 1937/39.

Ders., Prometheus, Studien zur Geschichte des deutschen Idealismus, Heidelberg 1947.

Ders., Wahrheit, Ein Versuch, Erstes Buch: Wahrheit der Welt, Einsiedeln 1947.

Ders., Verbum Caro, Skizzen zur Theologie I, Einsiedeln 1960.

Ders., Sponsa Verbi, Skizzen zur Theologie II, Einsiedeln 1961.

Ders., Kosmische Liturgie, Maximus der Bekenner, Einsiedeln ²1961.

Ders., Herrlichkeit, Eine theologische Ästhetik, Erster Band: Schau der Gestalt, Einsiedeln 1961.

Ders., Herrlichkeit, Eine theologische Ästhetik, Zweiter Band: Fächer der Stile, Einsiedeln 1962.

Baron R., Science et sagesse chez Hugues de Saint Victor, Paris 1957.

Barsotti D., Vie mystique et mystère liturgique, Paris 1954.

Ders., Christliches Mysterium und Wort Gottes, Einsiedeln 1957.

Bayer H. J., Untersuchungen zum Sprachstil weltlicher Epen des deutschen Früh- und Hochmittelalters, Berlin 1962.

Beck M., Finsteres oder romantisches MA, Aspekte der modernen Mediaevistik, Zürich 1950.

Beck W., Die Anfänge des deutschen Schelmenromans, Studien zur frühbarocken Erzählung, Zürich (Diss.) 1957.

von Beit H., Symbolik des Märchens, Versuch einer Deutung, 3 Bände, Bern 1952/57.

Benz E., Heilige Narrheit, Kyrios 3 (1938) 1—55.

Bloch E., Das Prinzip Hoffnung, 3 Bände, Berlin 1955/59.

Bezzola R. R., Le sens de l'aventure et de l'amour (Chrétien de Troyes), Paris 1947.

Ders., Liebe und Abenteuer im höfischen Roman, Hamburg 1961.

Ders., Les origines et la formation de la littérature courtoise en Occident (500—1200), drei Teile in fünf Bänden, Paris 1944/60/63.

Bindschedler M., Der Bildungsgedanke im MA, NSR (1954) 278—292.

Blomme R., La doctrine du péché dans les écoles théologiques de la première moitié du XIIe siècle. Louvain/Gembloux 1958.

Böckmann P., Formgeschichte der deutschen Dichtung, Erster Band: Von der Sinnbildsprache zur Ausdruckssprache, Der Wandel der literarischen Formensprache vom MA zur Neuzeit, Hamburg 1949.

Bösch B. u. a., Deutsche Literaturgeschichte in Grundzügen, Bern/München ²1961.

de Boor H., Die höfische Literatur; Vorbereitung, Blüte, Ausklang, 1170 bis 1250, München 1953.

Bouyer L., La spiritualité de Citeaux, Paris 1955.

Brinkmann H., Zu Wesen und Form mittelalterlicher Dichtung, Halle 1928.

Ders., Geschehen, Person und Gesellschaft in der Sprache des deutschen Rittertums, WW 2. Sonderheft (1953/54) 24—33.

Bruce J. D., The evolution of the Arthurian Romance from the beginnings down to the year 1300, Göttingen ²1928.

de Bruyne E., Etudes d'esthétique médiévale, 3 Bände, Bruges 1946.

Ders., L'esthétique du moyen âge, Louvain 1947.

Bumke J., Wolframs Willehalm, Studien zur Epenstruktur und zum Heiligkeitsbegriff der ausgehenden Blütezeit, Heidelberg 1959.

Chenu M.-D., La théologie au XIIe siècle, Paris 1957.

Ders., La théologie comme science au XIIIe siècle, Paris 1957.

Cilento V., Medio evo monastico e scolastico, Milano/Napoli 1961.

Cucuel E., Die Eingangsbücher des Parzival und das Gesamtwerk, Frankfurt 1937.

Curtius E. R., Europäische Literatur und lateinisches MA, Bern ²1948.

Ders., Gesammelte Aufsätze zur romanischen Philologie, Bern/München 1960.

Daniélou J., Origène, Paris 1948.

Davy M.-M., Théologie et mystique de Guillaume de Saint-Thierry, Band I: La connaissance de Dieu, Paris 1954.

Dies., Essai sur la symbolique romane (XIIe siècle), Paris 1955.

Dawson Chr., Die Gestaltung des Abendlandes, Eine Einführung in die Geschichte der abendländischen Einheit, Olten 1950.

Déchanet J.-M., Aux sources de la spiritualité de Guillaume de Saint-Thierry, Bruges 1940.

Ders., Guillaume de Saint-Thierry, L'homme et son oeuvre, Bruges/Paris 1942.

Deinert W., Ritter und Kosmos im Parzival, Eine Untersuchung der Sternkunde Wolframs von Eschenbach, München 1960.

Delarue P., Le conte populaire français, Catalogue raisonné des versions de France et des pays de langue française d'outre-mer, tome I, Paris 1957.

Delhaye Ph., L'enseignement de la philosophie morale au XIIe siècle, Medieval Studies (1949) 77 ff.

Ders., Le problème de la conscience morale chez Saint Bernard, étudié dans ses oeuvres et dans ses sources, Louvain/Lille 1957.

Ders., ‚Grammatica' et ‚Ethica' au XIIe siècle, Louvain/Lille 1959.

Ders., La philosophie chrétienne au moyen âge, Paris 1959.

Ders., Permanence du droit naturel, Louvain/Lille/Montréal 1960.

Ders., L'organisation scolaire au XIIe siècle, Louvain/Lille 1961.

Dempf A., Die Hauptform mittelalterlicher Weltanschauung, München/Berlin 1925.

Ders., Ethik des MA's, München/Berlin 1927.

Ders., Metaphysik des MA's, München/Berlin 1930.

Ders., Sacrum Imperium, Darmstadt 1954.

Ders., Die unsichtbare Bilderwelt, Zürich/Köln 1959.

Dilthey W., Von deutscher Dichtung und Musik, Leipzig/Berlin 1933.

Dumontier P., Saint Bernard et la Bible, Bruges/Paris 1953.

Eberle J., Psalterium profanum, Weltliche Gedichte des lat. MA's, Zürich 1962.

Eggers H., Wolframforschung in der Krise, WW 4 (1953/54) 274—290.

Ders., Symmetrie und Proportion epischen Erzählens, Studien zur Kunstform Hartmanns von Aue, Stuttgart 1956.

Eliade M., Das Heilige und das Profane, Vom Wesen des Religiösen, Hamburg 1957.

Evola J., Das Mysterium des Grals, München 1955.

Ehrismann G., Geschichte der deutschen Literatur bis zum Ausgang des MA's, 4 Bände (zitiert: 1, 2, 3, 4), München ²1954.

Ders., Märchen im höfischen Epos, PBB 30 (1905) 14 ff.

Ders., Über Wolframs Ethik, ZfdA 49 (1908) 405—465.

Ders., Wolframprobleme, GRM 1 (1909) 657 ff.

Ders., Studien über Rudolf von Ems, Beiträge zur Geschichte der Rhetorik und Ethik im MA, Heidelberg 1919.

Ders., Die Grundlagen des ritterlichen Tugendsystems, ZfdA 56 (1919) 137—216.

Ders., Dantes Göttliche Komödie und Wolframs Parzival, in: Idealistische Neuphilologie (Festschr. Vossler), Heidelberg 1922.

Emmel H., Formprobleme des Artusromans und der Graldichtung, Die Bedeutung des Artuskreises für das Gefüge des Romans im 12. und 13. Jahrhundert in Frankreich, Deutschland und den Niederlanden, Bern 1951.

Espenberger J. N., Die Elemente der Erbsünde nach Augustin und der Frühscholastik, Mainz 1905.

Faral E., Les arts poétiques du XIIᵉ et du XIIIᵉ siècle, Paris 1923.

Fechter W., Das Publikum der mhd. Dichtung, Frankfurt 1935.

Feurer G., Adam und Christus als Gestaltkräfte und ihr Vermächtnis an die Menschheit, Zur christlichen Erbsündelehre, Freiburg 1939.

Fierz-Monnier A., Initiation und Wandlung, Zur Geschichte des altfranzösischen Romans im 12. Jahrhundert von Chrétien de Troyes zu Renaut de Beaujeu, Bern 1951.

Flitner W., Europäische Gesittung, Ursprung und Aufbau abendländischer Lebensformen, Zürich/Stuttgart 1961.

di Fonzo L., Bibliografia di Jean Leclercq, Rom 1959.

Foucault M., Folie et déraison, Histoire de la folie à l'âge classique, Paris 1961.

Fourquet J., Wolfram d'Eschenbach et le Conte del Graal, Paris 1938.

Frappier J., Chrétien de Troyes, L'homme et l'oeuvre, Paris 1957.

Ders., Le roman breton: Les origines de la légende arthurienne: Chrétien de Troyes, Paris 1959.

Ders., Le roman breton: Perceval ou le conte de Graal, Paris 1959.

Génicot L., Das Mittelalter, Wien/Köln 1952.

Ders., La spiritualité médiévale, Paris 1958.

Gerhard M., Der deutsche Entwicklungsroman bis zu Goethes ‚Wilhelm Meister', Halle 1926.

de Ghellinck J., Patristique et moyen âge, Etudes d'histoire littéraire et doctrinale, 3 Bände, Bruxelles/Paris 1946/48.

Ders., Le mouvement théologique du XIIe siècle, Bruges/Paris 1948.

Ders., L'essor de la littérature latine au XIIe siècle, Bruxelles/Paris ²1955.

Gietmann G., Ein Gralbuch, Freiburg 1889.

Gilson E., La théologie mystique de S. Bernard, Paris 1947.

Ders., L'esprit de la philosophie médiévale, Paris 1948.

Ders., La philosophie au moyen âge, Paris 1952.

Ders., Les idées et les lettres, Paris 1955.

Glunz H. H., Die Literarästhetik des europäischen MA's: Wolfram, Rosenroman, Chaucer, Dante, Bochum 1937; Frankfurt a. M. ²1963.

Golther W., Parzival und der Gral in der Dichtung des MA's und der Neuzeit, Stuttgart 1925.

Ders., Parzival in der deutschen Literatur, Berlin/Leipzig 1929.

Grabmann M., Die Geschichte der scholastischen Methode, 2 Bde, Darmstadt ²1961.

Gross J., Entstehungsgeschichte des Erbsündedogmas, Von der Bibel bis Augustinus, München/Basel 1960.

Gruenter R., Parzivals ‚einvalt', Euph 52 (1958) 297—302.

Grundmann H., Religiöse Bewegungen im MA, Darmstadt ²1961.

Ders., Litteratus — illitteratus, Der Wandel einer Bildungsnorm vom Altertum zum MA, Archiv f. Kulturgesch. 40 (1958) 1—65.

Ders., Ketzergeschichte des MA's, Göttingen 1963.

Gsteiger M., Die Landschaftsschilderungen in den Romanen Chrestiens de Troyes, Literarische Tradition und künstlerische Gestaltung, Bern 1958.

Guardini E., Der Heilbringer in Mythos, Offenbarung und Politik, Stuttgart 1945.

Guénon R., Le roi du monde, Paris 1958.

Günter H., Die christliche Legende des Abendlandes, Heidelberg 1909.

Güntert H., Der arische Weltkönig und Heiland, Halle 1923.

Gutzwiller P., Der Narr bei Grimmelshausen, Basel (Diss.) 1959.

Haskins Ch. H., The renaissance of the twelfth century, Cambridge 1927.

Heckel H., Das ethische Wortfeld in Wolframs Parzival, Würzburg 1939.

Heer F., Aufgang Europas, Eine Studie zu den Zusammenhängen zwischen politischer Religiosität, Frömmigkeitsstil und dem Werden Europas im 12. Jahrhundert, Wien/Zürich 1949.

Ders., Die Tragödie des Heiligen Reiches, Stuttgart 1952.

Ders., Das Mittelalter von 1100 bis 1350, Zürich 1961.

Helbling H., Saeculum Humanum, Ansätze zu einem Versuch über spätmittelalterliches Geschichtsdenken, Neapel 1958.

Henzen W., Das 9. Buch des Parzival, Überlegungen zum Aufbau, in: Erbe der Vergangenheit (Festgabe K. Helm), Tübingen 1951, 189—217.

Ders., Zur Vorprägung der Demut im Parzival durch Chrestien, PBB 80 (1958) (West) 422—443.

Hilpich St., Die Torheit um Christi willen, Z. f. Asz. u. Myst. (1931) 121 ff.

Hönigswald R., Vom erkenntnistheoretischen Gehalt alter Schöpfungserzählungen, Stuttgart 1957.

Ders., Abstraktion und Analysis, Ein Beitrag zur Problemgeschichte des Universalienstreites in der Philosophie des MA's, Stuttgart 1961.

Hofer St., Chrétien de Troyes, Leben und Werke des altfranzösischen Epikers, Graz/Köln 1954.

Huizinga J., Herbst des MA's, Stuttgart 71953.

Javelet R., Psychologie des auteurs spirituels du XIIe siècle, Strasbourg 1959.

Jolles A., Einfache Formen, Darmstadt 21958.

Jung E. / von Franz M.-L., Die Graalslegende in psychologischer Sicht, Zürich/ Stuttgart 1960.

Kamlah W., Christentum und Geschichtlichkeit, Die Entstehung des Christentums, Stuttgart/Köln 1951.

Kampers F., Die deutsche Kaiseridee in Prophetie und Sage, München 1896.

Ders., Vom Werdegange der abendländischen Kaisermystik, Leipzig/Berlin 1924.

Keferstein G., Parzivals ethischer Weg, Jena 1937.

Kellermann H., Aufbaustil und Weltbild Chrétiens de Troyes im Percevalroman, Halle 1936.

Klapper J., Erzählungen des MA's, Breslau 1914.

Kobel E., Untersuchungen zum gelebten Raum in der mhd. Dichtung, Zürich (Diss.) o. J.

Köhler E., Ideal und Wirklichkeit in der höfischen Epik, Studien zur Form der frühen Artus- und Graldichtung, Tübingen 1956.

Ders., Trobadorlyrik und höfischer Roman, Aufsätze zur französischen und provenzalischen Literatur des MA's, Berlin 1962.

Kolb H., Schola Humilitatis, Ein Beitrag zur Interpretation der Gralerzählung Wolframs von Eschenbach, PBB (1956) (West) 65—115.

Kologrivof J., Essai sur la sainteté en Russie, Bruges 1953.

Koppitz H. J., Wolframs Religiosität, Bonn 1959.

Kraus A., Vom Wesen und Ursprung der Dummheit, Köln/Olten 21961.

Kremer K. R., Das Lachen in der deutschen Literatur des MA's, Bonn (Diss.) 1961.

Kundert-Forrer V., Raoul de Houdenc, Ein französischer Erzähler des XIII. Jahrhunderts, Zürich (Diss.) 1960.

Kuhn H., Dichtung und Welt im MA, Stuttgart 1960.

Ders., Die Klassik des Rittertums in der Stauferzeit, 1170—1230, in: Annalen der deutschen Literatur, herausgegeben von H. O. Burger, Stuttgart ²1962, 99—177.

Landgraf A., Das Wesen der läßlichen Sünde in der Scholastik bis Thomas von Aquin, Bamberg 1923.

Ders., Einführung in die Geschichte der theologischen Literatur der Frühscholastik, Regensburg 1948.

Ders., Dogmengeschichte der Frühscholastik, 5 Teile, Regensburg 1952 ff.

Leclercq J., La vie parfaite, Points de vue sur l'essence de l'état religieux, Paris/Turnhout 1948.

Ders., S. Bernard mystique, Bruges 1948.

Ders., L'amour des lettres et le désir de Dieu, Paris 1957.

Ders., Grammaire et humour dans les textes du moyen âge, Convivium 3 (1959).

Ders., Sancta Simplicitas, Collectanea Ord. Cist. Ref. (1960) 138—148.

Ders., Saint Pierre Damien, Ermite et homme d'Eglise, Rom 1960.

Ders., Vandenbroucke F., Bouyer L., La spiritualité du moyen âge, Paris 1961.

Ders., Etudes sur le vocabulaire monastique du moyen âge, Rom 1961.

Lehmann P., Die heilige Einfalt, in: Erforschung des MA's (5 Bde), Bd. III, Stuttgart 1960, 213—224.

von der Leyen F., Das Märchen, Ein Versuch, Leipzig ³1925.

Ders., Die Welt der Märchen, Düsseldorf 1953/54.

Ligier L., Péché d'Adam et péché du monde, 2 Bände, Paris 1960/61.

Löwith K., Weltgeschehen und Heilsgeschichte, Stuttgart 1953.

Loomis R. S., Arthurian tradition and Chrétien de Troyes, New York 1949.

Lottin, Psychologie et morale au XIIᵉ et XIIIᵉ siècles, bisher 6 Teile in 8 Bänden, Gembloux 1942/60.

Ders., Etudes de morale, Histoire et doctrine, Gembloux 1961.

Lowet R., Wolfram von Eschenbachs Parzival im Wandel der Zeiten, München 1955.

de Lubac H., Histoire et esprit, Paris 1950.

Ders., Der geistige Sinn der Schrift, Einsiedeln 1952.

Ders., Exégèse médiévale, Les quatre sens de l'Ecriture, bisher: première partie I und II; seconde partie I, Paris 1959/61.

Lüthi M., Die Gabe im Märchen und in der Sage, Bern (Diss.) 1943.

Ders., Das europäische Volksmärchen, Bern ²1960.

Ders., Märchen, Stuttgart 1962.

Ders., Es war einmal . . ., Vom Wesen des Volksmärchens, Göttingen 1962.

Ders., Volksmärchen und Volkssage, Zwei Grundformen erzählender Dichtung, Bern/München 1961.

Lukàcs G., Die Theorie des Romans, Ein geschichtsphilosophischer Versuch über die Formen der großen Epik, Berlin 1928.

Maisonneuve H., La morale chrétienne d'après les conciles des Xe et XIe siècles, Louvain/Lille 1962.

Marx J., La légende arthurienne et le Graal, Paris 1952.

Ders., Les littératures celtiques, Paris 1959.

Maurer F., Leid, Studien zur Bedeutungs- und Problemgeschichte, besonders in den großen Epen der staufischen Zeit, Bern/München ²1961.

Ders., Dichtung und Sprache im MA, Gesammelte Aufsätze, Bern/München 1963.

Mausbach J., Die Ethik des heiligen Augustinus, 2 Bände, Freiburg 1929.

Mergell B., Wolfram von Eschenbach und seine französischen Quellen, II. Teil: Wolframs Parzival, Münster 1943.

Ders., Der Graal in Wolframs Parzival, Entstehung und Ausbildung der Gralsage im Hochmittelalter, Halle 1952.

Metz J.B., Armut im Geiste, GuL 34 (1961) 419—435.

Michaud-Quantin P., Sommes de casuistique et manuels de confession au moyen âge, Louvain/Lille 1962.

Misch G., Wolframs Parzival, Eine Studie zur Geschichte der Autobiographie, DVjS 5 (1927) 213—315.

Ders., Geschichte der Autobiographie, bisher 6 Bände, Frankfurt 1949/62.

Mockenhaupt B., Die Frömmigkeit im Parzival Wolframs von Eschenbach, Ein Beitrag zur Geschichte des rel. Geistes in der Laienwelt des deutschen MA's, Bonn 1942.

Moeller Ch., Sagesse grecque et paradoxe chrétien, Louvain 1948.

Mohr W., Parzivals ritterliche Schuld, WW 2 (1951/52) 148—160.

Ders., Wandel des Menschenbildes in der mittelalterlichen Dichtung, WW 1. Sonderheft (1953) 37—49.

Ders., Hilfe und Rat in Wolframs Parzival, Festschrift Trier, Meisenheim 1954, 173—197.

Ders., Parzival und die Ritter, Von einfacher Form zum Ritterepos, Fabula 1 (1958) 201—213.

Ders., Parzival und Gawan, Euph 52 (1958) 1—22.

Ders., Einfache Formen, in: Reallexikon der dt. Literaturgeschichte, Berlin ²1958, Band I, siehe Stichwort.

Moser H., Dichtung und Wirklichkeit im Hochmittelalter, WW 5 (1955) 79 ff.

Müller G., Gradualismus, Eine Vorstudie zur altdeutschen Literaturgeschichte, DVjS 2 (1924) 681—720.

Müller M., Ethik und Recht in der Lehre von der Verantwortlichkeit, Regensburg 1932.

Neumann E., Zum ritterlichen Tugendsystem, WW 1. Sonderheft (1953) 49—61.

Ders., Der Streit um das ritterliche Tugendsystem, in: Erbe der Vergangenheit (Festgabe Helm), Tübingen 1951, 137—155.

Nolting-Hauff I., Die Stellung der Liebeskasuistik im höfischen Roman, Heidelberg 1959.

Nüsse H., Die Sprachtheorie Friedrich Schlegels, Heidelberg 1962.

Ohly F., Hohelied-Studien, Grundzüge einer Geschichte der Hoheliedauslegung des Abendlandes bis um 1200, Wiesbaden 1958.

Ders., Vom geistigen Sinn des Wortes im MA, ZfdA 89 (1958/59) 1—23.

Ders., Wolframs Gebet an den Heiligen Geist im Eingang des Willehalm, ZfdA 91 (1961) 1—37.

Ortega y Gasset J., Meditationen über ,Don Quijote', Stuttgart 1959.

Otto R., Das Heilige, Über das Irrationale in der Idee des Göttlichen und sein Verhältnis zum Rationalen, München 1947.

Panzer F., Gahmuret, Heidelberg 1940.

Paré G., Brunet A., Tremblay, La renaissance du XIIe siècle, les écoles et l'enseignement, Paris 1933.

Pieper J., Scholastik, Gestalten und Probleme der mittelalterlichen Philosophie, München 1960.

Ponsoye P., L'Islam et le Graal, Paris 1957.

Przywara E., Ringen der Gegenwart, 2 Bände, Augsburg 1929.

Ders., Humanitas, Der Mensch gestern und morgen, Nürnberg 1952.

Ders., Was ist Gott? Eine Summula, Nürnberg 1953.

Ders., In und Gegen, Stellungnahmen zur Zeit, Nürnberg 1955.

Ders., Mensch, Typologische Anthropologie, Band I, Zürich 1959.

Ders., Demut Geduld Liebe, Die drei christlichen Tugenden, Düsseldorf 1960.

Ders., Analogia Entis, Metaphysik: Ur-Struktur und All-Rhythmus, Einsiedeln 1962.

Rahn B., Wolframs Sigunendichtung, Eine Interpretation der ,Titurelfragmente', Zürich (Diss.) 1958.

Rahn O., Kreuzzug gegen den Gral, Freiburg 1933.

Ranke F., Gott Welt und Humanität in der deutschen Dichtung des MA's, Basel o. J.

Ders., Zur Symbolik des Grals bei Wolfram von Eschenbach, Trivium 4 (1946) Heft 1 20—30.

Ranke K., Betrachtungen zum Wesen und zur Funktion des Märchens, Studium Generale 11 (1958) 647—664.

Rahner K., Le début d'une doctrine des cinq sens spirituels chez Origène, Revue d'Asc. et Myst. 13 (1932) 113—145.

Ders., La doctrine des sens spirituels au moyen âge, en particulier chez saint Bonaventure, Revue d'Asc. et Myst. 14 (1933) 263—299.

Ders., Schriften zur Theologie, bisher 5 Bände, Einsiedeln 1960/62.

Riedlinger H., Die Makellosigkeit der Kirche in den lateinischen Hohelied-kommentaren des MA's, Münster 1958.

Ringbom L.-I., Graltempel und Paradies, Beziehungen zwischen Iran und Europa im MA, Stockholm 1951.

Röhrich L., Märchen und Wirklichkeit, Eine volkskundliche Untersuchung, Wiesbaden 1956.

Ders., Erzählungen des späten MA's und ihr Weiterleben in Literatur und Volksdichtung bis zur Gegenwart; Sagen, Märchen, Exempel und Schwänke mit einem Kommentar, Band I, Bern/München 1962.

Rosenfeld H., Legende, Stuttgart 1961.

de Rougemont D., L'amour et l'occident, Paris 1939.

Rupp H., Einiges Grundsätzliche zur deutschen Wortforschung, DU 3 (1951) Heft 1 53 ff.

Ders., Das neue Wolframbild, DU 5 (1953) Heft 2 82—90.

Ders., Neue Literatur zur höfischen Epik, DU 6 (1954) Heft 5 108—112.

Ders., Die Funktion des Wortes ,tump' im Parzival Wolframs von Eschenbach, GRM 7 (1957) 97—106.

Ders., Deutsche religiöse Dichtungen des 11. und 12. Jahrhunderts, Freiburg 1958.

Ders., Wolframs Parzival-Prolog, PBB (Ost) 82 (Sonderband) 1961, 29—45.

Ders., Einige Gedanken zum Menschenbild der deutschen höfischen Dichtung, DU 14 (1962) Heft 6 5—20.

Salmon P., Ignorance and awareness of identity in Hartmann and Wolfram, An element of dramatic irony, PBB (Ost) 82 (1960) 95—116.

Schirmer W., Die frühen Darstellungen des Arthurstoffes, Köln 1958.

Schlink E., Weisheit und Torheit, KuD 1 (1955) 1—22.

Schneider H., Heldendichtung, Geistlichendichtung, Ritterdichtung, Heidelberg 1943.

Ders., Parzival-Studien, München 1947.

Schnyder H., Sir Gawain and the Green Knight, An essay in interpretation, Bern 1961.

Schreiber G., Gemeinschaften des MA's, Recht und Verfassung, Kult und Fröm-migkeit, Münster 1948.

Schröder F. R., Parzivals Schuld, GRM 9 (1959) 1—20.

Schröder W. J., Der Ritter zwischen Welt und Gott, Weimar 1952.

Ders., Der dichterische Plan des Parzivalromans, Halle 1953.

Schröder W., Zum Wortgebrauch von riuwe bei Hartmann und Wolfram, GRM 9 (1959) 228—234.

Schwietering J., Die Demutsformel mittelhochdeutscher Dichter, Berlin 1921.

Ders., Typologisches in mittelalterlicher Dichtung, in: Ehrismann Festschrift, Berlin/Leipzig 1925, 40—55.

Ders., Wolframs Parzival, in: Von deutscher Art in Sprache und Dichtung, Band II, Stuttgart/Berlin 1941, 235—248.

Ders., The origins of the medieval humility formula, PMLA 69 (1954) 1279
— 1291.

Ders., Die deutsche Dichtung des MA's, Darmstadt ²1957.

Ders., Mystik und höfische Dichtung im Hochmittelalter, Darmstadt 1960.

Ders., Natur und art, ZfdA 91 (1961) 108—137.

Senn A. / Lehmann W., Word-Index to Wolframs Parzival, Madison/Wisconsin
1938.

Sertillanges R. P., Le problème du mal, 2 Bände, Paris 1948/51.

Siewerth G., Das Schicksal der Metaphysik, Von Thomas bis Heidegger, Einsiedeln 1959.

Simmel G., Philosophische Kultur, Potsdam ³1923.

von Simson O. G., Über das Religiöse in Wolframs Parzival, in: A. Berg-
strässer, Deutsche Beiträge zur geistigen Überlieferung, Band II, München
1953.

Singer S., Wolframs Stil und der Stoff seines Parzival, Wien 1916.

Ders., Wolfram und der Gral, Neue Parzival-Studien, Bern 1939.

Smalley B., The study of the Bible in the middle ages, Oxford ²1952.

Southern R. M., Gestaltende Kräfte des MA's, Das Abendland im 11. und 12.
Jahrhundert, Stuttgart 1960.

Sparnaay H., Verschmelzung legendarischer und weltlicher Motive in der Poesie
des MA's, Groningen 1922.

Spicq C., Esquisse d'une histoire de l'exégèse latine au moyen âge, Paris 1944.

Stammler W., Ideenwandel in Sprache und Literatur des deutschen MA's,
DVjS 2 (1924) 753—769.

Ders., ‚Edle Einfalt‘, Zur Geschichte eines kunsthistorischen Topos, in: Worte
und Werke (Festschrift Markwardt), Berlin 1961, 359—383.

Stauffer M., Der Wald, Zur Darstellung und Deutung der Natur im MA,
Zürich 1958.

Steinbüchel Th., Christliches MA, Leipzig 1935.

Ders., Vom Menschenbild des MA's, Darmstadt 1961.

von den Steinen W., Der Kosmos des MA's, Von Karl dem Großen zu Bern-
hard von Clairvaux, Bern/München 1959.

Strucks C., Der junge Parzival, Münster (Diss.) 1910/11.

Taubes J., Abendländische Eschatologie, Bern 1947.

Thompson St., Motif-Index of Folk-Literature, Bloomington 1933/36.

Thurneysen R., Sagen aus dem alten Irland, Berlin 1901.

Ders., Die irische Helden- und Königssage bis zum 17. Jahrhundert, Halle 1921.

Trier J., Der deutsche Wortschatz im Sinnbezirk des Verstandes, Band I: Von
den Anfängen bis zum Beginn des 13. Jahrhunderts, Heidelberg 1931.

Überweg F. / Geyer B., Die patristische und scholastische Philosophie, Darmstadt 1960.

Vann G., Der Lebensbaum, Studien zur christlichen Symbolik, Einsiedeln 1962.

Vignaux P., Philosophie au moyen âge, Paris 1958.

de Vries J., Betrachtungen zum Märchen, Helsinki 1954.

Ders., Kelten und Germanen, Bern/München 1960.

Ders., Keltische Religion, Stuttgart 1961.

Wapnewski P., Wolframs Parzival, Studien zur Religiosität und Form, Heidelberg 1955.

Ders., Deutsche Literatur des MA's, Ein Abriß, Göttingen 1960.

Weber G., Wolfram von Eschenbach, Seine dichterische und geistesgeschichtliche Bedeutung, Erster Band, Frankfurt 1928.

Ders., Der Gottesbegriff des Parzival, Frankfurt 1935.

Ders., Parzival, Ringen und Vollendung, Oberursel 1948.

Ders., Gottfrieds von Straßburg Tristan und die Krise des hochmittelalterlichen Weltbildes um 1200, 2 Bände, Stuttgart 1953.

Wehrli M., Der hist. Roman, Versuch einer Übersicht, Helikon 3 (1941) 89 ff.

Ders., Die Elegie Walthers von der Vogelweide, Trivium 1 (1943) Heft 3 12—29.

Ders., ‚Wär ich witzig, hieß ich nicht der Tell‘, in: Hortulus Amicorum (Festschrift F. Ernst), Zürich 1949, 187—194.

Ders., Zum Problem der Historie in der Literaturwissenschaft, Trivium 7 (1949) 44—59.

Ders., Besprechung von: Curtius, Europäische Literatur und lateinisches MA, in: AfdA 64 (1948/50) 84—91.

Ders., Wolframs Humor, in: Überlieferung und Gestaltung (Festgabe Th. Spoerri), Zürich 1950, 9—31.

Ders., Allgemeine Literaturwissenschaft, Bern 1951.

Ders., Besprechung von: de Boor, Geschichte der deutschen Literatur, in: AfdA 67 (1954/55) 93—98.

Ders., Wolfram von Eschenbach, Erzählstil und Sinn seines Parzival, DU 6 (1954) Heft 5 17—40.

Ders., Besprechung von: Wapnewski, Wolframs Parzival, in: AfdA 68 (1955) 111—119.

Ders., Vom Sinn des mittelalterlichen Tierepos, German Life and Letters 10 (1957) 219—228.

Ders., Besprechung von: E. Jung / M.-L. von Franz, Die Gralslegende in psychologischer Sicht, in: NZZ 5. Okt. 1960 Nr. 3380.

Ders., Strukturprobleme des mittelalterlichen Romans, WW 10 (1960) 334—345.

Ders., Vom literarischen Zürich im MA, Librium 4 (1961) 99—112.

Ders., Roman und Legende im deutschen Hochmittelalter, in: Worte und Werte (Festschrift Markwardt), Berlin 1961, 428—444.

Ders., Besprechung von: Bezzola, Les origines ..., in: NZZ 26. März 1961 Nr. 1120.

Ders., Tell, Bemerkungen zum Stand der Tellenforschung, NZZ 21. Okt. 1962 Nr. 4060.

Ders., Sacra Poesis, Bibelepik als europäische Tradition, Festschrift Maurer, Stuttgart 1963, 22—41.

Weigand J. H., A jester at the Grail Castle in Wolframs Parzival, PMLA 67 (1952) 485—510.

Wesle C., Zu Wolframs Parzival, PBB 72 (1950) 1—38.

Wessels P. B., Wolfram zwischen Dogma und Legende, PBB (West) 77 (1955) 112—136.

Wesselski A., Märchen des MA's, Berlin 1925.

Ders., Versuch einer Theorie des Märchens, Reichenberg 1931.

Wilckens U., Kreuz und Weisheit, KuD 3 (1957) 77—108.

Ders., Weisheit und Torheit, Eine exegetisch-religionsgeschichtliche Untersuchung zu 1 Kor 1 und 2, Tübingen 1959.

Willson B., Mystische Dialektik in Wolframs Parzival, ZfdPh 79 (1960) 57—70.

Ders., Das Fragemotiv in Wolframs Parzival, GRM 12 (1962) 139—150.

Wolf A., Christliche Literatur des MA's, Zürich 1958.

Wolfram-Jahrbücher, herausgegeben von W. Stammler, 1952—1955.

Wust P., Naivität und Pietät, Tübingen 1925.

Wyss H., Der Narr im schweizerischen Drama des 16. Jahrhunderts, Bern (Diss.) 1959.

Ziltener W., Chrétien und die Aeneis, Eine Untersuchung des Einflusses von Vergil auf Chrétien von Troyes, Graz/Köln 1957.

Zimmer H., Abenteuer und Fahrten der Seele, Der König mit dem Leichnam und andere Mythen, Märchen und Sagen, Zürich/Stuttgart 1961.

✱

Lumière du Graal, Etudes et textes, herausgegeben von R. Nelli, Paris 1951.

Les romans du Graal dans la littérature des XIIe et XIIIe siècles, Paris 1956.

Arthurian Literature in the Middle Ages, A collaborative History, herausgegeben von R. S. Loomis, Oxford 1959.

L'homme et son destin d'après les penseurs du moyen âge, Actes du premier congrès international de philosophie médiévale, Louvain/Bruxelles 1958, Louvain/Paris 1960.

La vita commune del clero nei secoli XI e XII, Atti della Settimana di studio: Mendola, settembre 1959, 2 Bände, Milano 1962.

Abkürzungen

AfdA	Anzeiger für deutsches Altertum und deutsche Literatur
BBSIA	Bulletin Bibliographique de la Société Internationale Arthurienne, Paris 1949 ff.
DTC	Dictionnaire de théologie catholique, Vacant/Mangenot, Paris 1909 ff.
DU	Der Deutschunterricht
DVjS	Deutsche Vierteljahrsschrift für Literaturwissenschaft und Geistesgeschichte
Euph	Euphorion, Zeitschrift für Literaturgeschichte ...
GuL	Geist und Leben, Zeitschrift für Askese und Mystik
GRM	Germanisch-romanische Monatsschrift
KuD	Kerygma und Dogma, Zeitschrift für theologische Forschung und Lehre
LfThuK	Lexikon für Theologie und Kirche, Buchberger/Höfer/Rahner, Freiburg 1957 ff.
NSR	Neue Schweizer Rundschau
NZZ	Neue Zürcher Zeitung
PBB	Paul und Braunes Beiträge zur Geschichte der deutschen Sprache und Literatur
PMLA	Publications of the Modern Languages Association
WW	Wirkendes Wort, Deutsches Sprachschaffen in Lehre und Leben
ZfdA	Zeitschrift für deutsches Altertum und deutsche Literatur
ZfdPh	Zeitschrift für deutsche Philologie

Texte des späten Mittelalters
und der frühen Neuzeit

Herausgegeben von **Wolfgang Stammler, Ernst Alfred Philippson**
und **Hugo Moser**, mitbegründet von **Arno Schirokauer** †

Zuletzt sind erschienen:

Heft 11: **Das Lied von Herzog Ernst**
Kritisch herausgegeben nach den Drucken des 15. und
16. Jahrhunderts
von K. C. K i n g
84 Seiten, 1 Bildtafel, DIN A 5, kartoniert DM 6,40

Heft 12: **Bonaventuras ‚Legenda Sancti Francisci‘**
in der Übersetzung der Sibilla von Bondorf
Herausgegeben von David B r e t t - E v a n s
212Seiten, DIN A 5, kartoniert DM 16,80

Heft 13: **Das Schachzabelbuch des Jacobus de Cessolis**
in mittelhochdeutscher Prosa-Übersetzung
Nach den Handschriften herausgegeben von Gerard F. S c h m i d t
160 Seiten, DIN A 5, kartoniert DM 12,60

Heft 14: **Pontus und Sidonia**
in der Verdeutschung eines Ungenannten aus dem 15. Jahrhundert
Kritisch herausgegeben von Karin S c h n e i d e r
266 Seiten, DIN A 5, kartoniert DM 19,60

Heft 15: **Berner Weltgerichtsspiel**
Aus der Handschrift des 15. Jahrhunderts
herausgegeben von Wolfgang S t a m m l e r
65 Seiten, DIN A 5, kartoniert DM 6,80

Heft 16: **Spätlese des Mittelalters**
I. Weltliches Schrifttum
Aus den Handschriften herausgegeben und erläutert
von Wolfgang S t a m m l e r
122 Seiten, DIN A 5, kartoniert DM 10,80

Heft 17: **Das Eisenacher Zehnjungfrauenspiel**
Herausgegeben von Karin S c h n e i d e r
50 Seiten, DIN A 5, kartoniert DM 6,80

Heft 18: **Das Buch der Erkanntnus des Theophrast von Hohenheim,
gen. Paracelsus**
Aus der Handschrift herausgegeben von Kurt G o l d a m m e r
58 Seiten, DIN A 5, kartoniert DM 6,80

Die Reihe wird laufend fortgesetzt!

ERICH SCHMIDT VERLAG